Best Wishes
Phil Richards

The Sky Is Not the Limit

Discovering the True North
for Your Life's Path

by

Phillip C. Richards, CLU, CFP, RHU

and

Jarrod Spencer, Psy.D.

Library of Congress Control Number: 2013958118

ISBN: 978-0-9912078-0-0

What People Are Saying About
The Sky Is Not the Limit

"I believe there are Three Lessons for Life: (1) Always give your best effort in everything you do. (2) Never be afraid to fail. Smart people learn from any failure. (3) Find something you have a love and passion for that can provide a living. Then learn all the fundamentals for whatever that may be so you have a solid foundation to build on. Don't be a person who gets up in the morning and isn't excited about what they do for a living. When you love what you do, it isn't work. This book captures the Three Lessons for Life."

—*Rick Barry, National Basketball Association Hall of Fame*

"This book is that rare inspiring event in your life when you are compelled to read every single word, think, and then take action. Its words will prompt you to say, 'I can do that; I will do that!' 'Nothing now can stop me!' 'I am so blessed!' 'I really can make a positive difference in this world!' 'True success can be accomplished by anyone!' 'The minute I change my outlook, I will change my life!' and 'Thank you for writing this book.' Your book has helped crystallize the belief in my life's purpose. I have always known from age nine that I am here for a purpose. My life has been an incredible adventure filled with continued successes, honors, and prestige. But all that only convinced me that I must accomplish more and leave a legacy. As Steve Jobs said, 'to put a dent in the Universe.' Your words have reaffirmed my belief in the mission. Many, many need to find their North Star!"

—*Dwight Carey, Professor, Senior Fellow, and Dean's Teaching Fellow,*
Temple University; Managing Member, American Productivity Group, LLC

"This book is a true masterpiece. Phil has been my mentor and a father to me the past two decades and is the wisest person I know. The true wisdom in this book is a gift to anyone who acts on it. I cannot imagine my or my family's life or this earth without the impact and influence of Phil Richards. Do something wonderful for yourself and drink often from this book."

—*Edward Deutschlander, CLU, CLF, CEO-Elect, North Star Resource Group*

"The lessons in this book apply to coaches in all sports who are dedicated to the coaching profession, which includes mentoring our youth of today both on and off the field. The ability of coaches to assess the talents of youngsters is extremely valuable for student athletes. This book will equip all coaches with the necessary tools for them to counsel their student athletes on the best career path and on the vocation that best suits their skill set. This is a must-read for all high school coaches, student athletes, and parents to make the right decisions concerning the future of the student athlete."

—*Robert Ferraro, Founder and CEO, National High School Coaches Association*

"Want to be a champion? Read Phil and Jarrod's book. It's a knockout!"

—*Larry Holmes, Former Heavyweight Boxing Champion of the World,*
International Boxing Hall of Fame, and World Boxing Hall of Fame

"What a great book Phil and Jarrod have assembled. Advice for a lifetime of happiness, satisfaction, and accomplishment. Simply full of great nuggets!"

—*Harry P. Hoopis, President and CEO, Hoopis Performance Network*

"This book unlocks the mystery of a successful life. Read it and you are sure to understand why Phil's life has morphed into a wild success both personally and professionally!"

—*Lewis Katz, Shareholder, New Jersey Nets,*
New Jersey Devils, and New York Yankees

"This book is a must-read for all managers and aspiring managers. Having been a manager for almost sixty years, I recognize the wisdom of Phil's and Jarrod's observations. Phil, who is the master modern manager himself, correctly recognized that loving what you do and being enthused by your daily activities is probably the single most important attribute for great success. I don't remember reading a book that made that truth so clear and relevant and then explains how to utilize that principle to achieve managerial success. It's brilliant and practical, and I wish someone had shared this concept with me sixty years ago. It would have saved me tons of time and money."

—*Norman G. Levine, CLU, ChFC, Motivational Speaker and Author of Eleven*
Books; Past President, GAMA, GAMA Foundation, LUTC, NAIFA

"*North*, south, east, or west—wherever you choose to go in life…let this book be your GPS!"

—*Eileen C. McDonnell, President and CEO,*
The Penn Mutual Life Insurance Company

"No matter where we are in our journey through life, we all seek guidance in finding our true direction. The wisdom shared by these two experts can help you hear God's whisper and understand His plan for your life."

—*Pat Santoro, Lehigh University Head Wrestling Coach;*
NCAA Champion Wrestler

"Whether you are just starting out or have decades of experience, *The Sky Is Not the Limit* has something for you. The valuable lessons Phil shares from a successful fifty-year career demonstrate his ongoing commitment to help others be successful."

—*Bob Senkler, CEO and Chairman, Securian Financial Group*

"I am pleased to acknowledge and commend everyone on this amazing book, *The Sky Is Not the Limit*. The reader will quickly discover this title to be far more than an excellent read. The book is an action plan for living significantly. Each chapter is brilliantly crafted by the authors, Phil Richards and Dr. Jarrod Spencer, as a virtual laboratory for lifelong learning. The book is not intended to be a 'quick' read. Each topic requires serious reflection and discernment. Those who have been blessed to know Phil and Scott Richards will recognize this work as essential biography. The words and stories become transparent. Each of the twenty-one chapters challenges readers to engage in a transformation process that will carry them to the place they want to be, with people whom they love, doing the things about which they are passionate. This is true for a young professional, a seasoned executive, a struggling artist, a committed missionary, or a senior citizen nearing retirement. Each will be inspired to consider their possibilities on the pages of *The Sky Is Not the Limit*."

—*Charles A. Smith, CLU, ChFC, AEP, CEO Emeritus, GAMA International*
John Newton Russell Award Recipient, 2005
GAMA International Management Hall of Fame Inductee, 2007
CEO, The Cumberland Financial Group, LLC

"Phil and Jarrod's book had me wishing I was beginning my career again! Whether a Navy SEAL, business leader, or college student, challenge yourself. Nothing but good will come from it!"

—*Ray Smith, Rear Admiral, US Navy (Ret.) and Navy SEAL Commander*

"In one's life, we pray that we are honored to know greatness in a person who elevates your life and the lives of many others in every important way under God that is good. In 1962, I met Phil and have been honored by his friendship and guidance over all of those years. He is, without a doubt, the most respected person in our great industry who has produced many outstanding people. He has exceeded production goals that many considered improbable and impossible. His life as a father and husband is beyond reproach, and his perseverance in some extremely difficult business and personal situations has proven his dedication and courage. Every person in our industry and in other endeavors must read this book and benefit from a truly great mind and man."

—*Maury Stewart, CLU, ChFC, CLF, Executive Consultant,*
The Penn Mutual Life Insurance Company

About Phil Richards's first book, *Twenty-Five Secrets to Sustainable Success*

"Years ago, I started a refuse business, and it was creating $38,000 of revenue. Reading Phil's first book, *Twenty-Five Secrets to Sustainable Success*, and visiting with him about it allowed me to increase my revenue to $500,000 per year."

—*Robert Rizzolino, CEO, RIZZ Containers & Disposal, LLC, Easton, PA*

To order *Twenty-Five Secrets to Sustainable Success* by Phillip C. Richards, which GAMA International published in 2007, please visit http://secure.gamaweb .com/public/GAMA/Store/Core/Orders/product.aspx?catid=4&prodid=216.

About the Authors

Phil Richards, CLU, CFP, RHU

Phil Richards is the Chairman of the Board and CEO of North Star Resource Group, the largest independently owned financial planning organization in the world. Phil's first book, *Twenty-Five Secrets to Sustainable Success*, has sold more than 10,000 copies and remains an industry Bible for building a company.

A winner of numerous industry awards, Phil was the 2005 inductee into the GAMA International Hall of Fame, and he is the only firm leader in the world to have received the International Management Award from GAMA International each and every year since the inception of that award forty years ago. In 2007, Phil was named the recipient of the sixty-sixth annual John Newton Russell Memorial Award, the highest honor in the insurance industry awarded by The National Association of Insurance and Financial Advisors.

Phil is an Adjunct Professor Emeritus for the Carlson School of Management at the University of Minnesota and a former Adjunct Professor at Central University of Finance and Economics in Beijing, China. He is a past president of GAMA International and the Minnesota/North Dakota Better Business Bureau, and he is a past chairman of the LIFE Foundation. Currently, he serves on the Board of Trustees for The American College and on the Mayo Clinic of Arizona Leadership Council. He also is the treasurer of the Arizona Heart Foundation's Board, and he chairs the Scott Richards North Star Charitable Foundation.

Phil has been a featured speaker in more than a dozen countries on topics including strategic planning, leadership, and alternate distribution systems in the financial services industry in the twenty-first century. He has addressed the annual meetings of more than one hundred companies. He was a speaker at

GAMA International's national LAMP meeting and its Canadian counterpart, and he was a main-platform speaker at meetings in Singapore, Taipei, and Manila. In addition, he has been a featured speaker at the Asian Pacific Conferences in Bangkok, Thailand; Beijing, Shanghai, and Singapore, China; Crete, Greece; and Sydney, Australia. He has been a lecturer numerous times at Beijing University and Shanghai University for Finance and Economics. He was a main-platform speaker for MDRT in Vancouver in 2010 and in Ireland in 2012.

Phil earned his BS degree in 1962 from Temple University, where he served as student body president and received the prestigious Sword Award as the outstanding senior classman. A recipient of a four-year wrestling scholarship, he served as team captain. He was inducted into the National Wrestling Hall of Fame in 2009 and the National High School Coaches Hall of Fame in 2010. He was elected to the Temple University Board of Trustees in 2009. Phil's firm was awarded the Community Service Award from *InvestmentNews* in 2010 and the Better Business Bureau's Integrity Award in 2011.

Jarrod Spencer, Psy.D.

MIND OF THE ATHLETE

Dr. Jarrod Spencer is a sports psychologist who is passionate about improving the emotional health of athletes. His forte is teaching athletes, coaches, and leaders how the mind works best. His central message is "clearer mind, better performance."

He is the president and founder of Mind of the Athlete, LLC, a sports psychology company committed to equipping athletes with skills and education on the mind and high performance. He is the creator of the Mind of the Athlete Program, a cutting-edge video and audio sports psychology curriculum.

Dr. Spencer conducts more than one hundred speeches each year nationwide to athletes and business leaders on peak-performance psychology. Annually, he provides nearly one thousand coaching sessions. Dr. Spencer works one-on-one with Olympic, professional, high school, and college athletes at such schools as the University of Michigan, North Carolina, Ohio State, Cal Poly, and Princeton. He is the sports psychologist for teams at the University of Maryland, Old Dominion University, Lehigh University, and Lafayette College.

Dr. Spencer is often heard on ESPN Radio explaining the psychology of current events in sports. He also starred in the TV Show "What the Heck Were They Thinking?!" with former heavyweight boxing champion Larry Holmes. He created and starred on the TV show "Mind of the Athlete." He frequently is a guest on morning-television news shows explaining the minds of athletes.

A graduate of Argosy University in Chicago, Dr. Spencer has extensive training and experience in the fields of health and sports psychology. He earned his master's degree in clinical psychology from West Chester University and his bachelor's degree in psychobiology from Lafayette College.

As an athlete, Dr. Spencer was an All-State High School wrestler and two-time captain of New Jersey State Championship wrestling teams. While in college, he was a tailback for Lafayette College's football team.

Dr. Spencer is a licensed psychologist in the states of Pennsylvania, Maryland, and Virginia. He is a member of the American Psychological Association, the Pennsylvania Psychological Association, and the Lehigh Valley Psychological and Counseling Association, and he is a credentialed speaker with the National Collegiate Athletic Association. He is actively involved with the Fellowship of Christian Athletes. Dr. Spencer resides in the beautiful Lehigh Valley of Pennsylvania with his wife and three children.

Dedication

This book is dedicated to our son, Scott Richards, who taught all of us that life is not about length but about breadth, that the only things we take from this life are those things we've given away. Scott, we'll see you in heaven.

Phil Richards, CLU, CFP, RHU

For Arthur Tron.
You taught me the way to treat people in life.
I am forever grateful.

Jarrod Spencer, Psy.D.

Contents

Foreword

Phil Richards and Dr. Jarrod Spencer are the perfect combination to write a book about your outlook on a professional career as well as an athletic career. It merges Phil's extraordinary career in the insurance and financial planning industry with Jarrod's experience and expertise in leading athletes to optimize their potential.

Phil's fifty years of experience and wisdom in the business world combined with Jarrod's ability to get athletes to believe in themselves is a recipe for success in any career, including parenthood.

They take a successful business model and apply it to everyday life. They get readers to see themselves in a way they never looked at themselves before. Phil and Jarrod give the reader a road map to get directly in touch with his or her soul. They give the reader a different perspective on how to set goals and, more importantly, how to achieve them.

They explain why you should never put limitations on yourself, no matter what you are trying to achieve. They make it clear that preparing properly to achieve goals maximizes your chances of achieving them. They also get you to understand that there is no substitute for commitment and hard work.

Phil and Jarrod illustrate why making things important in your life will make it easier for you to be successful in accomplishing them. In a unique way, the authors help athletes and team members prepare for professional careers. They also give coaches and managers a prescription for what they can do to help athletes and team members achieve goals.

The authors have captured the essence of encouraging people to become self-motivated.

—*Robert Ferraro, Founder and CEO, National High School Coaches Association*

Preface—So What Do I Do Now?

"True north is the internal compass that guides you successfully through life. It represents who you are as a human being at your deepest level. It is your orienting point—your fixed point in a spinning world—that helps you stay on track.... Your true north is based on what is most important to you, your most cherished values, your passions and motivations, the sources of satisfaction in your life."

Bill George
Author, *True North: Finding Your Authentic Leadership*

In navigational terms, the center of all direction is the North Star, Polaris, which marks the northern axis of the earth. For centuries, people have used the North Star as the starting point for finding their way. Despite the world's continuous transition, from day to night, from winter to spring, the North Star remains a comforting constant. Those who would set out on a journey would seek to find "true north" so that they could follow the right path to their ultimate destination.

In life, following your "true north" means finding the right path to follow in terms of your life's work, your vocation, the fulfillment of your God-given calling. The purpose of this book is to help you navigate the many choices you have so that you can find the most rewarding and personally satisfying path to happiness and contentment.

We live in a time of great uncertainty about the future. We all need a "true north" to guide us. In April 2011, a Gallup poll reported that 53 percent of non-retired Americans do not think they will have enough money to live comfortably in retirement, up sharply from about a third who felt this way in 2002.

Non-retired Americans now project that they will retire at age sixty-six, up from age sixty in 1995.[1]

Americans look to the economy for signs regarding how comfortably they will be able to retire. Continuing discussions about the economy and the fragility of the country's Social Security and Medicare programs have eroded Americans' confidence about the sufficiency of their monetary resources in retirement.

Having been in the insurance and financial services industry for fifty-one years, I have seen the market weather many storms. During the past few challenging years, while speaking with clients whose assets have diminished as a result of unfavorable market conditions, my advisors and I have heard this question many times: "So what do I do now?"

One strategy for coping with adversity is to focus on your strengths and delegate your areas of weakness to someone else. This strategy can help you whether you are managing a portfolio, training to run a marathon, building a business, or trying to advance in your career. There are actually quite a few parallels between business and sports; many businesspeople speak the sports language. In fact, a 2002 study by mutual fund company Oppenheimer found that male CEOs often have backgrounds in competitive sports and that 82 percent of executive businesswomen played organized sports after elementary school, vs. 61 percent of adult women in a separate Internet survey of the general population.[2]

Delegating your areas of weakness to someone else allows you to "hoard what you love." In July 2011, in a main-platform presentation that I delivered to four thousand attendees of the Asian Pacific Life Insurance Congress in Singapore, I discussed the concept of "hoard what you love, hire what you loathe." The idea gained great traction with the audience; they appreciated it and responded with extensive positive feedback and endless e-mails.

After returning from Singapore, I discussed the concept with three of my leading advisors who are perennial Top of the Table leaders: Shaun McDuffee, Todd Bramson, and Tom Haunty. They reinforced the merits of the concept and its use in accelerating the growth of a person's business, even for the very best of advisors.

---

1. "In US, 53 Percent Worry about Having Enough Money in Retirement," Gallup.com, April 25, 2011, accessed August 10, 2011, http://www.gallup.com/poll/147254/worry-having-enough -money-retirement.aspx.

2. Del Jones, "Many Successful Women Also Athletic," USAToday.com, last modified March 26, 2002, accessed August 15, 2011, http://www.usatoday.com/money/covers/2002-03-26-women -sports.htm.

The overwhelming validation I have received about this concept led me to partner with sports psychologist Dr. Jarrod Spencer to write a book on the idea. He is passionate about teaching people how their minds work. In doing so, he helps improve individuals' emotional health and ultimately, their performance. He works with several universities across the country as well as with national champions, world champions, Olympians, and high-school hopefuls. He likes to say that he equips athletes with the necessary tools for their psychological toolbox in sports and life.

I am certain of the concept's validity but thought it would lend additional credibility to the book if a trained professional collaborated with me in validating the data leading to the conclusions that I have come to. Someone once said, "That works in practice, but it'll never work in theory." With Dr. Jarrod Spencer's contributions, this idea works both in practice and in theory! We have identified Dr. Spencer's material in italics throughout this book. When you see italicized material, you will know it is attributed to him. When you see non-italicized material, you will know it is attributed to me.

While the book might appear to be geared to businesspeople, I believe its usefulness extends to just about anyone—senior citizens who must return to the work force, high school and college coaches, athletes, college seniors, corporate CEOs and managers, advisors in the insurance and financial services industry, and anyone else who is striving to better their situation in some way.

Acknowledgments

Phil Richards, CLU, CFP, RHU

Five organizations have contributed significantly to my half-century journey leading up to this book, and I would like to recognize and thank each of them:

1. The **National High School Coaches Association** and its members, in honor of John Maitland, a high school wrestling coach who saw far more in me than I did in myself and pushed me to a college degree that was clearly not on my radar screen. Their 350,000 members selflessly do likewise with our youth every day.

2. **Temple University**, which gave this tenement dweller a four-year free ride as it does so many others who can't afford it, changing the trajectory of their lives for the better, forever.

3. **GAMA International**, whose mission of growing leaders who grow the financial services industry has succeeded in helping millions of beneficiaries who don't even know it exists.

4. The **National Association of Insurance and Financial Advisors**, whose members, for more than a century, have focused on and helped widows, widowers, and orphans in their darkest hour and have helped save jobs and businesses.

5. **The American College of Financial Services**, whose 140,000 graduates have demonstrated their commitment to excellence in serving Americans in profound ways and who represent the very best in the financial services industry. Their imminent transition to university status is a testimony to the excellent leadership of their visionary president and CEO, Dr. Larry Barton. Their Chartered Life Underwriter and Chartered Financial Consultant designations are the gold standard of our industry.

These five organizations have occupied the higher moral ground in my life, and my hope is that you'll accept my profits from this book as an insufficient token of my appreciation for all you have done for me and the beliefs I hold dear.

I also wish to thank my co-author, Dr. Jarrod Spencer, without whose contributions this work simply wouldn't have happened. Additionally, Libbye Morris, as she did with my first book, selflessly provided the laborious writing and editing that could have occurred only with her many gifts and talents. My assistant, Jacci Umphress, and my team member, Lacey Struckman, have proven to be the forces behind the scene without whose help this manuscript would still be on the drawing board. And finally, to my wife and partner, Sue, whose patience and support are well known to family and friends alike, and whose faith is an inspiration to everyone.

Jarrod Spencer, Psy.D.

Above all else, I want to thank God for clarifying my calling in life and blessing me with this path.

To Phil Richards—I am grateful for this opportunity you have given me to write this book with you.

To Libbye Morris—Your positive energy throughout this project has been inspiring. Thank you.

To my best friend and wife, Abby Spencer—Your presence beside me strengthens me daily. I love you.

To Dr. Glenn Asquith—Your guidance has helped me follow my true north. Thank you.

To the Mind of the Athlete staff—Our mission and ministry thrive because of you. Thank you.

To the people of Fellowship of Christian Athletes—Your fellowship along this journey matters most. I am grateful.

Introduction—For Everyone Who Seeks Their Calling

Psychologist Ernest Becker said, "Psychotherapy is such a growing vogue today because people want to know why they are unhappy."

We believe that many people are unhappy because they are spending the better part of every day—and 60 percent of their lives—in the wrong profession or vocation. As you'll discover in Chapter 2, those who "live where they want with the people they love, doing the right thing, on purpose" are more likely to be happy than those who do not. "Doing the right thing" includes doing whatever energizes you and makes you eager to get out of bed every day so that you can participate in a job or activity that you love.

In this book, we provide a simple exercise to help you find the vocation that will fulfill you and make you happy—your "true north."

Who Is This Book For?

College Students and Recent Graduates

People who are beginning their careers often do so with little guidance. Choosing a major in college is often done on a whim, according to a loved one's suggestion, or through a modest amount of trial and error. Few people purposefully assess their vocational likes, dislikes, and aptitude before entering the workforce. This book is for those young people who are embarking on their life's work and searching for a vocation that will fulfill them—not just financially, but also mentally, spiritually, and emotionally.

A lot of us, myself included, stumbled into our careers. I stayed in the insurance and financial services industry because I loved it, but that was serendipitous. It certainly wasn't a plan that I had. In fact, I recently completed a survey for Dwight Carey, a Fox School of Management professor who is writing a book about successful Temple University graduates. One of the questions in his survey was "Did you have a plan for your working life when you graduated from undergraduate school?" Absolutely not! Most people don't. In fact, I've seen studies indicating that many young people graduating from college plan to take any job for two years or less just to get some experience. If they would complete the exercise in Chapter 1 of this book, they could move right into a fulfilling career that makes them happy instead of wasting two or more years in a job they may hate or that may provide experience that proves useless in their future vocation.

Very few people are fortunate enough to fall into the type of work they love. For most, self-reflection is required to determine life's true calling. This book helps you through that process.

Senior Citizens Who May Be Working Longer

It's never too late to discover your passion. At any time and at any age, you can reassess your life's work and make a change. In fact, many middle-aged and older Americans may be forced to continue their careers because of the current economic climate or individual circumstances. Today, millions who thought they could retire are staying in the workforce or entering second careers. Most believe they can't change vocations for any one of a number of reasons. We believe they can. We also believe that "can't" is a word of victimization and that we always have choices. Believing this opens many doors that the word "can't" slammed shut.

According to a September 2011 article in *The Wall Street Journal*, the percentage of US households with heads ages sixty to sixty-four who have primary mortgages has almost doubled, from a little over 20 percent to 40 percent. More Americans are reaching their sixties with so much debt they can't afford to retire.[3] Many have seen their 401(k) plans reduced to 201(k) plans due to the markets. Because so many of us are living longer, either the amount we must save has increased dramatically or we must work longer. Stretching for higher returns on our savings usually involves added risk and is generally imprudent for those close to retirement.

The housing crash has made things worse. A few years ago, homeowners in their sixties with big mortgages could sell their homes for a profit and buy a smaller place or rent. But the drop in housing values means that many homeowners have

---

3. E. S. Browning, "Older Americans Held Hostage by Mortgages," *The Wall Street Journal*, September 7, 2011, A1.

little equity, and some now owe more than their houses are worth. Many have little choice but to keep working.[4]

Why not work in a fulfilling and energizing career, especially if your former career was pure drudgery? This book is also intended for those people who are being forced to work longer than they had anticipated, as well as those middle-aged and older Americans who do have resources but who have retired and are looking for fulfillment as they embark on the next phase of their lives—a second calling.

The Half of the American Workforce That Is Unhappy

Sister Mary Loretta said, "To be successful, the first thing to do is to fall in love with your work. In other words, the secret to happiness, success, satisfaction, and fulfillment in our work is not doing what one likes but in liking what one does. When all else fails, listen to the advice of the seven dwarfs: Whistle while you work."

Unfortunately, the number of people who are unhappy in their jobs is staggering. In 1990, *Boardroom Report* indicated that upwards of 70 percent of all white-collar workers were dissatisfied with their jobs. Of those, 40 percent said they would be happier working someplace else. More than one-third of 1,100 middle managers surveyed had been in touch with a job-search company in the previous six months. More than half said that they had recently updated their résumés. Another survey of five hundred people found that one-third of sales reps surveyed were on the verge of quitting their jobs. Another 40 percent said that they were only moderately happy with their positions. Furthermore, the American Bar Association found that one-fourth of the three thousand lawyers it surveyed planned to change jobs in the next two years. In addition, in a survey conducted by the Wilson Learning Corporation, 1,500 people were asked, "If you had enough money to live comfortably for the rest of your life, would you continue to work?" Seventy percent said they would continue to work, but 60 percent of those said they would change jobs and seek more satisfying work.[5]

More recently, in 2010, the Conference Board Research Group found that only 45 percent of Americans were satisfied with their work. That was the lowest level ever recorded by the group in more than twenty-two years of studying the issue. In 2008, 49 percent of those surveyed reported satisfaction with their jobs. That means that 55 percent of Americans are unhappy in their jobs. Workers have grown steadily less happy for a variety of reasons, one of which is the fact that

---

4. Ibid.

5. *Boardroom Report*, April 1990, 398.

fewer workers consider their jobs to be interesting.[6] These unhappy workers are likely asking themselves an important question posed by Michael Gerber, author of the renowned book *The E-Myth Revisited*: "How can I spend my time doing the work I love to do rather than the work I have to do?"[7]

People who know what they like to do and are good at it will most likely find their jobs interesting; as a result, they will be happy in their jobs.

This book is for those people who are unhappy in their jobs—those whose mantra is "I'll do my eight and hit the gate."

Coaches, Especially Those Growing Our Youngsters at the High-School Level

Identifying youngsters' natural abilities and gifts at an early stage can be crucial to their success, as well as to that of the team. The lessons and examples found in this work can be very useful to a "conscious competent" coach in guiding our youth to the sport(s) or positions in which they can truly excel. While the financial rewards of coaching may be limited, the satisfaction that accompanies the great guidance of youngsters can provide purpose and can be a game changer.

Professionals Who Are Building Businesses

This book is for anyone who is building a business, including financial planners, professional medical providers, and aspiring entrepreneurs.

For businesses, the consequences of an unhappy workforce are costly. The Research Institute of America conducted a study for the White House Office of Consumer Affairs in 1985. Their findings should provide ample food for thought for CEOs and managers who are apathetic about customer service. Here are the findings:

- The average business will hear nothing from 96 percent of unhappy customers who receive rude or discourteous treatment.

---

6. "Survey: More Americans Unhappy at Work," CBSNews.com, last modified January 5, 2010, accessed September 19, 2011, http://www.cbsnews.com/stories/2010/01/05/national/main6056611 .shtml.

7. Michael E. Gerber, "Your Business Can Be More than Just a Job," Inc. website, last modified March 9, 2012, accessed November 28, 2013, http://www.inc.com/michael-gerber/your-business -can-be-more-than-just-a-job.html.

- Also, 90 percent of customers who are dissatisfied with the service they receive will not come back or buy again.
- Each of those unhappy customers will tell his or her story to at least nine other people, and 13 percent of those unhappy former customers relate their stories to more than twenty people.

Today, using the Internet, a dissatisfied customer can communicate that dissatisfaction to thousands or tens of thousands quickly with horrific potential consequences.

Additional research indicates that for every complaint received, the average company has twenty-six customers with problems, six of which are serious problems. Only 4 percent of unhappy customers bother to complain. For every complaint we hear, twenty-four others are never communicated to the company but are communicated to other potential customers. Of the customers who register a complaint, between 54 and 70 percent will do business again with the organization if their complaint is resolved. That figure rises to 95 percent if the customer feels the complaint was resolved quickly. Sixty-eight percent of customers who quit doing business with an organization do so because of company indifference. It takes twelve positive incidents to make up for one negative incident in the eyes of customers.

Hiring people who love what they do will do wonders for your company's customer service ratings. In Chapter 3, we provide interview questions that will help you select people with the attitude and aptitude to succeed in your organization. Later in this book, we describe in detail the mission of Zappos Shoes, which is "delivering happiness"—one of the reasons why Amazon bought the online shoe company for $850 million.

The Small-Business Owner

If they're successful, small-business owners eventually will need to hire someone to help them with their business. Every business reaches the point where it's going to expand because one person can't do it all. This book is for them, too. The exercise in Chapter 1 will help them determine not only what their own strengths are, but also the ideal type of support staff to seek.

In the insurance and financial services industry, we tell our salespeople to hire well *before* they can afford it. If people waited to expand their companies based on the cost of labor and when their profits justified it, very few businesses would expand successfully. Our own advisors are encouraged to hire interns, sometimes unpaid, to expand their practices before cash flow enables this expansion. As an aside, the interns are tested beforehand to determine if they will qualify as an advisor in the future. We do this to remedy the mistake we've made so often in the past—namely, falling in love with the young person, only to find that he or she is unqualified when later tested. In those instances in which we hired the person anyway, we experienced horrible results. Testing them before they're hired as interns eliminates this unwanted outcome. It also is the charitable thing to do for the young person who is spared the loss of a year or so of his or her life spent in the wrong vocation.

People Who Are Suffering from Stress-Related Illnesses

Being in the wrong line of work can and often does cause one to experience immense stress, which, in turn, leads to illness and, in many cases, premature death.

Dr. Paul J. Rosch is president of The American Institute of Stress, Clinical Professor of Medicine and Psychiatry at New York Medical College, and Honorary Vice President of the International Stress Management Association. He said, "In most instances, it's not the individual or the job that causes burnout. Rather, burnout is the result of a mismatch between the personality or the goals of the worker and the job description or the expectations of the workplace." He goes on to say, "Realize that stress is an unavoidable consequence of life. But stress is not burnout. Burnout is burnout. When was the last time you woke up totally refreshed, ready for the day? How long did you remain energized, excited, and exuberant about the day's activities? For far too many people, the stressors of life have zapped their ability to do their best, be their best, and enjoy their daily activities. Consider for a moment that one million Americans have a heart attack each year; thirteen billion doses of tranquilizers, barbiturates, and amphetamines are prescribed yearly; eight million Americans have stomach ulcers; and there are an estimated fifty thousand stress-related suicides each year. And we have twelve million people struggling with alcoholism in this country."

Stress accounts for two-thirds of family doctor visits and half the deaths of Americans under the age of sixty-five, according to the US Centers for Disease Control and Prevention. The American Medical Association concurs, saying that stress is a factor in more than 75 percent of all illness and disease today.

Imaging research at the University of Florida showed how mental stress can decrease someone's blood flow to the heart. A report in Circulation: Journal of the American Heart Association *equated stress with bad cholesterol and smoking as risk factors for coronary heart disease patients.*

Could you be suffering from a stress-related illness? If so, is being in the wrong profession the source of that stress? If it is, this book can help. Discovering what you love to do and do not love to do can be cathartic and freeing. You don't have to accept your fate in a vocation that leaves you unfulfilled and stressed. You can change your career path and commit to your lifelong dream at any age.

It's important to try to enjoy your work, even if you're not yet able to engage in the work you really want to do. There is a story about a Zen master who worked at a train station. His job was to clean, so he would clean and polish everything he could until it was shiny and beautiful. The work was mundane and tedious, yet he considered it an act of service, of being in the moment. He saw the beauty in his work. He found meaning in what he was doing, but it came from a spiritual plane.

While you're on that journey, even if you're in a position you're not thrilled about, try to make it about something more than just the tasks you're expected to complete. Be in awe of, and in service to, God. Make a stellar contribution wherever you are.

Many people have endured their less-than-ideal vocations for years, subscribing to B. C. Forbes's belief that "Whether we find pleasure in our work or whether we find it a bore depends entirely on our mental attitude toward it, not upon the task itself." But wouldn't it be better to enjoy your work instead of just enduring it?

We hope this book will help you identify what you do and do not enjoy doing so that you can spend your time doing what you love. That will lead to more contentment, better health, and a more fulfilling and rewarding life.

It's Not about the Money

In Srully Blotnick's *Getting Rich Your Own Way*, 1,500 people were divided into two groups and followed for twenty years. Group A, made up of 83 percent of the sample, embarked on careers chosen for the reason of making money now so that they could do what they wanted to later. Group B, the other 17 percent, chose their careers based on what they wanted to do now; they would worry about the money later. The data revealed some startling discoveries. At the end of twenty years, 101 of the 1,500 candidates had become millionaires. Of the millionaires, all but one were from Group B, the group that had chosen to pursue what they loved. According to this research, people who set out to make their million without serious consideration of their philosophy of life or which career would bring meaning and fulfillment are apt to be disappointed.[8]

---

8. Srully Blotnick, *Getting Rich Your Own Way* (Playboy Paperbacks, 1982).

It's not about the money, though. Think of the many people who had money but died miserable—sometimes long before they should have. Setting out to achieve wealth alone is a hollow experience in the end. Henry Ward Beecher said, "Very few men acquire wealth in such a manner as to receive pleasure from it. As long as there is the enthusiasm of the chase, they enjoy it. But when they begin to look around and think of settling down, they find that that part by which joy enters in is dead in them. They have spent their lives in heaping up colossal piles of treasure, which stand at the end like the pyramids in the desert, holding only the dust of things."

Instead, find your true passion and calling in life, your true north. That will ensure that every day is rewarding in and of itself. The sky is not the limit in terms of what you can achieve. Follow the guidelines in this book, and you can discover the potential that lies deep within you.

Chapter

1

Focus on Your Strengths, Delegate Your Weaknesses

*Success is achieved by developing our strengths, not by
eliminating our weaknesses.*

Marilyn vos Savant
American Journalist and Columnist

When I wrestled competitively in high school and college, I was a "counter-wrestler." I wasn't fast enough for a strong offensive approach, but I was quick enough to react defensively. My strategy was to wait for my opponent to make a mistake and then capitalize on it by making a counter-move against him. I knew I'd never be fast, so I didn't waste time trying to become faster. Instead, I honed my defensive skills to make them even stronger. This concept applies to management and leadership, too.

A Story about Chinese Table Tennis

One day in 1973, I was asked to give a presentation on this concept to a group of John Hancock managers in Atlanta. The presentation was titled "The Art of Management in an Age of Uncertainty," and I had been giving it to various groups for a number of years. In the presentation, I advised managers to find out what they really loved doing and to backfill the things they didn't like to do by hiring people who were good at those things.

My contact at John Hancock was a regional vice president named Roy Diliberto, who later became the first president of the Financial Planning Association. Roy and I attended Temple University together and have been friends since. At the reception following the presentation, Roy said, "You know, Phil, the subject of your presentation is the philosophy behind an article I recently read about Chinese table tennis." That piqued my interest, and I asked him to tell me more about it.

According to the article, South Korea dominated table tennis in the mid-twentieth century, but at the world championships, the Chinese fielded a team at the international level for the first time ever. They didn't just beat the Koreans in the finals—they embarrassed them. After the tournament, a sportswriter from the United States approached the coach of the Chinese table tennis team and asked, "How did you do that?"

"It's very easy," the coach replied. "We practice eight hours a day."

We practice only the things we're good at, and we ignore the things we don't do well.

The writer said, "Come on, now. Everybody here practices at least eight hours a day. There must be more to it than that."

"We practice differently," the coach said. "You see, we practice only the things we're good at, and we ignore the things we don't do well. So if we have a player who wins a regional table tennis championship in Guangdong Province and makes it to the nationals because she has a strong serve, we focus on improving her serve and not her weak backhand. We believe that if we can make her strengths strong enough, her weaknesses will not matter."

What an epiphany! Now I had a compelling metaphor that I could use to illustrate this important concept.

Over the years, I have shared that presentation with hundreds of companies in more than a dozen countries. I began telling people, "Write down the things you're good at and then focus on those things." That led to "Write down the things you hate to do." And just two years ago, I began telling my audiences, "Why don't you write down the top fifteen to twenty-one functions in your job description that allow you to succeed. Then place a '1' in front of the task you love to do the most and a '21' in front of the task you hate to do the most." At the Asian Pacific Life Insurance Congress in Singapore in 2011, I shared this exercise with the four thousand attendees and observed the universality of its application to citizens of many Southeast Asian countries.

My own top advisors have told me that the exercise has helped them focus more on the things they're good at and enjoy doing. They are able to become "conscious competents." They're consciously doing the things they really love to do, and they're offloading most or all of the things they don't like to do. The result is that both their income and their enjoyment have increased.

Recently, while giving a presentation in Bangkok, Thailand, through an interpreter, I had an interesting experience. As I was speaking, I sensed that the audience wasn't getting the point of my Chinese table tennis story, and I struggled to find a way to bring the point home. Then, as if from heaven, a story from my childhood came to me. It not only helped me make my point about focusing on your strengths but generated a lot of discussion after my presentation.

I told my audience that in junior high school, I played football, baseball, and basketball. One day, it occurred to me that I was one of the slower members of every team I was on, but I knew that I wanted to excel in athletics. I had been a pretty good boxer in New York City where I grew up, but boxing was not available at my high school or college in Pennsylvania. So I began thinking, *What can I do?* I realized I had not been beaten in street wrestling to that point. I also realized that my feet were very big. When I was in the tenth grade, I wore a size 12 shoe, and I was only 5'9". Big feet are an asset in wrestling, especially if you are a leg wrestler, which I became. The leg is six times stronger than the arm. To be a good wrestler, you need not have super-strong legs because weak legs are still much stronger than another wrestler's arms. I also noted that quickness is a major asset in wrestling, and even though I was a slow runner, I was extremely quick at hand–eye coordination games and on the wrestling mat.

So I rediscovered wrestling and succeeded at it. I am convinced that I would never have excelled in any other sport that I know of. Not only did the decision to wrestle get me a four-year full wrestling scholarship to Temple, but in 2010, it resulted in my being inducted into the National Wrestling Hall of Fame. That story at the Singapore presentation got a standing ovation from the thousands of people in the audience. *Not bad for a short, slow guy with big feet,* I thought. Believe me when I say I was grateful for the heavenly impromptu inspiration that allowed me to make the point that you must focus on what you are good at and marginalize your shortcomings.

Before that moment, while speaking to that Bangkok audience, I had never thought of or verbalized that story, but it helped me clarify my point that you've got to find out what your talent is, and sometimes it happens by experimentation and soul searching. I did that, however, as an unconscious incompetent. Today I would recommend that parents think about what their kids are good at and about how they can help their children discover and leverage their strengths and gifts.

It Works in Baseball, Too

Many athletes abide by this concept of focusing on your strengths.

Minnesota Twins pitcher Jim Kaat once traced his success back to spring training in 1966. The Twins had acquired a new pitching coach, Johnny Sain, who silently watched the pitchers perform. One by one, he called them in for a personal chat.

"Jim," said Sain, "I've been watching you pitch. What are your four best pitches?"

Kaat, knowing his pitching ability well, responded, "My best pitch is my fastball, then come my curve, my slider, and my changeup."

"What pitch do you spend the most time practicing?" asked Sain.

"My slider and changeup," said Kaat. "If I can improve on those two pitches, I know I'll have a good season."

Sain looked at Kaat, pondered his comments, and then responded, "I see it a little differently, Jim. I want you to take a different approach. Work on your fastball. I know it's your favorite pitch, so go out there and practice during warm-ups and games and concentrate on your fastball. Throw your fastball eighty to ninety percent of the time all year, and you'll win a lot of ball games."

Kaat left Sain's office stunned. He had expected expert tips for improving his changeup or slider. He thought that Sain could have at least provided technical advice for smoothing out his curveball. But telling him to do more of what he already did best didn't make much sense.

During that season in 1966, Jim Kaat threw fastball after fastball. He said he thought his arm was going to fall off, but he heeded the advice of his coach. In 1966, Kaat won twenty-six games and went on to become the American League's Pitcher of the Year.[9]

---

9. Leo Hauser, *Leo Hauser's Five Steps to Success* (Wayzata, Minnesota: Hauser Productions, 1993), as cited in Glenn Van Ekeren, *Speaker's Sourcebook II* (New York: Penguin Putnam Inc., 1994), 7.

Whether you're in sports or in business, you will excel by focusing on your strengths and marginalizing your weaknesses.

Peter Drucker's Feedback Analysis

To focus on your strengths, you first need to know what they are. Renowned business author and management consultant Peter Drucker believed that people are more likely to know what they're not good at than to know the areas in which they excel. "And yet, one can only perform with one's strengths," he said. "One cannot build performance on weaknesses, let alone on something one cannot do at all. People...have to know their strengths so that they can know where they belong."[10]

Drucker suggested that the best way to find out what your strengths are is to complete what he called the feedback analysis.

> To focus on your strengths, you first need to know what they are.

"Whenever one makes a key decision, and whenever one does a key action, one writes down what one expects will happen. And nine months or twelve months later, one then feeds back from results to expectations.... Within a fairly short period of time, maybe two or three years, this simple procedure will tell people first where their strengths are—and this is probably the most important thing to know about oneself. It will show them what they do or fail to do that deprives them of the full yield from their strengths. It will show them where they are not particularly competent. And finally, it will show them where they have no strengths and cannot perform."[11]

After completing the feedback analysis, Drucker asked the reader to consider several conclusions. "The first, and most important, conclusion: Concentrate on your strengths. Place yourself where your strengths can produce performance and results. Second: Work on improving your strengths. The feedback analysis rapidly shows where a person needs to improve skills or has to acquire new

---

10. Peter F. Drucker, *The Essential Drucker: The Best of Sixty Years of Peter Drucker's Essential Writings on Management* (New York: Harper Paperbacks, 2008), 218.

11. Ibid., 218–219.

knowledge. It will show where existing skills and knowledge are no longer adequate and have to be updated. It will also show the gaps in one's knowledge."[12]

Finding Your Strengths

Millions of people have used an assessment tool called StrengthsFinder to discover their top five talents. In 2001, Gallup introduced the first version of the tool in the book Now, Discover Your Strengths; *it spent more than five years on various best-seller lists.*

In 2007, the Gallup Press published a sequel to the book, StrengthsFinder 2.0,[13] *which introduced a new and improved version of its popular assessment. The book contends that throughout our lives, we devote more time to fixing our shortcomings than to developing our strengths. It also states that people who have the opportunity to focus on their strengths every day are six times as likely to be engaged in their jobs and more than three times as likely to report having an excellent quality of life in general.[14]*

When you're looking for somebody to
propel your business or your athletic ability
to the next level, you should be partnering
with someone who has the skills
you don't have.

Hiring to Backfill Your Weaknesses

Once you find out what your strengths and weaknesses are, that tells you where you need help. You need to hire people who excel in your areas of weakness. But we tend to get that backwards—we hire people not only whose values are the same as ours, but whose likes, dislikes, and skills are the same as ours. That works great when you're looking for a friend or a mate. But when you're looking for somebody to propel your business or your athletic ability to the next level, then you should be partnering with someone who has the skills you don't have.

---

12. Ibid., 219.

13. Tom Rath, *StrengthsFinder 2.0* (New York: Gallup Press, 2007).

14. Ibid., iii.

Ellen Voie, CAE, president of the Women in Trucking Association, said it well: "I've learned to admit that I'm not the best in some areas, but I find great employees who excel in those spaces."

I recommend that you list your top twenty-one job functions, in order of what you like to do the most all the way down to what you like to do the least. The bottom items (items 16–21, for example) on that list become the job description of the first person you're going to hire. Then the least-liked aspects of your job will be done by someone else, and you'll be doing the top fifteen. If you hire a second person, he or she should be good at items 11–15 on your list, for example. Your third hire should be good at items 6–10 on your list. That will free you up to focus on items 1–5. For new coaches, advisors, or businesspeople, consider hiring a college intern as your first hire and using your twenty-one un-numbered tasks as your selection device.

Our minds are hardwired to look favorably on others who share our values and enjoy the same things we do. That's the mistake most of us make. Sharing common values is important, but focusing on similar likes in business causes conflicts, and it challenges both parties in accomplishing the tasks at the lower end of the list, since neither person really wants to do those.

Phil Richards's Twenty-One Job Functions

1. Growing leaders
2. Being a visionary
3. Industry relations
4. Institutional memory
5. Strategic planning
6. Recruiting
7. Selection
8. Marketing
9. Management
10. Supervision
11. Handling legal issues
12. Human resources
13. Meeting planning
14. Employee benefits
15. Client relations management
16. Compliance
17. Accounting
18. Financials
19. Technology
20. Detailed paperwork, reports
21. Sales

At age seventy-three, I am often asked when I am going to retire. Why would I want to retire? After a career of figuring out what I am good at and enjoy doing, I am now focusing on only the first four items on my list of twenty-one tasks—

growing leaders, being a visionary, industry relations, and institutional memory. I am working in the dream job of a lifetime. The seventeen things I don't like to do or hate to do have no part of my day—I have delegated them to others who enjoy doing them and, quite frankly, are better at them than I am. This is a pathway to happiness and fulfillment. As my colleague Todd Bramson often says, "Work less, earn more, have more fun." That's living the dream. Try it.

Dr. Jarrod Spencer's Twenty-One Job Functions

1. *Professional speaking*
2. *Sharing psychology via media (video, audio)*
3. *Preaching*
4. *Preparing speeches*
5. *Learning about the mind*
6. *One-on-one coaching*
7. *Mentoring*
8. *Consulting*
9. *Vision casting*
10. *Writing*
11. *Strategizing*
12. *Marketing*
13. *Business development*
14. *Developing relationships*
15. *Attending athletic events*
16. *Sending e-mails*
17. *Sales*
18. *Administration*
19. *Office management*
20. *Charting*
21. *Financials*

Focusing on your strengths is a winning strategy that many successful people abide by. In an article in the August 13, 2012, issue of the *Star Tribune*, based in Minneapolis, my friend Harvey Mackay, *New York Times* number-one best-selling author of *Swim with the Sharks without Being Eaten Alive* and nationally syndicated columnist, invited Darren Hardy, publisher of *Success* magazine, to make a presentation to a group of businesspeople he was mentoring. In his presentation, Hardy noted that a distinction of super-achievers is that they become world-class at a few tasks instead of trying to be great at a lot of things.

"What are your vital functions?" Mackay writes. "What are the three vital functions that only you can do? What are the three functions that contribute the most to the success of your business or job? If you take the time to write them down, it will force you to focus your attention on what it is you should be doing every day." Hardy's personal goal is to spend 90 percent of his time on his top three functions.[15]

---

15. Harvey Mackay, "The Secrets to Success? You Might Be Surprised," *Star Tribune*, August 13, 2012, D3.

Author and performance consultant Dr. Kevin Elko has similar advice. He says there are two "knowings" that are placed in you: (1) what your gift is and (2) what you are to do with it. He says everybody has a gift, and sometimes people make the mistake of thinking they have many gifts and trying to develop all of them. Or they try to develop one they wish they had. "It is about getting honest with what your best gift is, developing it, and letting it shine," Elko says. "You are called to do the work that is rightfully yours—just do that work. Do not desire to be anybody else—all the mystery and power you need is in that rightful work. We are to love nothing other than that which comes to us, woven in the pattern of our destiny. What could better fit our needs?"[16]

Supporting the Technician in All of Us

In *The E-Myth Revisited*, Michael Gerber contends that everybody who goes into business is actually three people in one: an entrepreneur, a manager, and a technician.[17] He adds that the typical small-business owner is 10 percent entrepreneur, 20 percent manager, and 70 percent technician.[18] The entrepreneur is the person who dreams up the business and is willing to finance it and take risks. The manager is the numbers person who keeps the venture afloat and is able to make payroll. The technician—or what I like to call the carpenter or artist—is the one who does the actual work. When new business owners start out, they can't afford to hire anyone, so they personally fill all three roles.

> Everybody who goes into business
> is actually three people in one: an
> entrepreneur, a manager, and a technician.

Gerber provides an example of a pastry-shop owner who is first and foremost a baker (the artist). She bakes every day at two o'clock in the morning, keeps the books, and makes all of the business decisions. As the business grows, she realizes she can't do everything, so she hires someone—but it has to be the right person. She needs to hire somebody who's going to be the entrepreneur and the marketer, raise the money, handle the financing, and do the books.

---

16. Dr. Kevin Elko, "Five Questions That Will Change Your Life," accessed on June 10, 2012, drelko.com/.

17. Michael E. Gerber, *The E-Myth Revisited: Why Most Small Businesses Don't Work and What to Do About It* (New York: HarperCollins, 1995), 19.

18. Ibid., 29.

That artist, carpenter, or baker has to *do things right*. The businessperson, on the other hand—the entrepreneur or CEO—has to *do the right things*. It's a critical difference. If you're a carpenter and you don't do things right, you're out of business. If you're an entrepreneur and you don't do the right things, you're out of business, just the same, but for different reasons. All Michelangelo had to do was be able to paint beautifully. The decision regarding where and how he should paint fell to Pope Julius II, who had to do the right thing. He wanted the Sistine Chapel ceiling painted over the objections of Michelangelo. He could have had Michelangelo paint on the side of a stone wall, but history shows that would have been the wrong thing to do, especially because the elements probably would have eroded the painting by now.

> To have that efficient, effective business,
> you first need to know which role you
> are best suited for—that of entrepreneur,
> manager, or technician.

Gerber goes on to say that you have to build your business as if you were franchising it. Picture five hundred or one thousand businesses just like yours. If you manage it right, then it will be transferable—someone else could run your business efficiently and effectively, even if you weren't there to guide it. Gerber suggests hiring the person who is least qualified to do the job you want done successfully. You don't want a PhD flipping hamburgers at McDonald's because someday he or she will leave you. For that job, you want the least-educated, least-qualified person who is capable of flipping hamburgers properly because, chances are, he or she is less likely to be able to get a job anywhere else and will be more grateful for the job long term, so you're going to have better stability in your workforce and greater profitability.

To have that efficient, effective business, you first need to know which role you are best suited for—that of entrepreneur, manager, or technician. Embrace that role—do what you love and are good at—and complement your skill set by hiring people who are good at those tasks you don't like to do.

WWJD?

When addressing audiences, I frequently tell leaders and managers to suppose that Jack Welch—the chairman and CEO of General Electric between 1981 and

2001—came to work for your company as the chief executive officer or chairman of the board. What changes would he make? What would Jack do?

It's Your Turn

Exercise 1-1: What are your strengths and weaknesses?

Write down twenty-one functions that are vital to the successful performance of your job. Rank them in order of your preferences, with number one being the thing you love/enjoy doing the most and number twenty-one being the function you dislike/hate doing the most.

1. _____   12. _____
2. _____   13. _____
3. _____   14. _____
4. _____   15. _____
5. _____   16. _____
6. _____   17. _____
7. _____   18. _____
8. _____   19. _____
9. _____   20. _____
10. _____   21. _____
11. _____

Exercise 1-2: Who are you?

Michael Gerber, author of *The E-Myth Revisited*, believes that every business-person is three people in one: an entrepreneur, a manager, and a technician. Of these three roles, which one describes you best, next best, and least? Hint: Look at your twenty-one activities above.

1. _____
2. _____
3. _____

If you are in business for yourself and are more of a technician than an entrepreneur or manager—in other words, if you are an accountant, financial services advisor, writer, caretaker, or artist—then you'll need to hire someone to handle the entrepreneurial and managerial sides of the business. Don't hire someone else who is good at what you do.

Exercise 1-3: What if you were your biggest competitor?

Ask yourself the following questions to improve your business or game and position yourself for success:

If you were your biggest competitor, what would you do? How would you attack your business?

_____

_____

_____

_____

What changes should you make to your business to insulate it from those attacks?

_____

_____

_____

_____

Exercise 1-4: What changes would consultant Jack Welch advise in your business or life that you should execute?

_____

_____

_____

_____

2

Living Purposefully

*The high prize of life, the crowning fortune of man, is to
be born with a bias to some pursuit which finds him in
employment and happiness.*

Ralph Waldo Emerson
American Poet

I believe that purposeful living is a requirement for happiness. Legendary executive coach Richard J. (Dick) Leider[19] says that the four components of happiness are to live where you want, with the people you love, doing the right thing, on purpose.

The Ten-Thousand-Hour Rule

In his 2011 book *Outliers*, Malcolm Gladwell repeatedly mentions the "ten-thousand-hour rule," claiming that the key to success in any field is, to a large extent, a matter of practicing a specific task for a total of about ten thousand hours. "Ten thousand hours is the magic number of greatness," he says.[20] In another 2011 book titled *Bounce*, however, Matthew Syed contends that spending ten thousand hours on an endeavor contributes to a person's skill level only if they are purposeful hours.[21]

---

19. Dick Leider's website, "Living on Purpose," accessed on November 28, 2013, www.richardleider .com.

20. Malcolm Gladwell, *Outliers: The Story of Success* (New York: Little, Brown & Company, 2011), 41.

21. Matthew Syed, *Bounce: Mozart, Federer, Picasso, Beckham, and the Science of Success* (New York: HarperCollins Publishers, 2011), 92.

Syed, the table tennis champion of Great Britain, argues that many of us have driven ten thousand hours in a car, but that doesn't make us great drivers. It's because those hours were not spent driving purposefully. He also gives an example of his mother, who typed 70 words per minute consistently for thirty years. She typed for more than ten thousand hours, yet she never improved her speed. But researchers conducted an experiment in which typists were provided with many hours of purposeful practice. Some of them eventually increased their speed to 140 words per minute. "That is the thing about purposeful practice: It is transformative," Syed says. "And that is true whether you're into table tennis, tennis, soccer, basketball, football, typing, medicine, mathematics, music, journalism, public speaking—you name it."[22]

> What is actually required is ten thousand hours of *purposeful* practice, and for practice to be truly purposeful, you need concentration, dedication, and access to the right training.

So the ten-thousand-hour rule is inadequate as a predictor of excellence. What is actually required is ten thousand hours of *purposeful* practice, and for practice to be truly purposeful, you need concentration, dedication, and access to the right training. Sometimes that means living in the right town or having the right coach. But always it is the result of a determined effort to excel, to try to be the best you can be.

Correcting Our Course

To be the best at what we do, we sometimes need to correct our course of action. In the 1960 book *Psycho-Cybernetics*, Maxwell Maltz, a cosmetic surgeon, likened the human brain and nervous system to an interceptor missile. The target or goal is known—for the missile, it's an enemy ship or plane. The objective is to reach it and hopefully destroy the target. The missile is equipped with radar and sonar sensors that propel it forward in the general direction of the target. These sensors tell the machine when it is on the correct course (positive feedback) and when it commits an error and gets off course (negative feedback). The missile does not respond to positive feedback; it simply stays on course. But if it receives

---

22. Ibid., 96.

negative feedback, the corrective mechanism automatically brings it back on course. "The torpedo accomplishes its goal by going forward, making errors, and continually correcting them," Maltz said—and that is also how humans make progress toward a goal.[23]

Only by making mistakes can we be successful and perfect our business or sports acumen. It's true in sales, too. I have calculated that, during the process of obtaining 350 clients, a financial services advisor will experience approximately twenty thousand rejections, either on the phone or in person. Advisors have no control over the number of rejections they will get, but they do have control over the duration of the pain associated with experiencing those rejections. They can learn to get their pain response out of the way in the first few years of their career so that they can really begin to enjoy the business, or they can stretch the pain out over ten or twenty years. We encourage them to jump right in and get their negative reaction to rejections over with in the first three years so that they're able to move on to a successful and enjoyable career serving others.

Encouragement and reassurance are powerful tools for helping people succeed. Some people have the luxury of a loving parent, mentor, or coach who said, "Don't worry about your mistake. I like that you were assertive," or "I like the fact that you tried something new. Get out there and try again." Encouraging effort is the key. The legendary UCLA basketball coach John Wooden never had his team's goal be to win the national championship but instead encouraged his players to be the very best they could be. They won ten national championships.

Many people, however, have never had the luxury of a positive role model to cheer them on and motivate them. Individuals who can encourage themselves even when they make mistakes, and reassure themselves even when they stray from the path forward, have a great advantage. Self-encouragement is a mindset that is incredibly valuable. We can learn how to encourage ourselves; it requires a conscious effort to acknowledge what we've done well and the areas where we need improvement.

Today, young people are often expected to select a single sport to play by the time they're freshmen in high school. They have to realize that they're good at a sport early on because, at the bigger schools, there is a lot of competition to be on the sports teams. It wasn't always like that.

Parents can encourage their children to find out, early on, where their strengths lie— and not just in the sports arena. Hearing those words "I see something in you" from a

---

23. Maxwell Maltz, *Psycho-Cybernetics: A New Way to Get More Living Out of Life* (New York: Simon & Schuster, 1960), 19, 20, 28.

role model early in life can be so powerful in shaping a child's path and setting him or her on the road to happiness. Praising someone, especially publically, is a tremendous tool and can serve as a game-changer in the life of a young person.

Intrinsic Motivation to Succeed

Thirty-year-old ice skater Shizuka Arakawa, now retired, was the 2006 Olympic Champion in Ladies Singles and the 2004 World Champion. During her career, she is estimated to have fallen down twenty thousand times. Each time, she got up and continued skating. She did not interpret falling down as failure. Armed with a growth mindset, she interpreted falling not merely as a means of improving, but as evidence that she was improving.[24]

The key is to have intrinsic, or internal, motivation.

Some individuals don't have the inner motivation to keep recovering once they've made a mistake. For some people, it's because they are paralyzed by the fear of success, which often can be more debilitating than the fear of failure. We tend to gravitate to what is familiar to us rather than what's preferred. An individual may understand intellectually that it would be good for him to become a state champion, but performing at the level required to accomplish that goal might put him outside of his comfort zone. He is bombarded with troublesome images and thoughts: If I'm the champion, then people will expect more of me *and* What happens if I don't win the next one? *Worse, this person may avoid the very best competitions for fear of losing and exposing himself as something other than a champion.*

To avoid this type of paralysis, you have to become accustomed to being successful. You have to get comfortable operating outside your comfort zone. In other words, you have to become comfortable being uncomfortable. That's a tough thing to do for some individuals.

The key is to have intrinsic, or internal, motivation. There are intrinsic and extrinsic motivations. Extrinsic motivation comes from an external source—wanting to get a promotion so that you can make more money, for example. Intrinsic motivation comes from an internal source—wanting to get that promotion because you love the feeling of having greater influence, serving people, and advancing. It's the intrinsic motivation

---

24. Syed, 127.

that makes you get up time and time again—that inner voice that encourages you to say, "Staying down is not an option." Intrinsic motivation is what keeps an individual striving to improve. It's what fuels people's drive to go after that greater purpose in life and discover what they are meant to do.

Everything that you do in this world is a manifestation of what you have already conceived in your mind. To paraphrase motivational author Napoleon Hill: "If your mind can conceive it, then you can achieve it." We learn doubt. We learn limitations. And we learn how to believe in ourselves—most children believe that anything is possible. The fear of rejection is a learned behavior. Children will repeatedly ask for candy, ice cream, cake, etc., often for as many times as it takes to wear us down until they get it; the rejection is meaningless to them and the reward worthy. It is later in life, unfortunately, that we learn to take rejection personally.

Seeking Purpose from God

Each one of us has talents that God bestowed on us. We flourish in certain endeavors because of our God-given talents. It is up to us to identify those talents, and we can discover them simply by entering into a personal relationship with God and being open to His guidance. As Rick Warren says in The Purpose-Driven Life, *"The purpose of your life is far greater than your own personal fulfillment, your peace of mind, and even your happiness. It's far greater than your family, your career, even your wildest dreams and ambitions. If you want to know why you were placed on this planet, you must begin with God. You were born by His purpose and for His purpose."[25]*

Working with athletes today, I like to ask two questions. The first is "How is your relationship with your father?" That can tell me a lot. A lot of times, the dad is busy or not around, and that can be tough on a young person. The other question is "How is your relationship with your heavenly Father?" All too often, that relationship has been fractured somewhere along their journey. Today, 92 percent of Americans believe in God, down only slightly from the 1940s.[26] I believe that young people crave a spiritual foundation and that it leads to happiness. Spiritual people feel more alive and fulfilled, and they are better able to identify their God-given talents because they're connected with God.

---

25. Rick Warren, *The Purpose-Driven Life: What on Earth Am I Here For?* (Grand Rapids, Michigan: Zondervan, 2012), 23.

26. Frank Newport, "More Than Nine in Ten Americans Continue to Believe in God," last modified June 3, 2011, accessed on December 3, 2013, http://www.gallup.com/poll/147887/Americans-Continue-Believe-God.aspx.

Three Factors Related to Success

Sometimes, being good at something and passionate about it just isn't enough to propel you to success. According to author Jim Collins, success can be predicted based on three factors—what you can be the best in the world at, what you are deeply passionate about, and what drives your economic engine.[27] I have a sailboat and am a good sailor, and I am passionate about sailing. But no one is going to pay me for it. So it would not be wise for me to try to make a living at sailing. Collins calls the intersection of your answer to those three questions your Hedgehog Concept (sometimes defined as doing one thing well, based on the hedgehog's one successful strategy of rolling into a ball to foil any type of predator). Identifying what you are passionate about, could be the best in the world at, and would get paid handsomely for is the challenge...and the opportunity.

Self-Actualizing by Finding Your Talents

On Maslow's Hierarchy of Needs, living where you want, with the people you love, doing the right things, on purpose is a manifestation of the highest level of achievement: self-actualization. Most people will seek to discover their strengths only after they have satisfied their physiological, safety, love/belonging, and esteem needs.

Many high-functioning people don't realize how much capability they truly have until someone encourages them or until they realize they have the power within themselves to achieve great things.

Setting Realistic Goals

Living purposefully is a grand ideal. Sometimes reality keeps you from living that ideal. Living where you want to live with the people you love may be impossible at a certain point in time because of economics, family situations, or other barriers, but we can strive to reach that ideal. It gives us a goal to aim for. We have to remind ourselves constantly that success is not a destination but the progressive realization of a worthy ideal.

In the financial services industry, I visit with advisors who are making as little as $30,000 a year, but almost every one of them has the ability to earn many

---

27. Jim Collins, *Good to Great: Why Some Companies Make the Leap and Others Don't* (New York: HarperBusiness, 2001), 96.

hundreds of thousands of dollars a year. I work at convincing them of their worth and encouraging them to realize that they can reach beyond the sky if they just do the right things and believe in themselves and the advice they give.

We can tell people to think good thoughts, and that's simply an ideal or a goal. But in reality, negative thoughts are going to creep into their minds on occasion. Again, that's where self-encouragement comes in. They can encourage themselves to be aware that negative thoughts will occur, realize that those thoughts are not healthy, and dispense with them to the best of their ability.

> **Identifying what you are passionate about, could be the best in the world at, and would get paid handsomely for is the challenge...and the opportunity.**

When I was the student-body president at Temple University, the young man who was my vice president was Lewis Katz, who remains one of my best friends today. Lewis earned a bachelor's degree in biology at Temple. Then he went on to Dickinson Law School at The Pennsylvania State University and graduated number one in his class. He recently gave $15 million to Dickinson and $25 million to Temple.

Lewis is a former principal owner of the New Jersey Nets and the New Jersey Devils and a former member of the board of governors of the National Basketball Association. He also was a co-managing partner of the YankeesNets. He is a current shareholder of the Nets, the New York Yankees, and the YES Network. Lewis loves children, so he built a youth center in Camden, New Jersey. He then built a boys' club in Camden for 1,200 kids. The first day, the maximum of 1,200 kids signed up, and he said, "No problem. We'll build another one." And he did!

In his meetings with other NBA owners, he repeatedly proposed a rule that would require a young person to be at least twenty-three years old before he can play in the NBA. The majority of the other owners didn't agree with him, and that frustrated him greatly, though he did succeed in getting the others to refrain from drafting youngsters until a year after high school. He wants to see young people get their education, and it makes his heart cry to see the millions of kids in big cities across this country who do not study because they believe they will play in the NBA someday. Only a minuscule few make it to the NBA, and millions of kids who have their sights set on that goal will be sorely disappointed. Worse yet is their forfeiture of their education because of this unrealistic goal from a macro vantage point. Somebody needs to coach them in a different direction and tell them that their ticket out of poverty and distress is studying, not thinking they are going to be among the elite few who make it to the NBA.

> ## Most kids never try swimming, tennis, or table tennis. They need to try a lot of different sports and activities to find out what they can excel in.

I just recommended the book *Bounce* to a parent whose son is in that very same place in his life. I told the parent, "If your son is quick and fast but is not going to be big, the NBA isn't going to happen for him. So you have to find out what talents he does have." Most kids never try swimming, tennis, or table tennis. They need to try a lot of different sports and activities to find out what they can excel in. My childhood Jewish friends excelled at different endeavors, in my opinion, because their parents and their culture encouraged them to try just about everything until they hit on their passion or their long suit and uncovered their individual blessings.

That's why coaching is so important. You can't tell kids very much, but you can *coach* them to consider the reality of their situation and then let their good minds figure it out.

The Science of Happiness

Shawn Achor, author of *The Happiness Advantage*, grew up in Waco, Texas. He graduated magna cum laude from Harvard University and earned a master's degree from Harvard Divinity School in Christian and Buddhist ethics. He spent more than a decade at Harvard, where he won numerous distinguished teaching awards for his work. In 2006, he was Head Teaching Fellow for "Positive Psychology," the most popular course at Harvard at the time.

In 2007, Shawn founded Good Think Inc. to share his research with a wider population. When the global economy collapsed in 2008, the world's largest banks immediately called him in as an expert to help restart forward progress. Today, he travels around the world giving presentations on positive psychology to Fortune 500 companies, schools, and nonprofit organizations. He has worked with doctors in California, executives in Hong Kong, and teachers in

South Africa, using positive psychology to enhance individual achievement and cultivate a more productive workplace. His presentations on the science of happiness and human potential have received attention in *The New York Times*, the *Boston Globe*, *The Wall Street Journal*, and on CNN and NPR.[28]

Thanks to an invitation to One Day University from Lewis Katz, I attended Shawn's presentation titled "The Science of Happiness." He believes that humans are hardwired for sympathy—that can be either a positive or a negative thing—and that we must buffer our brains against negative influences. He says you can break students if you don't maximize their potential and their happiness simultaneously. Further, he says our environment is not predictive of happiness in the long run. Experiments demonstrate that 90 percent of the predictability of happiness is not dependent on our environment. "The belief that the external world causes happiness is plain wrong," he said, citing research conducted in forty different countries.

Shawn also noted that there are seventeen published articles dealing with negative topics for every positive article. He calls it the medical-school-freshman syndrome: "I have every illness I study." And he says that the rates of depression are increasing at alarming rates, despite the fact that our metrics are improving. For many people, their financial situation is better now than it was decades ago. Plus, we haven't been in a war that threatened our country, like World War II, in seven decades. We haven't had to crawl under desks as we did in New York City when I was in grade school because we were afraid the Russians were going to nuke us. Shawn also points out that the average age at which depression manifests itself was 29 in 1967, and in 2006, it was 14.5. Also, twice as many people were depressed in 2006 as four decades earlier, despite the improvements in affluence and standards of living.

Echoing that research, an article in 2011 from The New York Times *reported that the emotional health of college freshmen has declined to the lowest level since an annual survey of incoming students started collecting data twenty-five years ago.[29] That is an alarming statistic that suggests that depression is rampant, particularly among our young people.*

---

28. Big Speak website, "Shawn Achor," accessed November 29, 2013, http://www.bigspeak.com /shawn-achor.html.

29. Jacques Steinberg, "Pressures of High School and Economy Weigh on College Freshmen," *The New York Times* blog "The Choice," last modified January 27, 2011, accessed on December 3, 2013, http://thechoice.blogs.nytimes.com/2011/01/27/emotional-health/?scp=1&sq=depression%20 in%20college%20students&st=cse.

Social cohesion is an accurate predictor of happiness, yet we live in a world where narcissism is more common than social cohesion. More people have decks behind their homes than those who have porches in front of their homes, and they don't communicate verbally with their neighbors as much as people did in past decades. Church attendance, formerly a great source of community for most people, is also decreasing. In sports, too often the mindset is "me–we" instead of the optimal "we–me," which is necessary for social cohesion and athletic team success.

Today we are more technologically connected through texting, e-mailing, and social networking. While this technology has its benefits, I believe it has contributed to our being more emotionally disconnected than ever. This, too, is eroding social cohesion. Live, in-person, face-to-face verbal communication is still the best way to establish connectedness.

Larry Rosen, a psychologist at Cal State Dominguez Hills, has been studying the effects of technology on people for more than twenty-five years. He recently reported that teens and young adults who log on to Facebook constantly are more narcissistic than other young people. "The social network feeds into a narcissist's MO perfectly by allowing people to broadcast themselves 24/7 on their own terms," Rosen says. Among users of all ages, the more people use Facebook, the more likely they are to have antisocial personality disorder, paranoia, and anxiety.[30]

Narcissism, which is ever-increasing in our society, is the antithesis, the opposite, of gratitude. When a Supreme Being is part of your daily thinking, you have gratitude. You can't know of a Supreme Being who created you, your family, everything around you, every bit of happiness, and everything good about life and not feel grateful. I find it difficult to comprehend how depression and gratitude are easily compatible.

To reclaim our spiritual, emotional, and mental health, we need to discover our strengths. Here is a self-assessment I share with my advisors to help them do just that:

- What am I great at?
- What am I lousy at?
- What is going well/right?
- What is not going well/right?
- What do I need to *start* doing?

---

30. Daniela Hernandez, "Too Much Facebook Time May Be Unhealthy for Kids," *Los Angeles Times*, last modified August 6, 2011, accessed on December 3, 2013, http://articles.latimes.com/2011/aug/06/news/la-heb-facebook-teens-20110806.

- What do I need to *stop* doing?
- What do I need to do *differently*?
- What are my billable hours?
- If I were to write a book about financial planning, what would the executive summary say? (One message!)
- How much money is entrusted to me?
- What is the fairy tale, *the dream*?

When I was a senior at Easton High School in eastern Pennsylvania, I was named the sports editor of the school newspaper, *The Junto*. I had two assistant sports editors on my team. One of them, Larry Sobel, was going for the state championship in tennis. One day I asked him, "Larry, when you hit a tennis ball, given all the variables, can you really direct that ball right where you want it to go?"

He replied, "Phil, better than you could throw it there. That's how accurate I can be."

To reclaim our spiritual, emotional, and mental health, we need to discover our strengths.

The funny thing was that Larry was one of the least gifted athletes I had ever met. He was awkward and slightly pigeon-toed. But that year, he won the Pennsylvania Division I state tennis championship. Last year I had dinner with Larry; we hadn't seen each other for forty or fifty years. He went on to attend Harvard as an undergraduate and also graduated from Harvard Law School. He did what this book is about—he found out what he loved doing. He found out what his body enabled him to do and marginalized his short suits. He couldn't play football, play baseball, or run track. But through trial and error, he discovered that he could play tennis—in fact, better than any other high school player in Pennsylvania that year!

It's unfortunate when people fail to find out where their strengths lie. One of my good friends at Easton High School was Mario Capecci, who was an intelligent person and a really great high school basketball player—he was as fluid and athletic as anyone in that school, but he never played in college because, at 5'7", he was just too short. Had he excelled at another sport, he might have been able to get a college scholarship as many of his friends did. Today, Mario is the proud and successful owner of an Italian restaurant in Easton, yet I often wonder if he had taken a different road, if a different coach or teacher had intervened in Mario's life, might he have been the one to discover a cure for cancer? It is easy to see how one can become passionate about the mission of the National High School Coaches Association because coaches can have such a tremendous positive impact on young people.

Whether we find that motivation and encouragement externally or internally, it is critical that we find out where our strengths lie so that we can live where we want, with the people we love, doing the right thing, on purpose.

It's Your Turn

Exercise 2-1: Your three success factors

1. What can you be the best in the world at?

_____

_____

2. What are you deeply passionate about?

_____

_____

3. What drives your economic engine? (What will someone pay you to do?)

_____

_____

Exercise 2-2: Your purposeful-living factors

1. If you could live where you want, where would that be?

_____

_____

2. Which loved ones would you want to live near?

_____

_____

3. What does "doing the right thing" mean to you?

_____

_____

4. What does living "on purpose" mean to you?

_____

_____

3

Interviewing to Enhance Growth

I hire people brighter than me, and then
I get out of their way.

Lee Iacocca
American Businessman

Interviewing is a critical path to growth for any organization. Yet too often, managers either rush an interview or fail to ask questions that elicit a clear picture of a candidate's strengths, weaknesses, attitude, and fit with the organization's culture.

Hiring the wrong person is costly, and it happens all too often. According to a groundbreaking study by Leadership IQ, a firm that studied twenty thousand newly hired employees over three years,[31] 46 percent of new hires fail in the first eighteen months, and only 19 percent will achieve unequivocal success.

The study revealed that most interviewers focus on technical skills when interviewing candidates, yet coachability, emotional intelligence, motivation, and temperament are much more predictive of a new hire's success or failure. The study, reported in *Fortune* and *Forbes*, found that 26 percent of new hires fail because they can't accept feedback, 23 percent because they're unable to understand and manage emotions, 17 percent because they lack the necessary motivation to excel, 15 percent because they have the wrong temperament for the job, and only 11 percent because they lack the necessary technical skills. It is no surprise that turnover is as high as it is in America with employers focusing on the one thing that proves not to be the cause of failure—technical skills.

---

31. Mark Murphy, CEO of Leadership IQ, "Hiring for Attitude: Research and Tools to Skyrocket Your Success Rate," white paper, accessed on September 4, 2011, www.leadershipiq.com.

In addition, 82 percent of the managers who participated in the study reported that, in hindsight, their interview process with these employees had elicited subtle clues that they were headed for trouble. The managers also admitted that, during the interviews, they failed to heed the warning signs because they were too focused on other issues, too pressed for time, unsure of their interviewing skills, or lacked confidence in their interviewing abilities.

> ## The best way to determine a candidate's coachability, emotional intelligence, motivation, and temperament is to ask open-ended questions.

The best way to determine a candidate's coachability, emotional intelligence, motivation, and temperament is to ask open-ended questions (those that can't be answered with a simple yes or no) that delve into the candidate's psyche. Many experts refer to this as behavioral interviewing.

Preparation is important. Before the interview, write down the interview questions you want to ask your candidate. During the interview, write down (or have someone else write down) each candidate's answers to your questions. After the interview, evaluate the answers to try to determine if the candidate has initiative, long-term thinking, self-awareness, risk-taking ability and tolerance, honesty, integrity, and an attitude of gratitude. Tony Hsieh, CEO of Zappos, likes his recruiters to ask candidates, "On a scale of one to ten, how lucky are you?" People who consider themselves lucky tend to make great team members because they are always looking for opportunities—they're *expecting* luck to happen to them. Studies show that people who believe they are lucky are better prepared for opportunities and look for them. They just might feel happier as well.

A Critical Pre-Interview Exercise

The list of twenty-one job functions you developed in Chapter 1 is a valuable tool that not only helps you know yourself and your strengths better; it can help you find team members whose skill sets, likes, and dislikes complement your own.

When you are preparing to hire an administrative assistant, sales associate, manager, or other team member, simply e-mail your list of twenty-one job functions (without the numbering) to candidates. Ask them to number the items from one to twenty-one, with number one being the task they would enjoy doing the most and number twenty-one being the task they would enjoy the least. This will allow you to match each candidate's list against your own. If a candidate enjoys doing the same things you enjoy, he or she is probably not the right person for you to hire (although he or she may be a good candidate to be your friend). The candidate who enjoys doing the things you *dislike* doing is your ideal match. Interview only those candidates whose skill set is the opposite of yours or close to it.

Interview Questions That Reveal Character

I always ask the following four questions during an interview. Candidates' answers will speak volumes about their attitude, personality, and character:

1. What is your greatest personal asset?

2. What is your greatest personal liability? (In other words, what is the one thing about yourself you would most like to improve?)

3. What is your greatest business asset? (Or, if you are enormously successful in ten years, what characteristic do you have that would have made that success predictable?)

4. What is your greatest business liability? (Or, if you fail to meet your goals and objectives, what characteristic of yours may have caused that lack of success?)

Here are additional interview questions I have used successfully through the years to reveal a candidate's character:

1. Tell me about your dream job.

2. What are you looking for in this job?

3. What's more important to you—work or money?

4. What would your previous boss or supervisor say about your work if I called him or her?

5. How do you cope under pressure? Can you give an example?

6. Do your skills match another job better, and if so, which one?

7. How would you know if you were successful on the job?

8. If you were hiring the person for this job, what would you look for?

9. What qualities do you look for in a boss?

10. What's your biggest professional disappointment?

11. Tell me about a time when you really had fun on the job. What were you doing?

12. What have you learned from mistakes you've made in previous jobs?

13. What have you done to improve your knowledge in the past year?

14. Are you a team player?

15. What frustrates you in a job?

16. Have you ever had to let anybody go?

17. How do you deliver bad news?

18. When you disagree with a manager, what do you do? Can you give me an example?

19. Have you ever been asked to do the wrong thing, and if so, how did you react?

20. What are you grateful for?

21. How lucky are you? (Keep in mind that one definition of luck is when preparation meets opportunity.)

Notice that most of these questions require candidates to tell a story, thus revealing more about themselves than simple yes and no answers will reveal.

Before I conduct an interview, I have the above questions printed and placed under the glass that covers my desk so that I can refer to them easily.

Their Earliest Memory

Another question I always ask at North Star Resource Group is, "What is your earliest memory?" I have only anecdotal evidence—no psychological evidence—that this is a valid predictor of personality, but I believe that people who think positively will recount a positive memory. Likewise, I believe that stoics or negative people will retrieve a memory of a sad or traumatic occasion when asked this question. One person may say, "My earliest memory is that I got a beautiful new red bike for Christmas." Another might say, "My first memory is that I fell off my bike and had to go to the hospital to get a lot of stitches." All else being equal, I would be more likely to hire the person who shares a positive memory. This may be right or wrong, but it's worked for me for decades and has proven, in most cases, to be borne out by subsequent observations.

Alfred Adler (1870–1937) was an Austrian medical doctor, psychotherapist, and founder of the school of "individual psychology." He believed that people's first memories offer great insight into their attitude.

Adler wrote, "Most illuminating of all is the way the individual begins his story, the earliest incident he can recall. The first memory will show his fundamental view of life, his first satisfactory crystallization of his attitude. It offers us an opportunity to see at one glance what he has taken as the starting point for his development. I would never investigate a personality without asking for the first memory."[32]

This is not to say, however, that people who had traumatic occurrences in their childhood grow up to be negative people. On the contrary, I believe that many such people grow up to be resilient, optimistic individuals with positive attitudes.

Following the Energy

Another telling question is, "What energizes you?" You can separate the job functions or activities you enjoy into three categories. In the first category are the things you enjoy doing and are good at but drain your energy—for example, leading a board meeting. In the second category are those things you enjoy and are good at, and they have a neutral effect on you—they neither drain nor energize you. Supervising someone one-on-one is one example. In the third category are those things you do that energize and recharge you—you love doing them, you're good at them, and they energize you. You can't wait to engage in those activities more. For some, that activity is public speaking. For others, it's selling. It's obviously different for everyone.

Having candidates identify what energizes
them will reveal those activities that are
at the top of their list.

Having candidates identify what energizes them will reveal those activities that are at the top of their list. When people recognize what energizes them, they can spend more time working in that arena, the energy feeds off itself, and they can't wait to get up the next day to engage in that activity more.

---

32. *The Individual Psychology of Alfred Adler: A Systematic Presentation in Selections from His Writings*, edited by Heinz L. Ansbacher and Rowena R. Ansbacher (New York: Harper & Row, 1956), 351.

A Sense of Urgency

Another question I like to ask candidates is, "When was the last time you got a speeding ticket?" Sometimes people are reluctant to answer because it seems like a trick question—they don't want to admit that they've broken the law. But hopefully you're going to get a truthful answer. I actually like people who get speeding tickets because I like people around me who are in a hurry even when they don't have a particular reason to be. The energy they bring to a firm, a team, or a meeting is infectious.

> An attitude of gratitude is the perpetual
> mark of a person with humility.

When I was looking for an administrative assistant a few years ago, I asked one young woman that question, and she responded, "Never." She immediately asked if she had made a mistake by answering that way.

I replied, "You didn't make a mistake, but it wasn't the answer I'm looking for."

She asked why, and I replied, "Well, I'm looking for people who get speeding tickets even when there is no hurry."

She said, "You asked me if I got a speeding ticket. You didn't ask me if I got stopped by a cop for speeding. I did get stopped recently, but I talked my way out of it."

That was a good answer, and she subsequently got the job.

I wasn't asking the right question. It's important that we are precise in our word choice. I learned my lesson on that one.

An Attitude of Gratitude

At North Star Resource Group, we have begun focusing on gratitude and have, in fact, added gratitude to our values. We used to have four values, and they formed the acronym FIGS: faith, integrity, growth, service. We have since added gratitude to that list of values, which now forms the acronym FIGGS: faith, integrity, growth, gratitude, service. Downplaying these values as "only words" would miss the mark.

In October 2011, North Star Resource Group was blessed to receive the Integrity Award from the Minnesota–North Dakota Better Business Bureau. The firm was chosen from among more than two hundred large companies. Words matter, and values count. The values of a business define its culture.

What are your personal values? Are they similar to your business values?

I believe that the same number of good and bad things usually happen to all of us; it's how we react to them that counts. Neurologist, psychiatrist, and Holocaust survivor Viktor Frankl corroborates that in saying, "Forces beyond your control can take away everything you possess except one thing: your freedom to choose how you will respond to the situation. You cannot control what happens to you in life, but you can always control what you feel and do about what happens to you." If, as you look back, you're more grateful for the good things that have happened to you than you are angry about the unfortunate things, it makes other people want to be around you. Asking someone what they are grateful for will often reveal this quality. A bonus is that it is difficult, if not impossible, to be grateful and depressed at the same time.

An attitude of gratitude is the perpetual mark of a person with humility. In his book *Good to Great*, Jim Collins talks about Level 5 leadership, with Level 5 referring to the highest level on the hierarchy of executive capabilities. "Level 5 leaders embody a paradoxical mix of personal humility and professional will," he writes. "They are ambitious, to be sure, but ambitious first and foremost for the company, and not themselves."[33]

Frustration and Anger Management

Another revealing question to ask in an interview is "How do you manage frustration?" Candidates' answers will shed insight into how they will deal with those twenty thousand inevitable rejections they'll get if they enter a sales career.

Along the same lines, another question that is indicative of a candidate's emotional well-being is "How do you manage your anger?" Anger is simply a reaction to emotional hurt. A person may be experiencing some strong negative emotion, but we may not be able to label that emotion more specifically; it instead just manifests itself as the socially acceptable emotion of anger. So if you're angry, how is that emotion going to manifest itself in you? What will it look like? Some people become quiet and withdrawn. Other people become laser-focused and aggressive. Still others act out physically or verbally.

---

33. Collins, 39.

In an interview, a candidate is probably not going to admit that he becomes violent when he gets angry, but when we ask this question, we're looking for a certain degree of transparency and self-reflection. Like many of these questions, there's no right or wrong answer. Candidates' answers will indicate their depth of self-awareness about their own emotional well-being. If they have an issue with frustration or anger, have they spent any time working on it?

The Emotion of Excitement

The feeling that athletes should have prior to a competition is one of excitement. Sure, they're going to be nervous, but a person whose excitement overrides the nervousness is the person you want on your team. An athlete who says, "I just can't wait to get out there and help win the basketball game tonight" is a person who can handle pressure. He is the one who says, in the final minutes of the game, "Give me the ball!" That's the guy we want on our team and in our company.

To determine people's level of excitement about the tasks they enjoy doing, ask questions in an abstract way to test their ability to think on their feet. Ask them a question they probably haven't prepped for. Say, "Tell me about a time when you felt great energy, great excitement, about a project or an athletic event, and how that affected the outcome."

Most people can't lie very well when they're thinking on their feet. Now they're searching for some memories, digging deep for situations from their past. You'll elicit more information if you ask questions that begin with, "Paint me a picture," "Tell me a story," or "What might this look like?" The stories they tell you will help you gauge the level of their excitement.

Books and Music

Another indication of what people truly enjoy is how they spend their time away from work or school. If you ask candidates what book they're reading right now for personal enjoyment, what kind of music they listen to, or what activities they engage in, that will tell you what energizes them. It also reveals how they like to escape from reality and what missing pieces of life they're filling in with these activities.

Knowing what someone *doesn't* spend their time doing also reveals a great deal. My internist at the Mayo Clinic after many years asked me during one of my examinations, "How did you manage to fit so much into your life?" He was referring to my business success, sailing, charitable work, family time, speaking, and all the other things I love doing. Out of the blue, I said this: "There are two things I don't do. I don't play golf, and I don't read novels. That has given me a lot of time to do the things I am interested in." It also has provided time for the really important things like family and friends. It has always made sense to me to have not only a "to do" list but to have a "not to do" list as well. Never eating desserts and never drinking alcohol before noon are on that list.

> ## Knowing what someone *doesn't* spend their time doing also reveals a great deal.

Whatever people have made a conscious effort *not* to do reveals to you what's at the bottom of their list—what they don't enjoy doing.

It takes time and effort to find out what people excel at and discover their true personalities, attitudes, and motivations. Vow to become a master interviewer, and you will surround yourself with people who complement your own skill set, share your values, and fit well into your corporate culture. While there are numerous books on the art of interviewing, this chapter will give you a framework and a beginning toward that end.

It's Your Turn

Exercise 3-1: What energizes you?

_____

_____

_____

_____

_____

_____

_____

_____

Exercise 3-2: What are you grateful for?

1. _____
2. _____
3. _____
4. _____
5. _____
6. _____
7. _____
8. _____
9. _____
10. _____

Exercise 3-3: Do you have a daily "to do" list? Do you write it out the night before you need to refer to it?

_____

_____

_____

_____

_____

_____

_____

_____

Exercise 3-4: Do you have a "not to do" list? If so, what types of activities are listed on it?

_____

_____

_____

_____

_____

_____

_____

_____

Chapter

4

Inspect What You Expect

Good men prefer to be accountable.

Michael Edwardes
South African Businessman

The US Navy SEALs (Sea, Air, Land) were established by President John F. Kennedy in 1962 as a small, elite maritime military force to conduct Unconventional Warfare. They carry out the types of clandestine, small-unit, high-impact missions that large forces with high-profile equipment (such as ships, tanks, jets, and submarines) cannot. Navy SEALs are trained to operate in all the environments (sea, air, and land) for which they are named.

Among the people who have directed Navy SEAL training is Rear Admiral Ray Smith. He achieved the highest graduation rate in the fifty-year history of the course. Admiral Smith was a Navy SEAL for thirty-one years and achieved extraordinary success through focused, participatory leadership. During his four-year tenure as Commander of the 2,300-man SEAL force, Admiral Smith raised personnel retention to a level three times the navy average. As a navy captain, he led the Navy SEALs in Operation Desert Storm, conducting more than two hundred operations of strategic significance while incurring no casualties.

Today, Admiral Smith is widely regarded as one of the navy's most inspirational leaders. He told me a story that is a testament to the value of coaching and mentoring. "I enlisted to be a sailor but failed to make it," he said. "A changing point in my life was that while I was in boot camp, a chief petty officer asked me if I had ever thought about going to the naval academy. I didn't realize I could. He told me that if I did well on the test, which one hundred people were going to take, then after boot camp, I could qualify to go to a prep school on the East Coast. That officer saw potential in an eighteen-year-old who didn't see it in himself. And that is how I became a navy officer and a SEAL."

Incidentally, Admiral Smith is the only SEAL to have had two sons and a nephew become Navy SEALs.

He has spoken extensively on his leadership experiences to a wide range of audiences, including corporate, political, military, and civic leaders. During his presentation titled "Teaching Moments," he shows a video excerpt of the Navy SEALs' "Hell Week."

Hell Week is the defining event of Basic Underwater Demolition (BUD/S) training. It is held early on, before the navy makes an expensive investment in an individual's Navy SEAL operational training. Hell Week consists of five and a half days of cold, wet, brutally difficult operational training on fewer than four hours of sleep. The experience tests physical endurance, mental toughness, pain and cold tolerance, teamwork, attitude, and the ability to perform work under high physical and mental stress and sleep deprivation. Above all, it tests determination and desire. On average, only 25 percent of SEAL candidates make it through Hell Week, the toughest training in the US military. "It is often the greatest achievement of their lives, and with it comes the realization that they can do twenty times more than they ever thought possible," the Navy SEALs website says. "It is a defining moment that they reach back to when in combat. They know that they will never, ever quit or let a teammate down."[34]

We have to build accountability into our systems to help our athletes, team members, and children succeed.

I feel blessed to have befriended Ray Smith at the National High School Wrestling Championships over the past few years—we both attended many of them, as guests of The National High School Coaches Association and its CEO, Bob Ferraro. One day, when we were discussing the discipline required in the sport of wrestling, Admiral Smith told me that 40 percent of the wrestlers who attempt to become SEALs are successful and that, as a group, wrestlers have the highest percent of graduates. The hard-rock conditioning in the wrestling world seems appropriate for the rigors of the SEAL program.

As you can imagine, individuals who endure Hell Week become quite introspective during their grueling training. As he is being broken down physically and mentally, each SEAL begins to take a hard look deep into his soul. And he finds out what he is made of.

---

34. Navy SEALs website, "Hell Week," accessed on November 29, 2013, http://navyseals.com/nsw/hell-week-0/.

A SEAL who has been forced to inspect *his soul and mind knows* what to expect—*he knows he can go 115 hours without sleeping. He knows he can maintain a high level of physical performance during difficult training exercises, even though he is wet, cold, and exhausted.*

As leaders, we have to *inspect* what we *expect*, too. That means we have to build accountability into our systems to help our athletes, team members, and children succeed.

Accountability Helps Drive Performance

Admiral Smith says that the three legs of the "stool" of leadership are responsibility, authority, and accountability. Accountability is the main element we should focus on to become effective leaders. Building accountability into our businesses increases the likelihood that our people will succeed. When we fail to build checkpoints into our team members' jobs, we are doing them a disservice.

As the saying goes, "Authority plus responsibility equals accountability." It's like turning in your homework. If you know that your homework is due at eight o'clock in the morning, you're going to do whatever it takes to have it ready by that time. But if the homework is assigned without a deadline, it's not as likely to get done. A goal without a deadline is just a dream. Indeed, some goals, when missed, can be nightmares. To truly have a goal, you need a deadline.

Admiral Smith uses the metaphor of a sailboat. "It's not the lofty sail but the unseen wind that moves the ship. You are the sail, and your team members are the unseen wind." The more accountability you give those you are supervising, the straighter their path toward success will be. In the end, too-kind management might actually be cruel management.

In the insurance and financial services business, when assigning tasks to people, I always ask, "Is this something we can have back within forty-eight hours?" That creates a deadline, a sense of urgency. It's that urgency that helps people overcome procrastination or a lack of energy.

Success is always predicated on discipline. For Navy SEALs, much of the discipline they need is created externally. Thus, even if a Navy SEAL doesn't have the internal discipline to complete a task (granted, an unlikely situation), the system provides discipline and accountability to help him succeed. Most of us don't live in the world of the SEALs, though; we live in a world of choices. We're constantly confronted with the choice of whether or not to excel. But accountability is the tool that we, as leaders, can use to hold one another to task so that we can accomplish necessary work and excel.

Accountability requires deadlines or standards, as well as consequences for not meeting them. At North Star, for example, all of our newer people are required to have their activity reports in by ten o'clock on Monday mornings. If they don't, then two things happen: First, they will hear from a superior who will ask them for the report and ask why it was not e-mailed on time. Second, their scholarship payment for that two-week period will be withheld until they turn the report in. They don't lose the scholarship, but the money will not be paid to them until the requirement is met. That definitely motivates people to get their reports in on time. That's accountability.

When you are building a business, you will help others succeed if you build into the system some automatic checkpoints that have consequences attached to them. Those checkpoints are one of the key drivers in most businesses, especially the insurance and financial services industry. Without those checkpoints, or inspections, our advisors would not be anywhere near as successful as they are because this business has a lot of free will and independence attached to it.

Some people, for whatever reason, come into an organization implementing their own checkpoints—they determine what they need to do on a daily basis that permits them the luxury of going home at the end of the day. In fact, it has been determined that 20 percent of the people hired into an organization will succeed without regard to its leadership. These winners would succeed in any organization, no matter how poorly it might be run.

Another 60 percent of the people we hire will require leadership and guidance to succeed, and that's where we'll need to spend our time. The middle 60 percent generally want to be in the top 20 percent. Our job as leaders is to educate them, provide them with accountability, and help them discover the things they love to do. Furthermore, in keeping with the purpose of this book, it is our job to help them backfill into those strengths assistants who will do the things our advisors dislike doing.

I believe that the bottom 20 percent of the people who come into our organizations were placed there by God to test us! They will not succeed, regardless of how much time we spend with them. These are the quitters, and efforts to help them should be considered to be in the charitable-contribution category. Civility dictates that we attempt to figure out what they should be doing, perhaps by using the twenty-one-point test in this book, and helping them get there.

Quarterly Reviews Serve as Checkpoints

One of the checkpoints we use in the insurance and financial services industry is the quarterly review. Every ninety days, we meet with our advisors to determine how well they are performing in terms of various metrics related to selling insurance, securities, and financial services to clients. Half a year is too long a period of time to go before checking their performance, and a month is too short a period of time to measure results. Activity can be measured on a monthly basis, but you can't measure results in any complex business in which there is a long lag time between the effort and the final result. (In our business, that is normally 90 to 120 days.) Manage activity on a monthly basis, but monitor results on a quarterly basis.

> ## You need a tool like the quarterly review to determine if your expected results have been achieved.

In the first week following a quarter, we look at the quantification of each individual's performance. It's at that point that—just like the interceptor missile we discussed in Chapter 2—you can make the necessary corrections in a person's career to get him or her back on course. If the results that were agreed upon were not achieved, then you will have to modify the activity requirements. If someone's results were supposed to be 100, for example, and she achieved 80, she will need 120 units to bring her average up to 100 for the two quarters. Unless this is done, goals for the year will have to be reduced to reflect the results achieved thus far. To do otherwise will be to fly in the face of that famous definition of insanity—namely, doing the same thing over and over again and expecting a different result.

You need a tool like the quarterly review to determine if your expected results have been achieved. These checkpoints are like a gyroscope—they help you maintain direction by getting your team members' performance back on course.

In addition to reviewing advisors' metrics during a quarterly review, I also ask the following questions to help determine how confident an advisor is at that juncture:

- What deliverables do you expect from us (the company)?
- What are your deliverables in return?

- What is your opinion of your performance?
- What do I need to change for you to deliver?
- Most importantly, how do you want me to hold you accountable?

The beauty of these reviews is that we have them built into our calendar, and my assistant sets them up on days when she knows I will be in the office. Once you have a system in place, you're like Frank Sinatra—you just show up to sing, and you don't move the piano!

Once you have a system of checkpoints in place that works for you, don't change it. I heard recently that Tony Bennett left his heart in San Francisco more than fifteen thousand times. He is estimated to have sung that song publicly fifteen thousand times, but he didn't leave his heart in other cities or countries. He always left his heart in one place—San Francisco—because that was what was selling. If he had changed the name of that city, it would have ruined the song. If it's working, don't change it. But, as Admiral Ray Smith says, "If you're in a hole that you don't want to be in, stop shoveling. Don't dig any deeper." In other words, if what you're doing is not working, stop and try another approach.

> If we serve as the inspiration to convince
> them that neither the sky nor anything
> else can limit them, we have served
> our purpose.

Without checkpoints—without inspecting what you expect—people lose direction, and their performance suffers. Author Ron Willingham discusses what he calls the Law of Limited Performance: "People soon discover the level of performance their managers will settle for and then gravitate to that level. Managers then assume that's all that people are capable of achieving, so they accept it as fact and quit challenging their people to do better. So both reinforce what the other believes."[35] The more we ask of people, the more we are helping them be all they want to be. The less we ask of them, the less they'll give. If we serve as the inspiration to convince them that neither the sky nor anything else can limit them, we have served our purpose.

---

35. Ron Willingham, *The People Principle: A Revolutionary Redefinition of Leadership*, (New York: St. Martin's Press, 1997), 77–78.

Inspection Can Reveal Inefficiencies

Inspecting your business from varying angles often reveals surprises. Recently, North Star was under siege from an onslaught of computer viruses. Our IT professionals determined that 38 percent of the viruses that attacked our computer system came from Facebook. Accordingly we declared Facebook out of bounds—we now have a block on Facebook on all company computers. Our advisors and associates have to wait until they go home to visit their Facebook pages or to use a personal device such as an iPhone to access them. Some of the Facebook activity that was going on was business-related, but much of it was not.

We discovered that most of our team members had been on Facebook for more than half an hour every day. Now that we have blocked Facebook access, you can imagine what the anticipated efficiencies will be within the company. Plus, it sometimes took our IT team a full day to eliminate viruses from each computer affected, negatively impacting everyone in the firm. Now they no longer have to spend their time chasing down computer viruses, at least from that source.

Inspecting What You Expect in Sports

Inspecting what you expect also applies to athletics. During the summer, collegiate athletes are required to work out and train consistently. In August, when they regroup on their campuses, these athletes undergo multiple conditioning tests. The coaching staff will inspect the physical skills and abilities of each of their athletes. They expect them to come back to school in shape, at the level that will enable them to have great practices, few injuries, and a winning season.

The more that coaches inspect their returning players' physical conditioning and endurance, and the higher their expectations are, the better results they'll get. That's how championships are won.

It's no surprise that many of our Navy SEALs, Rangers, and State Troopers come from a sports background. These positions require a lot of the self-discipline that is learned through sports.

Inspecting What We Expect from Our New Hires

In Chapter 3, we discussed how important it is to hire people who enjoy doing the things you don't enjoy doing. Ideally, you want to hire people who are good at items 6–21 on your list of twenty-one job functions. That allows you to do what you enjoy doing—items 1 through 5—and delegate the other job functions to someone else. We must inspect our candidates' performance in those areas—via a thorough interview and reference checks, for example—to ensure that they excel in the areas you need help with. Any written tests that you are already using may also be helpful.

If it turns out that they only somewhat enjoy doing the job functions you've numbered 6 through 21 on your list, but they don't love doing those things, you are not going to see peak performance in those areas.

It's like putting a football player who loves to play the position of wide receiver into the game as a defensive back. You probably won't get the same level of athletic performance from him. He may be able to play the defensive-back position at an acceptable level, but if he doesn't love it, he won't excel at it. If he loves being a wide receiver, let him play in that position and make the biggest contribution to the team that he possibly can.

Leading People Becomes Easier

If people are doing what they love to do, their energy will drive their performance, and you can focus on managing that energy. Jim Loehr says in his book *The Power of Full Engagement*, "Manage energy, not time," and Rear Admiral Grace Hopper advised us to "Manage things, lead people." The things we love to do energize us, and to the extent that someone is already energized to do certain tasks, then the leader's job is to simply guide the direction of that energy, not to *create* the energy. The energy is created by the individual who says, "These are the things I really love and enjoy doing."

People who spend their time doing what they love to do have intrinsic motivation. As a manager, coach, mentor, or businessperson, you won't have to worry about inspiring or motivating that person extrinsically—for example, with a hefty salary—because it's not the salary that's driving him or her. The legendary Al Granum says, "Motivation is like a cattle prod—it works, but the effects are brief."

There are 168 hours in a week. Someone who works forty hours a week spends about 24 percent of his or her time at work, so it makes sense that it should be a happy place to be. The easiest way to make that happen is to allow people to do what they love to do. If you have a company full of people who enjoy their work, then you'll have a company full of high achievers who need little extrinsic motivation. If the saying "The whole is equal to the sum of its parts" is valid, your company's performance will reflect the highly motivated team members who work and play there.

But sometimes even high achievers have complaints. Encourage those you're leading to approach their manager and say, "This is what I'm unhappy about. Is there anything you can do about it?" Coworkers are not in a position to do something about the problem. So complaining horizontally, to coworkers, is not healthy for any organization, and it shouldn't be tolerated.

> The leader's job is to simply guide the direction of that energy, not to *create* the energy.

Internal Preparation Gets Spectacular Results

Often when I give a presentation on the Mind of the Athlete, I open with this quote from Muhammad Ali: "The fight is won or lost far away from the witnesses, behind the lines, in the gym, and out there on the road, long before I dance under those lights." In sports, it's commonly known that your fights are never won or lost in the ring. It takes a great deal of mental as well as physical preparation to win a game or fight—before we ever engage in the competition.

Sharon Adele Wood, a Canadian mountaineer and guide who was the first North American woman to reach the summit of Mount Everest, would agree. She said, "It's not the mountains that we have to conquer, nor the elements. But rather it's those self-imposed barriers, those limitations, in our mind."

For Best Results, Couple Discipline with Warmth

In sports, accountability goes hand-in-hand with discipline, which is most effective when it's coupled with a key ingredient—warmth. We know this from the parenting world. There are four main parenting styles, and these styles contain varying combinations of two elements: discipline and warmth.

- ***Laissez-faire parenting style**—This is the style exhibited by parents who provide little discipline and little warmth. Children who grow up in this environment receive little guidance or support.*

- **Passive parenting style**—*This style is low in discipline but high in warmth. This is the type of home in which kids might party during high school. Their parents say it's OK; they want to be cool.*

- **Authoritative parenting style**—*This style is high in discipline and also high in warmth. An authoritative parent will tell his child, "You will be home at eleven p.m.— no ifs, ands, or buts about it, and there will be a consequence if you're not. And when you come in the door, I'll give you a hug and a kiss and tell you I love you." That's the optimal environment in creating healthy high performers.*

- **Authoritarian parenting style**—*This style is high in discipline and low in warmth. Children raised in this type of environment may do all the right things and excel for a while (often through high school), but eventually they often struggle under the weight of heavy discipline with little emotional support. It's difficult to thrive in that kind of environment.*

People develop self-discipline because of an environment of discipline around them. So if we look at the sports culture, the teams that really thrive are those that have very high discipline coupled with the most important ingredient, which is warmth. Football coach Tony Dungy, who became the first black American head coach to win the Super Bowl when his Colts defeated the Chicago Bears in 2007, led his teams this way. He radiated warmth but at the same time ran a very tight ship. The best coaches often have that mix.

<blockquote>

You can help those in your charge tremendously by providing them with accountability and discipline plus warmth.

</blockquote>

Whether you're a coach, a parent, or a manager, you can help those in your charge tremendously by providing them with accountability and discipline plus warmth. That's what athletes, children, and team members look to us for—guidance in a tumultuous world full of conflicting priorities and distractions. It is our job to help them discover what they love to do, then keep them on a path that will lead them to success.

An Example of Why This Concept Is Important

At North Star recently, we were screening applicants for a key position in the company, part of an initiative intended to transform its financial dynamic. One of our staff members referred a candidate to us, and the candidate was approved and recommended by each person he interviewed within our company.

We found out that this person had previously worked for another financial firm whose senior vice president happened to be a good friend of mine. The candidate asked us not to contact the employer because he said he was still with the company. But something told me to do some more checking. So I made a casual phone call— not to the senior vice president of the company, but to one of his staff members, who also happens to be a friend. I asked, "Are you familiar with this person?"

He said, "Oh, yes, he used to work for us."

"What do you mean he *used* to work for you?"

"Oh, he was let go in October."

"Oh, really? I'm shocked," I said. "Can you tell me anything about him?"

"Oh, yes. We let him go because he had a bad attitude. That's all I am able to tell you."

This is a perfect example—a drastic example—of inspecting what you expect. As you can imagine, there were a lot of red faces in our company when I told our team members that the person they had vetted and wholeheartedly accepted had been let go from his former company six months earlier! We must challenge assumptions. The assumption was that this candidate was still working at another firm and was honest about everything he told us. Look for background information to validate your decisions. Inspect what you expect, and expect only what you inspect! Remember that a candidate for a job will never, ever look better to you than he or she does during that job interview.

It's Your Turn

Exercise 4-1: What can you inspect?

In your work, coaching, athletic competitions, or life in general, what do you intend to inspect so that you can expect positive results?

_____

_____

_____

_____

_____

_____

Exercise 4-2: Accountability

Whose performance would improve if you held them accountable? Are you growing others by asking them, "How do you want me to hold you accountable?"

_____

_____

_____

_____

_____

_____

_____

_____

Chapter

5

Be Open to Your Life's Calling

"Don't impose your puny human limits on Creation."[36]

Psalm 138:8 says, "The Lord will fulfill His purpose for me." God has a plan for each of us, and it is up to us to find out what it is. Dream big; don't let anyone impose "puny, human limits on Creation and interfere with the plan He has for your life." The clues about that plan surround us. We need to seek them out and be open to them.

Many times, those clues manifest themselves as a result of a religious upbringing.

At Temple University, I was the only Christian brother in a national Jewish fraternity called Pi Lambda Phi. They even elected me president of the senior class, possibly because they wanted me to feel accepted. The people I got along with best, and the best friends I had when I went to Temple, were either in that fraternity or pledging it. Pi Lambda Phi, founded at Yale University in 1895, is described as the first non-sectarian fraternity in the United States, "accepting men of good character without regard to race or religion." Although it was non-sectarian, it was predominantly Jewish until the end of World War II.

Through my many friendships with Jewish people from childhood on, my experience with their culture taught me that many Jewish parents encourage their children to try a lot of different life experiences until they find something they're really good at. In areas like athletics, Jews seem to become great at a disproportionate rate, from the phenomenal Jewish boxers of the early twentieth century to Sandy Koufax, legendary pitcher for the Dodgers, to Mark Spitz, with seven Olympic gold medals in swimming. I don't know whether Spitz could have gotten a gold

---

36. The quote is humorously attributed to Copernicus by author Dava Sobel in *A More Perfect Heaven: How Copernicus Revolutionized the Cosmos* (New York: Walker & Company, 2011).

medal in any other sport; he may have. We'll never know. But we do know that somehow, maybe because of being exposed to a diversity of activities, he found that swimming was something God had gifted him with talents for, and he spent ten thousand hours developing that talent.

In the Jewish culture, this emphasis on diversity and totality in terms of activity seems to give young people a better probability of finding out what it is that they can be great at. Earlier I referred to my high school friend, Larry Sobel, who was not gifted athletically but still won the Pennsylvania High School Tennis Championship. His dad, Morton, a great defensive end for New York University in the 1930s, encouraged him in all sports until they found the one he could excel at.

> Many Jewish parents encourage their children to try a lot of different life experiences until they find something they're really good at.

If someone is good at something, then chances are, they enjoy it, and that makes it easier to put in ten thousand hours into that activity than if they were trying to excel in an area they didn't like or only marginally liked.

In Europe during the Middle Ages, land was the commodity that helped people gain wealth. But laws prevented Jews from owning land. Therefore, they had to make their way in the world in areas other than land ownership. They became great alchemists, jewelers, doctors, and bankers. Both the Fuggers in Germany and the Medicis in Italy were Jewish, and they created two great banking empires of the Middle Ages. They gained success in that area partly because they were precluded from enjoying the stores of wealth that everybody else in society was entitled to.

The Jewish community does a great job of positioning the next generation to succeed. Upon turning thirteen years old, a Jewish boy automatically becomes a bar mitzvah and participates in a ceremony in his synagogue. He may be required to read from the Torah; chant the haftarah, the weekly prophetic portion; lead some or all of the congregational service; and offer a personal interpretation of the weekly Torah portion, called a d'var Torah. Leading up to the ceremony, the boy must demonstrate proficiency in Hebrew and a commitment to Judaism. During this coming-of-age process, Jewish boys typically receive an outpouring of support from their families and synagogue community.

We believe that these educational requirements, and the discipline that goes along with them, give Jewish young people a solid start in terms of the learning process.

You also see this discipline among Mormon (Church of Jesus Christ of Latter-day Saints, or the LDS Church) young people. Mormons are required to spend two years doing missions work. Commonly referred to as Mormon missionaries, most LDS Church missionaries are single young men in their late teens and early twenties and are assigned to a mission of the church that is usually far from their home. LDS missionaries serve voluntarily. They do not receive a salary for the work they undertake; most support themselves or are supported by their families. This effort requires a great deal of self-discipline, an awareness of God, a servant leadership mentality (rather than imposing authority, servant leaders share power, put other people's needs first, and empower others to develop and perform at the highest levels possible), and humility, not to mention support from family and the church community. While the purpose may be to convert people to Mormonism, the by-products of that purpose are pretty significant in molding young people's minds and habits.

Look for Early Childhood Clues

For many people, there are clues during childhood about what their life's calling should be. We can see early signs in some people's lives that they loved something and gravitated to it. Maybe it's a little girl who is interested in bugs and later on becomes a scientist who loves the environment and earth science. The people who follow these early inclinations—and who are lucky enough to have parents who support them—are likely to find their true north early in life and excel in their chosen profession or vocation at an early age.

A great example is a young man named Sage Karam from Nazareth, Pennsylvania. By eighteen years old, he successfully completed the Road to Indy program to become one of the youngest Indy car drivers ever. After a successful stint in karting as a kid, Karam won the 2010 US F2000 National Championship. The following year, he moved up a level and won Rookie of the Year honors in the 2011 Star Mazda Championship. In 2013, Sage moved up again to the next level of racing and won the Indy Lights championship, which included a million-dollar scholarship toward his dream of being an Indy car driver.

Nobody has been on this pace and has had this kind of dominance in the sport of racing at such a young age. Sage was listed among Sports Illustrated's *Ten Sportskids of the Year in 2011. It was a unique situation; Sage could drive a car at 150 miles an hour on the racetrack, yet he couldn't drive a car on the streets in the Lehigh Valley because he didn't have a license yet.*

Sage was in Colorado for the Operation Smile convention in 2010, telling people how important it is to try to find that thing you love and that you're really good at. He's one example of somebody who found his niche early in life.

When the Karams lived in Easton, Pennsylvania, and Sage was just a boy, he had a little motorized car that he would race around their unfinished basement. Then his parents had a home built in Nazareth, and while it was in progress, he would race his car around the property. He also loved to study racing videos—in particular, he liked to watch driver Aryton Senna.

Before Sage could consciously understand what a life's calling was, he resonated with racing. And, as serendipity would have it, when his parents built their home in Nazareth, guess who their neighbors were? Legendary Indy car driver Mario Andretti and his family.

Pay Attention to Circumstances

Many times, people end up in certain situations and have something revealed to them. We believe it is God's way of turning our attention in a different direction than we're headed. The following story is an example of what I'm talking about.

Recently, because of the thoughtfulness of my friend, Bob Savage, I had the privilege of visiting with Dr. Lloyd A. Jacobs, the president of The University of Toledo, home to 22,000 students in Toledo, Ohio. He is an amazing person. After high school, he joined the Marine Corps and served for four years, then decided to go to Miami University, where he earned a BA in chemistry. He then went to medical school at Johns Hopkins University and became a vascular surgeon. He began his appointment as The University of Toledo's sixteenth president in 2006, when the former Medical University of Ohio, which he was president of for approximately three years, merged with The University of Toledo. He is a quintessential leader with a vision and a plan. When he talks about measuring the performance of physicians at the medical school there, he says, "I am going to measure them based on what the Toledo infant mortality rate is in coming years."

Dr. Jacobs told me the story of how he ended up at Toledo Medical School. Years ago, he interviewed for a position at Northwestern University in Chicago. He and his wife drove from Toledo to Chicago. After the interview, he was offered the position and all but verbally accepted it, pending a little more thought over the weekend. In the car, driving through Chicago, he ended up in a traffic jam on Interstate 94 and got stuck in traffic for more than two hours, during which time his frustration served as a tipping point, causing him to decide not to take that job in a traffic-congested city.

God has a plan for our lives.
There are no accidents.

I think that both the university and the City of Toledo have benefited tremendously because one man got stuck in a traffic jam. Any maybe, just maybe, a few children are alive today because of Dr. Jacobs's metrics regarding infant mortality.

God has a plan for our lives. There are no accidents. We need to pay attention to these occurrences and follow the path God has created for us.

Often in life, like Dr. Jacobs's trip to Chicago, things don't go as planned, and we spend a significant amount of effort, energy, and time sorting out a difficult scenario. We need to face those challenges head-on, pray for God's guidance, figure out what we need to do about it, and make it right. And often, during that process, we discover a lot about ourselves, including what we do and do not want to do and where we do and do not belong. It is during that discovery and renewal process that we often experience newfound clarity and vision about God's purpose for us.

Other Ways to Discover Your Calling

We believe that completing the exercise in Chapter 1—listing twenty-one activities and ranking them from what you love to do down through what you dislike doing—will help you make tremendous progress toward finding your true north so that you can spend your life doing what you love. There are myriad other tools that can help you in your quest to discover your calling, too. We have listed some additional ways to be open to His calling.

Pray for God's Guidance

Because we believe that God knows every individual's calling before he or she is even born, we also believe it's critical to pray for God to reveal His plan for your life. In the book The Power of a Whisper: Hearing God, Having the Guts to Respond, *author Bill Hybels says, "I've come to believe that hearing the quiet whisper of the transcendent God is one of the most extraordinary privileges in all of life—and potentially the most transforming dynamic in the Christian faith. When people hear from heaven, they are rarely the same again. . . . Without a hint of exaggeration, I can boldly declare that God's low-volume whispers have saved me from a life of sure boredom and self-destruction. They have redirected my path, rescued me from temptation, and reenergized me during some of my deepest moments of despair.*[37]

At any age, we can all benefit from training, mentorship, apprenticeship, and higher education.

Spend Time in Self-Reflection

If you don't already do so, make it a point occasionally to rise before dawn and spend time, before you commence your busy day, in self-reflection while you take a walk or drink your coffee. Before dawn, there's a stillness, a peace to the world. This quality time will allow you to gain self-awareness and psychological insight as you pray, meditate, reflect on your life situation, and gain clarity that you might not be able to attain while your mind is preoccupied with work, school, or taking care of children.

Take a Personality Profile

Tools like the Myers–Briggs Personality Indicator® can help you discover your personality type, which affects all aspects of your life. Knowing more about your type can help you communicate with people, plan your future, and get to know yourself better. CPP, Inc., the exclusive publisher of the MBTI instrument, offers personal profiles and interpretations online at https://www.mbticomplete.com/en/index.aspx.

Make a Commitment to Lifelong Learning

We are never too old to learn. At any age, we can all benefit from training, mentorship, apprenticeship, and higher education. Taking courses later in life may expose us to subjects that we were never able to explore at a younger age. Reading some of your favorite books from past years is a great learning experience.

---

37. Bill Hybels, *The Power of a Whisper: Hearing God, Having the Guts to Respond* (Grand Rapids, Michigan: Zondervan, 2010), 16–17.

Although the book hasn't changed, you have, usually in profound ways that allow you to see things you missed the first time around.

Hire a Life Coach

Psychologists, life coaches, counselors, and spiritual advisors help us see our unique set of circumstances in new ways. Many athletes use coaches, and many CEOs use executive coaches, to help them optimize their potential. Today, anyone can benefit from the counsel of a professional to help them embark on a new career, improve relationships, or achieve financial freedom. Even if you live in a small town or remote area, you can conduct counseling sessions via phone, Skype, and e-mail. With a counselor, you can gain insight as well as the support that is so critical to success.

According to a review in Psychotherapy Networker, *a magazine for professionals in the psychotherapy field, about ten thousand life coaches of various types are working in the United States alone. They usually begin by asking extensive, specific questions and honing in on a precise set of goals. Homework may include writing in a journal, doing exercises such as building a "life blueprint," and reporting on progress with various action plans.[38] It is an unregulated field, and practitioners are not required to obtain credentials. Before hiring a life coach, ask people you know for referrals, and check references.*

As the old saying goes, "Plans fail for a lack of counsel, but with many advisors, they succeed."

Keep a "Calling Journal"

In the book *Whistle While You Work: Heeding Your Life's Calling*, authors Dick Leider and David Shapiro suggest keeping a "calling journal." They write, "When we record the details of our yearnings, we are more likely to connect at a deeper level with the Source of our calling. Keeping track of our dreams, ideas, and insights can give us the extra push we need to heed our calling."[39]

Practice Creative Visualization

In her book *Visioning: Ten Steps to Designing the Life of Your Dreams*, Lucia Capacchione says that visioning is rooted in the idea that you can design your own

---

38. Karen S. Peterson, "Life Coaches All the Rage," *USA Today*, accessed November 29, 2013, http://www.usatoday.com/news/health/2002-08-04-lifecoach_x.htm.

39. Richard J. Leider and David A. Shapiro, *Whistle While You Work: Heeding Your Life's Calling* (San Francisco: Berrett-Koehler Publishers, Inc., 2001), 40.

life and that it is within your power to design the life of your dreams and vision your dream into reality. The process begins by naming your heart's desire and translating it into pictures and words on paper.[40]

Plan a Personal Retreat

In their book *Who Are You? What Do You Want? Four Questions That Will Change Your Life*, authors Nick Ukleja and Robert Lorder recommend taking a two-day retreat in a quiet setting and following a series of exercises to help you focus on determining your life's path. They recommend using the forty-eight-hour "Who Am I and What Do I Want?" Personal Retreat either privately or in corporate retreat settings.[41]

Gain Inspiration from Others

Each month on the NBC's *TODAY* show titled "Life Reimagined TODAY," and in features at AARP.org/Jane, Emmy-award-winning journalist Jane Pauley and AARP shine a spotlight on people who, both by choice and necessity, are reinventing themselves. These people are starting new careers, learning new skills, changing how they live, and, after years of waiting, finally pursuing their dreams. A live radio show is featured as part of the series, too. Seeing how others have discovered their life calling may give you ideas and inspiration.

Take a Fourteen-Question Quiz

At http://www.theonequestion.com/test/1.php/ is a fourteen-question quiz you can take to "find your purpose in life and live your passion." The fourteen questions are as follows:

1. What are you naturally curious about?
2. What would you like to change about the world?
3. What would you love to accomplish before you die?
4. What would you do if you could not fail?
5. What would you do if you would not be limited by money?
6. What would you like to hear at your funeral?

---

40. Lucia Capacchione, *Visioning: Ten Steps to Designing the Life of Your Dreams* (New York: Tarcher /Putnam Books, 2000), 16–17.

41. Nick Ukleja, PhD, and Robert L. Lorber, PhD, *Who Are You? What Do You Want? Four Questions That Will Change Your Life* (London: Penguin Books, Ltd., 2009), 105.

7. What are the things you currently enjoy doing?

8. What were the activities or tasks you were doing when you felt most empowered?

9. What would you most like to be acknowledged for so far in your life?

10. If you had only one wish, what would it be?

11. Whose life do you want to be living?

12. What ideas are you most inspired by? Why?

13. With whom do you like to surround yourself?

14. Do you take responsibility for what is happening to you?

Write Down Your Goals

Instead of just thinking about what you'd like to accomplish, write your goals down and share them with someone else. A study conducted at Dominican University revealed that people who write their goals down, record their progress regularly, and send their commitments to a friend accomplish significantly more than people who do not follow these steps.[42]

> Instead of just thinking about what you'd like to accomplish, write your goals down and share them with someone else.

Further Reading

A question we hear over and over again is, "Can you refer me to some books on the topic of finding your life's calling?" In addition to this book, we have put together a list of books that will introduce you to the insight and philosophies of many authors who have investigated this topic.

- Captain D. Michael Abrashoff, *It's Your Ship: Management Techniques from the Best Damn Ship in the Navy*, Warner Books, 2002

- Larry Barton, PhD, *Crisis Leadership Now*, McGraw-Hill, 2008

- Srully Blotnick, *Getting Rich Your Own Way*, Doubleday, 1980

---

42. "Goals Research Summary," accessed November 29, 2013, http://www.goaltrak.com/files /articles/researchsummary2.pdf.

- Gregg Braden, *The Divine Matrix: Bridging Time, Space, Miracles, and Belief*, Hay House, 2007

- Kevin Brennfleck and Kay Marie Brennfleck, *Live Your Calling: A Practical Guide to Finding and Fulfilling Your Mission in Life*, Jossey-Bass, 2005

- Marcus Buckingham and Donald O. Clifton, *Now, Discover Your Strengths*, The Free Press, 2001

- Lucia Capacchione, *Visioning: Ten Steps to Designing the Life of Your Dreams*, Tarcher/Putnam Books, 2000

- Jim Collins and Jerry I. Porras, *Built to Last: Successful Habits of Visionary Companies*, HarperBusiness, 2004

- Jim Collins, *Good to Great: Why Some Companies Make the Leap and Others Don't*, HarperBusiness, 2001

- Stephen R. Covey, *The 7 Habits of Highly Effective People*, Free Press, 2004

- Chris Crowley and Henry S. Lodge, MD, *Younger Next Year: Live Strong, Fit, and Sexy—Until You're Eighty and Beyond*, Workman Publishing Company, 2007

- William Damon, *The Path to Purpose: How Young People Find Their Calling in Life*, Free Press, 2008

- Ed Deutschlander and Rich Campe, *Be the First Believer: Leadership Life Lessons*, Bethany Press International, 2013

- Diane Dreher, *Your Personal Renaissance: Twelve Steps to Finding Your Life's True Calling*, Perseus Books, 2008

- Peter F. Drucker, *The Essential Drucker: The Best of Sixty Years of Peter Drucker's Essential Writings on Management*, Harper Paperbacks, 2008

- Tony Dungy, *The Mentor Leader: Secrets to Building People and Teams That Win Consistently*, Tyndale House Publishers, 2010

- Martha Finney and Deborah Dasch, *Find Your Calling, Love Your Life*, Simon & Schuster, 1998

- Viktor E. Frankl, *Man's Search for Meaning*, Simon & Schuster, 1963

- Bill George, Andrew N. McLean, and Nick Craig, *Finding Your True North: A Personal Guide*, Jossey-Bass, 2008

- Bill George, *True North: Finding Your Authentic Leadership*, Jossey-Bass, 2007

- Michael E. Gerber, *The E-Myth Revisited*, HarperCollins, 1995, 2001

- Malcolm Gladwell, *Outliers: The Story of Success*, Little, Brown & Company, 2011

- Malcolm Godwin, *Who Are You: 101 Ways of Seeing Yourself*, Penguin Books, 2000

- Martin Grunburg, *The Habit Factor: The Science of Behavior Meets the Art of Achievement*, Equilibrium Enterprises, 2010

- Leo Hauser, *Leo Hauser's Five Steps to Success*, Hauser Productions, 1993

- Tony Hsieh, *Delivering Happiness: A Path to Profits, Passion, and Purpose*, Hachette Book Group, 2010

- Bill Hybels, *The Power of a Whisper: Hearing God, Having the Guts to Respond*, Zondervan, 2010

- Lawrence Pearsall Jacks, *Education through Recreation*, 1932

- Michael Jordan, Mark Vancil, and Sandro Miller, *I Can't Accept Not Trying: Michael Jordan on the Pursuit of Excellence*, Harper, 1994

- Jeremie Kubicek, *Leadership Is Dead: How Influence Is Reviving It*, Howard Books, 2011

- Richard J. Leider and David A. Shapiro, *Whistle While You Work: Heeding Your Life's Calling*, Berrett-Koehler Publishers, Inc., 2001

- Norman G. Levine, *A Passion for Compassion: The Formula for Successful Financial Advisors*, La Gesse Stevens Publishers, 2001

- Norman G. Levine, *Past Is Prologue: Timeless Techniques for Financial Advisors in the 21st Century*, National Underwriter Company, 2008

- Alan Lew, *This Is Real and You Are Completely Unprepared: The Days of Awe as a Journey of Transformation*, Little, Brown & Company, 2003

- Maxwell Maltz, *Psycho-Cybernetics: A New Way to Get More Living Out of Life*, Simon & Schuster, 1960

- Leon Martel, *Mastering Change: The Key to Business Success*, Simon & Schuster, 1986

- John C. Maxwell, *Everyone Communicates, Few Connect: What the Most Effective People Do Differently*, Thomas Nelson, Inc., 2010

- Harvey B. McKay, *Swim with the Sharks without Being Eaten Alive: Outsell, Outmanage, Outmotivate, and Outnegotiate Your Competition*, HarperBusiness, 2005

- Dan Millman, *The Four Purposes of Life: Finding Meaning and Direction in a Changing World*, New World Library, 2011

- Dan Millman, *Way of the Peaceful Warrior: A Book that Changes Lives*, H. J. Kramer, 2006

- Norman Vincent Peale, *You Can if You Think You Can*, Fireside/Simon & Schuster, 1986

- M. Scott Peck, MD, *The Road Less Traveled: A New Psychology of Love, Traditional Values, and Spiritual Growth*, Touchstone, 1978

- Thomas J. Peters and Robert H. Waterman, *In Search of Excellence: Lessons from America's Best-Run Companies*, Warner Books, 1982

- Paul Zane Pilzer, *Unlimited Wealth: The Theory and Practice of Economic Alchemy*, Crown, 1991

- Tom Rath, *StrengthsFinder 2.0*, Gallup Press, 2007

- Phillip C. Richards, *Twenty-Five Secrets to Sustainable Success*, GAMA International, 2007

- Mark Sanborn, *The Fred Factor: How Passion in Your Work and Life Can Turn the Ordinary into the Extraordinary*, Doubleday, 2004

- Kurt Senske, *The Calling: Live a Life of Significance*, Concordia Publishing House, 2010

- Art Sepulveda, *How to Live Life on Purpose: Discover Your Calling and How You Can Fulfill It*, Harrison House, Inc., 2004

- Robin Sharma, *The Leader Who Had No Title: A Modern Fable on Real Success in Business and in Life*, Free Press, 2010

- Fred Sievert, *God Revealed: Revisit Your Path to Enrich Your Future*, Morgan James Publishing, 2014

- Artie Sposaro, *Sacred Flow: Discovering Life in the Divine Current*, Missional Press, 2011

- Charles F. Stanley, *God Has a Plan for Your Life: The Discovery That Makes All the Difference*, Thomas Nelson, 2008

- Maury Stewart, *The Miracle Business: A Lifetime of Lessons on Leadership*, GAMA International, 2012

- Paul G. Stoltz, PhD, *Adversity Quotient @ Work: Make Everyday Challenges the Key to Your Success—Putting the Principles of AQ into Action*, HarperCollins, 2000

- Jim Stovall, *The Ultimate Gift*, David C. Cook Publishers, 2001

- Richard A. Swenson, *Margin: Restoring Emotional, Physical, Financial, and Time Reserves to Overloaded Lives*, NavPress, 2004

- Matthew Syed, *Bounce: Mozart, Federer, Picasso, Beckham, and the Science of Success*, HarperCollins Publishers, 2011

- *The Individual Psychology of Alfred Adler: A Systematic Presentation in Selections from His Writings*, edited by Heinz L. Ansbacher and Rowena R. Ansbacher, Harper & Row, 1956

- Nick Ukleja, PhD, and Robert L. Lorber, PhD, *Who Are You? What Do You Want? Four Questions That Will Change Your Life*, Penguin Books, Ltd.

- Rick Warren, *The Purpose-Driven Life: What on Earth Am I Here For?* Zondervan, 2012

- Ron Willingham, *The People Principle: A Revolutionary Redefinition of Leadership*, St. Martin's Press, 1997

It's Your Turn

Exercise 5-1: What did you love to do as a child?

What you enjoyed doing as a child provides clues about where your life's calling lies. Think back to your childhood. What did you enjoy doing?

1. _____
2. _____
3. _____
4. _____
5. _____
6. _____
7. _____
8. _____

Exercise 5-2: Who can you mentor or help grow by requiring accountability?

_____
_____
_____
_____
_____
_____
_____

Chapter

6

The Importance of Self-Awareness

He who knows others is wise. He who knows himself
is enlightened.

Lao Tzu
Chinese Taoist Philosopher

Self-awareness is defined as a clear understanding of your strengths, weaknesses, beliefs, inclinations, habits, motivations, emotions, and values, and it is an important factor in achieving success. Self-awareness is the first step in creating what you want in life. Having clarity about who you are, what you want, and why you want it empowers you to make those desires a reality consciously and actively.

The better you know yourself, the better you will be able to make changes to improve yourself. Knowing yourself well also makes it easier for you to complete the exercise in Chapter 1, in which you rank your activities or job functions from those you like the most to those you like the least.

Not knowing who you are stunts your personal and professional growth, keeps you embroiled in internal struggles and ruts, and leads to unfulfilling or difficult relationships.

Many philosophers, psychologists, and writers throughout the centuries have commented on the importance of self-assessment:

- "I know I'm not seeing things as they are; I'm seeing things as I am." Author Laurel Lee

- "A loving person lives in a loving world, and a hostile person lives in a hostile world. Everyone you meet is your mirror." Ken Keyes Jr. said this in his *Handbook to Higher Consciousness*.

- "As you are on the inside, you are on the outside."

- "You become what you think about." American motivational speaker and author Earl Nightingale said that in 1956 in *The Strangest Secret*, and it's as true today as it was then.
- "A man is but the product of his thoughts; what he thinks, he becomes." Mahatma Gandhi
- "Garbage in, garbage out." Silicon Valley maxim
- "The unexamined life is not worth living." Socrates
- "Introspection with an emphasis on growth and change will help us to achieve a full and fulfilled life." Sir John Templeton said this in *Discovering the Laws of Life.*
- "Know thyself." Greek proverb

Why Self-Awareness Is Rare

Why don't more people engage in self-examination to take a hard look at who they are? Often it's because self-reflection is not something that is modeled to us; we didn't learn it from our parents or teachers. Another reason people don't engage in self-reflection is that our pre-conscious mind is flooded with a lot of trauma and drama, and we want to keep that all hidden from the world—and from ourselves. We avoid the process of self-examination and self-reflection because we want to avoid finding anything negative or unpleasant. Emotionally it could overwhelm us. So we go day by day, week by week, not engaging in self-examination. Some people would like to self-examine but just haven't found the person to do it with, the time to do it, or the emotional wherewithal to turn inward because we're afraid of what we're going to see.

We avoid the process of self-examination
and self-reflection because we want to avoid
finding anything negative or unpleasant.

Another reason we don't self-reflect is because we want to be in control of everything. The exercise we've proposed in Chapter 1 requires that you rank twenty-one activities or job functions from the ones you enjoy the most down to the ones you enjoy the least, then delegate those functions at the bottom of your list to other people. But many people are reluctant to delegate tasks to others because they fear the job won't get done properly. It's a pride or control issue. Sometimes, to be the most effective, we have to let go of some duties and focus on those that we enjoy the most—and that pay us the most.

There are people out there who will say, "I can do all twenty-one of these tasks better than anybody else, so why would I want to delegate them?" The answer is because if you focus on the activities that you love to do and that produce the most revenue, you'll get a lot more done, you'll make more money, and you'll have a lot more fun. Given a finite amount of time, you ought to be focusing on those things that you enjoy doing and that you're really good at.

Frequently, we teach our advisors to focus on relationships and raising revenue and to let our support staff handle the $10- and $20-an-hour work. One such advisor, Ted, who earns more than $1 million a year, is really good at what he does. He has six full-time team members. Ted is a great delegator and delegates everything to these six people. But when he gets their work back, he goes over every last comma and every last piece of arithmetic. In my quarterly reviews with him for more than a quarter of a century now, I have told him, "Why don't you let them all go? Why are you paying them? You're doing all their work for them in the final analysis anyway."

Ted can't or won't change because he's a perfectionist. His professionalism compels him to make sure it's right. Well, here's what happens. Maybe his assistant makes two mistakes per hundred cases, and Ted is so good that he makes only one mistake per hundred cases. He winds up doing a lot of $10- and $20-an-hour work in time that he could be using to meet with high-revenue-producing clients. If he were to let his assistants' work go without checking behind them, it would mean apologizing to two clients a year instead of only one. That said, he is a true professional and a great advisor.

When I was a youngster, one of my teammates asked our wrestling coach why he should stop smoking if Mickey Mantle smoked—and look how good Mickey Mantle is. Our coach replied, "Just think how good Mickey Mantle would be if he didn't smoke." That's the point—just think how good Ted would be if he focused only on the things he loved doing, such as managing relationships and building even more trust with his clients by allowing them to see just how trustworthy he is. One thing is for sure: He'd enjoy what he does more that way.

The saying goes, "Perfectionism can be a life of misery, but excellence is a life of bliss." You can always strive to be excellent, but you can never be perfect. That's why the Oakland Raiders' motto is "A tradition of excellence," not a tradition of perfection. If we just shift our mindset a little, we could release ourselves from feeling compelled to attain perfection. It's just not possible, so why set yourself up for defeat?

How Others' Perceptions Mold Us

Many times, we have a distorted view of who we are based on what others have told us. As children, we begin to build up a self-image through how others see us, and we develop unique strategies to gain approval, acceptance, and love. Our parents, teachers, and peers all had their own warped viewpoints created by their own upbringing. They could not reflect on who was in front of them, only on what their own conditioning allowed them to. Many times, we try to adjust our behavior to conform to that distorted image that others have of us. Admiral Ray Smith, the former Navy SEALs trainer we mentioned earlier, said, "Personal myths born of youth, which form the foundation of adult personalities, are almost completely devoid of facts and logic!" Taking the time to find out who we really are helps us live an authentic life that is void of the distorted images that others impose on us. It is liberating to know who you are and to live the life you were meant to have.

In some cases, others tell us we're capable of much more than we can actually accomplish. I know of some parents who had unrealistically high expectations for their child. They put incredible pressures on her, and it created tension in the home. Finally they put the child through some psychological and IQ testing and found out that her IQ was average. They realized that the child had been operating within her realm of ability. At that point, they recognized that they had been expecting too much of her. A lot of parents do this—they develop an expectation that their children are going to attend Princeton or play in the NBA, yet some children don't have the aptitude for that level of performance. Assessing their abilities can shed light on their capabilities, thus allowing parents and teachers to maintain realistic expectations of them.

In other cases, people expect too little of us. Victor Serebriakoff (1912–2000) was born in the slums of east London, the son of a Russian father and a Cockney mother. He dropped out of school and got a job as an office clerk at a lumber company, but he was soon dismissed for lack of attention to detail. He then worked as a manual laborer, with periods of unemployment during the Depression. He signed up for the army during World War II. On the standardized army intelligence test, he learned that he had an IQ of at least 161, as high as the scale went. The army assigned him to train recruits in its teaching corps.

He later joined Mensa, the high-IQ society that is open to people who have attained a score within the upper 2 percent of the general population on an approved intelligence test that has been properly administered and supervised. After being named secretary in 1954, he helped the organization grow from four members who shared dinners together to a worldwide organization boasting more than 100,000 members. Enthusiastic about the organization, he helped build membership by sending out brochures, appearing on television, approaching universities, and introducing supervised testing as an entry requirement. Serebriakoff became the Honorary International President of Mensa in 1982.

But until he had a reliable, valid self-assessment done, no one knew how intelligent he was and therefore didn't expect much of him. Had he never gotten that test done, he would have been held back his entire life by an erroneous perception of his capabilities.

A Plethora of Self-Assessment Tests

In addition to IQ tests, many self-assessment tests are available online and through psychologists and career counselors to help adults determine their strengths, weaknesses, goals, interests, and personality type. Most of them are intended only for informal use and enlightenment; few of them could stand up in a court of law.

Tests that a career counselor may administer include the Minnesota Importance Questionnaire (MIQ), the Survey of Interpersonal Values (SIV), and the Temperament and Values Inventory (TVI).

> Many self-assessment tests are available online and through psychologists and career counselors to help adults determine their strengths, weaknesses, goals, interests, and personality type.

A popular interest inventory is the Strong Interest Inventory (SII), formerly known as the Strong–Campbell Interest Inventory. The SII is administered by a career development professional, who also scores it and interprets the results. Other interest inventories include the Kuder Occupational Interest Survey and the Self-Directed Search (SDS), which you can take on your own. SDS was developed in accordance with National Career Development Association (NCDA) guidelines. An online version that is published by PAR (Psychological Assessment Resources, Inc.) is available at http://www.self-directed-search.com/how -much-is-it-. After completing the assessment, you will receive a printable report containing a list of occupations that most closely match your interests. You can also try O*Net Interest Profiler, a free tool that can help you discover your interests. It's available at http://www.mynextmove.org/explore/ip.

The Enneagram is another well-known system for learning about yourself and others. The Enneagram test reveals which of nine "type descriptions" you fall under: The Reformer, The Helper, The Achiever, The Individualist, The Investigator, The Loyalist, The Enthusiast, The Challenger, or The Peacemaker. Some tests are free on the Enneagram Institute's website (http://www.enneagraminstitute.com/), but there is a fee for others. The Enneagram is not commonly taught or researched in academic psychology. It has been promoted widely in both business-management and spiritual contexts. In business contexts, it is generally used as a typology to gain insights into workplace dynamics; in spirituality, it is more commonly presented as a path to higher states of being, essence, and enlightenment. It has been described as a method for self-understanding and self-development but has been criticized as being subject to interpretation, making it difficult to test or validate scientifically.

Numerous other self-assessment resources are listed at http://www.rileyguide.com/assess.html.

Quieting the Mind

Self-awareness is best achieved when the mind is quiet. Those who meditate are well aware of the benefits of meditation, which is known to reduce stress, lower blood pressure, reverse heart disease, reduce pain, and enhance the body's immune system, enabling it to fight illness. Some studies have found a direct correlation between meditation and the performance level of sports professionals.

> "Internal chatter" often gets in the way of prayer.

According to a Psychology Today article, meditation brings about a higher level of self-acceptance and insight about oneself. The physical act of meditation generally consists of simply sitting quietly and focusing on one's breath and a word or phrase. Many people can't seem to get the hang of it, no matter how often they try, because it is a struggle to overcome the internal chatter that we all experience.[43]

That "internal chatter" often gets in the way of prayer, too. Rabbi Alan Lew said that often, when we attempt to pray, our minds become filled with thoughts that interfere with our prayers. He wrote, "The thoughts that carry our attention away [during

---

43. Cary Barbor, "The Science of Meditation," *Psychology Today*, last modified May 1, 2001, accessed on November 30, 2013, http://www.psychologytoday.com/articles/200105/the-science -meditation.

prayer or meditation] are never insignificant thoughts, and they never arise at random. We lose our focus precisely because these thoughts need our attention and we refuse to give it to them. This is why they keep sneaking up on our attention and stealing it away. This is how it is that we come to know ourselves as we settle deeply into the act of prayer [or meditation].[44]

What bombards our minds are the situations we've been blocking out and not dealing with. As soon as we quiet ourselves, those thoughts compete for our attention. It's the work of the pre-conscious mind. It's important for us to pay attention to those thoughts and deal with them regularly because they block the flow of energy from within us. When we process that information and deal with it, then we begin to feel lighter, and our minds are clearer. Things begin to flow and click. We can listen better. We can meditate or pray more easily and hear God's whisper more readily. Then we are better able to self-reflect and gain self-awareness.

I recently attended my nineteenth Jesuit religious retreat in which participants are silent for four days. We are allowed to speak to one another during the opening dinner on Thursday night and during the closing dinner on Sunday night, but I choose not to speak even then. The purpose of the retreat is pure introspection and reflection, and it gives people an opportunity to get their priorities straight and to solidify their relationship with God. During every retreat, I come away with an "a-ha!" realization. Two "a-ha!" realizations came to me during the 2013 retreat—first, that "Christian indifference" allows me to accept whatever cards I'm dealt, even though I've prayed for a different outcome, and second, that God's plan for each of us is long-term, not short-term. In 2012, my "a-ha!" realization was that the greatest gift that God gives us is forgiveness. We continue to sin, and He continues to forgive us. At another silent retreat, my "a-ha!" realization was "Don't let somebody else's actions determine your behavior." I realized that if you do so, you're a puppet and they're a puppeteer. That was worth four days of my life. From that point on, whenever something happens that I don't like, I think about how important it is not to allow someone else's incivility to determine my behavior.

Richie Pastorella is a boyhood friend of mine from the lower east side of Manhattan who became a policeman in New York City. When my wife, Sue, and I were on our way to Europe one year, we had dinner with Richie and his wife in New York. In his car as we were driving through Brooklyn, suddenly a car came up behind us, and the driver began tailgating us and flipping his high beams on and off because Richie was going the speed limit or slower. Richie was talking,

---

44. Alan Lew, *This Is Real and You Are Completely Unprepared: The Days of Awe as a Journey of Transformation* (New York: Little, Brown & Company, 2003), 69.

but he never took his attention off of the road or what he was saying. I was sitting in the front seat with Richie and looking at the flickering light coming into the car. He could see that I was distracted and said, "You know, that guy behind me is trying to tick me off and get my attention, but I'm just going to ignore him." I thought, *Here is a detective in the New York City Police Department with a gun on him (New York policemen are required to have their guns with them 24/7) who is quite capable of taking two men out with his bare fists, and he is ignoring this rude (lucky) driver. There is no anger, there is no being upset, there's no road rage. Nothing.* Richie was a guy in control, a man who knew himself. He refused to let the other driver's incivility determine his behavior.

In my first book, *Twenty-Five Secrets to Sustainable Success,* I tell Richie's story of being blown up by a bomb on December 31, 1981, at the courthouse in lower Manhattan when he was a detective and member of the New York City Bomb Squad. Though he endured hundreds of operations and lost sight in both eyes and 95 percent of his hearing, I never heard him say an unkind word about the FALN, the Puerto Rican terrorist group that had planted the bomb. Richie went on to get two master's degrees and to devote his life to giving consoling presentations throughout America to the surviving family members of police officers and firefighters who have died on duty. Once again, he refused to allow the incivility of others to determine his behavior. Dealt a bad set of cards, he totally controlled his reaction to that personal tragedy. He continues to lead a life worth living. Today, both of his sons, Mark and Richard, are detectives in the NYPD.

Sports Help Reveal Your True Character

When you're involved in athletics, you really find out what you're made of. Sports reveal character. You can't hide out there on the field, court, or mat. As you engage in challenging physical competitions, you'll see what's on the inside, and you'll get a very clear assessment right away as to what you're good at and what you're not good at. The key is being open to coaching, hearing evaluations, and receiving guidance and feedback.

In sports, you can't let random thoughts ruin your concentration. In wrestling, you could be winning 12–0, and in one split second, if you lose your attention, you're on your back, and you've just lost the bout. It's the same if you're a defensive player on a football team. With one lapse of concentration, one misstep, you suddenly have a receiver two or three feet behind you, and you've just given up a touchdown. You have to know your abilities and maintain consistent concentration.

Learning from Our Losses

A lot of times, we learn more from our losses than we do from our wins, both in sports and in life. We become aware of who we are through our pain. Rear Admiral Ray Smith says, "Sometimes the brightest light comes from a burning bridge." Those epiphanies we experience after a failure can tell us a lot about ourselves. They also help us avoid making the same mistake again, which, in turn, leads us closer to achieving our goals and finding our true north.

> Those epiphanies we experience after a failure can tell us a lot about ourselves.

In sports, it's all about in-game adjustments. In a basketball game, the athletes and coaches determine the adjustments they can make immediately to have a better outcome. That's self-awareness. The more we're able to learn from our losses and make those adjustments quickly in life, the more we're going to find out what we're called to do—the things that we love to do and that give us enduring energy.

Listening to Intuition

Albert Einstein said, "The really valuable thing is intuition." When I think back on my life and on all the choices I regret, there was often a visceral intuition that I ignored, and I wish in hindsight that I had had greater awareness of it and that I had given it more time, attention, and thought. If I had done so, things probably would have turned out differently. It's important that we "listen to our gut." Intuition is a powerful guide, but we often ignore it.

One of the reasons we drown out that intuition is that we overload our schedules and become stressed. The book Margin *explains how to build margins into all aspects of our lives so that we're not overloaded and stressed. Written by a Christian doctor named Richard Swenson, the book talks about how important it is to create financial, time-related, and emotional margins.*[45] *Building in that extra space allows us to be more reflective and self-aware.*

---

45. Richard A. Swenson, *Margin: Restoring Emotional, Physical, Financial, and Time Reserves to Overloaded Lives* (Colorado Springs, Colorado: NavPress, 2004).

Sometimes clues abound regarding who we are and what our life's calling is, but because we are not self-aware, we cannot see, hear, or heed those clues. Being more self-aware can help us pay attention to the clues that are directing us toward our ideal life's path.

> Being more self-aware can help us pay
> attention to the clues that are directing us
> toward our ideal life's path.

Self-Awareness on the Job

According to an article on *Inc.* magazine's website, self-awareness is probably one of the least-discussed leadership competencies but possibly one of the most valuable. In a work environment, self-awareness is being conscious of what you're good at while acknowledging what you have yet to learn. This includes admitting when you don't have the answer and owning up to your mistakes. To increase self-awareness, the article suggests the following:

1. Solicit feedback about your work performance, either informally or through 360-degree assessments, through which superiors, peers, and those reporting to you anonymously provide feedback on all aspects of your behavior. Then make necessary improvements and adjustments.

2. Reflect on each day's events, including how people reacted to you and how fluidly you were able to work with or manage others. To do this effectively on your own requires a high degree of emotional intelligence, or EQ, which is defined as awareness of your own and others' emotions and how they are impacted by situations.

3. Conduct regular "post-mortems" on every project you're involved in. This requires that you ask good questions and listen to others without justifying or defending your actions.[46]

We all become conditioned by the events and people around us. In some cases, our habits, values, and desires are shaped by the influence others have had on us for years or even decades. Being self-aware puts us in control of our own lives and empowers us to discover what genuinely motivates us. It can help us make better decisions. It takes courage to analyze ourselves because the process often reveals

---

46. Chris Musselwhite, "Self-Awareness and the Effective Leader," Inc.com, accessed on November 30, 2013, http://www.inc.com/resources/leadership/articles/20071001/musselwhite.html.

aspects of our character that we need to change. But taking that important step and then making improvements and adjustments will lead us to more opportunities in life and a higher level of fulfillment. The sky is not the limit. There is little that we can't accomplish if we are keenly aware of our own strengths and weaknesses!

It's Your Turn

Exercise 6-1: How self-aware are you?

Self-awareness is the first step in creating what you want in life, and it requires that you have a clear understanding of your strengths, weaknesses, beliefs, inclinations, habits, motivations, emotions, and values.

1. My strengths include

_____

_____

2. My weaknesses include

_____

_____

3. I believe that

_____

_____

4. I know that I am inclined to

_____

_____

5. My habits include

_____

_____

6. I am motivated by

_____

_____

7. My values include

_____

_____

Exercise 6-2

How much do you allow the incivility of others to determine your behavior?

_____

How can you improve in this area? How important is that to you? To your loved ones?

_____

_____

_____

_____

_____

_____

Chapter

7

Let Good Habits Guide Your Path

Habit is either the best of servants or the worst of masters.

Nathaniel Emmons
American Theologian

Developing good habits and forgoing bad habits can help you become who and what you are meant to be.

Back in 1960, cosmetic surgeon Dr. Maxwell Maltz contended in his book *Psycho-Cybernetics* that it takes about twenty-one days to dissolve an old mental image and adopt a new one.[47] Since that time, many experts have agreed that it takes twenty-one days to establish a new habit.

Martin Grunburg, author of *The Habit Factor*, believes it can take up to three months to develop a new habit and that the most important factor in the formation of any habit is consistency over time. He also believes that developing good habits is good for us. "Science has proven that habits can help to keep us safe and make our life easier," he says. "When habit is engaged, we save precious energy as we accomplish worthwhile and practical tasks without conscious thought."[48]

A Big Enough "Why"

Business consultant Brian Tracy says that the speed of new-habit pattern development is largely determined by the intensity of the emotion that accompanies the decision to begin acting in a particular way. For example, he notes that many

---

47. Maltz, *Psycho-Cybernetics*, xiii.

48. Martin Grunburg, *The Habit Factor: The Science of Behavior Meets the Art of Achievement* (La Jolla, California: Equilibrium Enterprises, 2010), 57.

people think and talk about losing weight and resolve to lose weight and become physically fit, and this may go on for years. Then one day, the doctor says, "If you don't get your weight down and improve your physical condition, you are in danger of dying at an early age." Suddenly, the thought of dying can be so intense or frightening that the individual immediately changes his diet, begins exercising, stops smoking, and becomes a healthy and fit person. Psychologists refer to this as a "significant emotional experience" or SEE.[49]

We have to understand the "why," the motivation, behind our actions.

Similarly, I believe that if you have a big enough *why*, you'll figure out the *how*. Whether the goal is losing weight, becoming a champion weight lifter, or some other life change, it will be easier to put the habit-formation process in place if it's meaningful enough to you. I always marvel at women who are engaged to be married and decide to lose weight so that they can look great in their wedding dress. That's a big "why." It's really important to them to look good on what many consider to be the most important day of their life. They succeed because of the big why.

It's very difficult for us to develop habits if we're not passionate about what we're doing. Why would I want to get up and run at five o'clock in the morning? Why is it worth it to me? Again, we have to understand the "why," the motivation, behind our actions. It is critical in developing habits. It's really about tapping into those God-given talents we have, those things inside of us that make us special and unique. And many times, we need to build good habits, not for money or fame, but just because we can, because we realize that it's a gift, and because when we do it, we feel closer to God, and we feel energized. We feel alive. It's easier to develop good habits if we know that this is leading some place that only we can go and if we feel deep inside of ourselves that we are meant to go there.

One of the reasons I love sports is because at that moment of truth, when you're out there on the playing field, it's very difficult to hide if you've cut corners and failed to maintain good habits. Sooner or later, on the bigger stage, you and everyone else will know if you did all the right things or not. If you ate healthy foods, if you lifted weights effectively, if you were in shape and pushed as hard as you could on your runs, then those are the good habits that are going to give you confidence—and victory—in those moments of truth.

---

49. "Seven Steps to Developing a New Habit," Brian Tracy International, last modified October 4, 2011, accessed on December 3, 2013, http://www.briantracy.com/blog/personal-success/seven-steps-to-developing-a-new-habit/.

Good Habits Are Liberating

A good habit is really about freedom. You might think you would feel imprisoned by a habit, but just the opposite is true—if you have a good habit, you do it without thinking. It's automatic. For example, my wife says to me frequently, "I'm just amazed at the fact that you have to shave every morning." But I don't even think about shaving. It became a habit for me long ago. In fact, I shave even if I'm at home alone over a weekend. Habits liberate you. They give you freedom. The businessperson who has to make a lot of calls or invest time in a task does those things automatically. They may seem painful to others, but to the businessperson doing them, they're non-events because he or she has formed the proper habits.

We have a thirty-ninth-floor condominium in Florida with a railing around the deck. How many people would walk out on that deck if there were no railing? The railing is a tool of containment as well as a permission slip to view the ocean. I think if people understood that, they would be more prone and willing to invest the time and effort it takes to develop a good habit. Habits set you free!

Understanding the Trade-Off

Everything in life is a trade-off. Nobody likes getting up early in the morning to exercise; however, the trade-off is that if you can get out of bed and get out the door, then you get the intrinsic reward of being outside early in the morning, running or walking, when the world is still. You get to sweat out toxins and experience the serotonin release that comes with exercise. We should all try more often to tolerate the discomfort of exercise long enough to get the reward out of it. People who are able to manage the trade-offs consciously have a greater ability to establish good habits.

Good Habits Lead to Success

Developing good habits can lead to success. Albert E. N. Gray, an official of the Prudential Insurance Company of America, had thirty years of continuous experience, both as an agent in the field and as a promoter and instructor in sales development. In a 1940 talk, Gray said, "The common denominator of success— the secret of success of every person who has ever been successful—lies in the fact that they formed the habit of doing things that failures don't like to do."

There is a story of a father who wrote to his son in Vietnam for 635 days in a row. He told that story to some friends over dinner, expecting an overwhelming reaction of disbelief. But it never came. Why? He realized that, to the others, it was obvious that a habit had been formed, and that after the first thirty days or so, it was just natural for him to sit down and do it. The father was like a railroad engine on a track that had built up the momentum that acted like a flywheel, driving it forward in a seemingly effortless way.

We All Have Choices

The pain of losing is greater than the pain of the determination needed to form the right habits so that you don't lose. In our business, we modify that as, "The pain of regret is greater than the pain of rejection." It's all about choices. The problem is that most people don't recognize that we always have choices. As Holocaust survivor and psychiatrist Viktor Frankl said, "Everything can be taken from a man but...the last of the human freedoms—to choose one's attitude in any given set of circumstances, to choose one's own way."[50] So the one thing that can't be taken away from us is the way we perceive things, that inner peace that we can have regardless of our situation. It matters not what torture or what pain others deliver; we have the choice of being able to view that in a way we want, not in the way that others are intending.

Nelson Mandela, former president of South Africa, maintained great habits while he was in prison for twenty-seven years. While imprisoned, he continued a disciplined eating regimen that he had begun as an athlete in the 1940s, as well as early-morning exercise. Years later, as a free man, Mandela was up by 4:30 a.m., regardless of how late he had worked the previous evening. By 5:00 a.m., he began his exercise routine, which lasted at least an hour. He ate breakfast by 6:30 a.m. and read the day's newspapers. Mandela chose to make the best of his situation.

I like definitions, and the definition of "choice" that I often share with athletes is "giving up something you want for something else you want more." Even high-functioning leaders have to pass up a lot of really good things to create the margin in their life for the great things. And if good is the enemy of great, you don't want to have good habits; you want to have great habits. You want to have great choices. You want great things. So you must let go of a lot of choices that are actually pretty good.

---

50. Viktor E. Frankl, *Man's Search for Meaning* (New York: Simon & Schuster, 1963), 104.

Determination Helps Form Habits

It's all about determination. That engaged woman is very determined. She'll do whatever it takes and develop whatever habits she needs to in her quest to lose weight before her wedding day. She has determination. A wrestler who really wants to win a state championship or a boxer who wants to win the Golden Gloves will pay whatever price he needs to in an effort to reach his goals. A financial planner will decide on a goal in writing and will execute the plan to cause her to achieve it.

> The pain of losing is greater than the pain of the determination needed to form the right habits so that you don't lose.

Bill Cosby Committed to His Dream

Dropping out of Temple University as a junior, Bill Cosby became a starving comedian, but he made a commitment to be successful at it. His education and training as a comedian included staying up until all hours of the night talking to seasoned comics, researching material, and working on new routines. Quoted in the *Dallas Times-Herald*, Cosby had this to say: "Anyone can dabble. But once you've made that commitment, then your blood has that particular thing in it, and it's very hard for people to stop you. Once again, we're faced with the prerequisite to success—commitment. Is there any way around it? It is doubtful."[51]

When attending Temple University, my friends Bobby Marshall, Lew Katz, and I worked with Bill Cosby. Lew, Bill, and I had grant-in-aid scholarships at Temple, and each of us worked twenty hours a week in the coat room in Mitten Hall, which was the Student Union Building. Cosby was funny as a college student, really funny! He was naturally funny, but he worked hard to perfect it. He paid the price of investing the ten thousand hours in purposeful practice that we discussed earlier. He was years into his profession before he felt a need to have others write his material, a rare phenomenon, probably caused more by time constraints than by a need for better material.

As president of the student council at Temple University, it was my job to schedule speakers for the student body as part of the "lecture and convocation

---

51. *Speaker's Source Guide No. 2*, 66.

series." On one such occasion in 1962, I arranged to have Eleanor Roosevelt, former First Lady, speak to the student body. She was quite advanced in age by then, had Parkinson's disease, and characteristically drooled a bit, very common for that disease. Knowing she was a somewhat dry speaker at that late stage of her career, I invited Cosby to speak first. He had the audience in stitches with his demeanor and jokes. He made the occasion a tremendous success by disposing the audience to Ms. Roosevelt's words of wisdom. The two of them made a great team.

> Even high-functioning leaders have to pass up a lot of really good things to create the margin in their life for the great things.

One night a few months later, some of us working in Mitten Hall after we closed tried to convince Bill not to opt out of school after his junior year. We were unsuccessful. He convinced us that he had to leave, saying, "Hey, guys, I know you're trying to be helpful. But right now, I am very funny, and I don't know why. It's a gift. If I stay in school, complete my senior year, and lose whatever it is that's allowing me to be funny, I won't know how to get it back."

Bill Cosby spoke irrefutable words of wisdom. He knew what he was good at and passionate about. He committed to making it his life's work and didn't let anything stand in his way—not even putting off a college degree. He followed his instincts and, as a result, is one of the most successful comedians, as well as leaders, of all time. Cosby went on to receive a doctorate in education from Temple. We find it interesting that others like Bill Gates and Steve Jobs made similar choices.

Negative Emotion Creates Good Sparks but Bad Fuel

In the instances just mentioned, it's positive emotional energy that is prompting a behavior change. In some cases, negative emotion (anger or an emotional void, for example) can create the impetus for behavior change. Negative emotion creates good sparks to initiate a behavior change, but it is not good at fueling that behavior change over a sustained period of time. So negative emotion creates good sparks but bad fuel.

You Need Only One Win to Break a Bad Habit

It's great when you're entrenched in a good habit. But when you're entrenched in a bad habit, it can be close to impossible to break it. I used to smoke up to five packs of cigarettes a day. Giving up cigarettes was the toughest thing I ever had to do in my life. In my many failed attempts to quit, I tried everything. I institutionalized myself, tried hypnosis, and endured the torture of being in a phone booth with little oxygen replaced by smoke. I failed to quit well over one hundred times. Usually I would make the decision to quit on a Saturday night at midnight, and I would begin smoking again by noon on Sunday. But I was determined to quit. I knew that, unlike in athletic competition, in this game you need to win only once. If your record is one win and one hundred losses, you've won. Holding on to that thought—that I needed to win only once—was what enabled me to get through the pain each time, until I finally quit smoking. The pain was so intense that, to this day, whenever I see someone smoking, I pray for them. The pain still causes me to have nightmares that I am smoking again, even though it has been thirty-six years since I have had a cigarette.

Why is it that we slip back into bad habits after we think we have gotten rid of them? I believe it's because we get overextended, and that causes us to get emotionally overwhelmed. That margin in our life begins to shrink, and we begin to scale back on the things we should do for ourselves. Under stress we regress.

In terms of getting back on the wagon—getting back into the habit of eating healthy foods, exercising, or getting better sleep—a lot of it is a deeply inside-out process, not the other way around. During the times when I've fallen off from my good habits the most, turning it around really starts with my spirit, from the inside. I have to get better connected with God. On one such Sunday, it was something as simple as going to church that helped. That felt good, and from there I started to have a better Sunday. Then my mind started feeling better, which, in turn, empowered me to exercise. Subsequently, my body eventually began feeling better, and I was able to get back into my overall good habits.

Twenty-One Good Habits to Adopt

We have created a list of good habits that we believe will lead to success and help you stay on track as you discover the true north for your life's path.

1. **Listen.** The most important habit of a successful person is to listen.
2. **Read.** Leaders are readers. It's important to expand your pool of knowledge regularly. Today's readers are tomorrow's leaders!

3. **Write things down.** Whether it's a to-do list or a life plan, it's important to get it down on paper. For some reason, we're hardwired to think that we're going to remember everything, but the facts often prove otherwise. In her book *Write It Down, Make It Happen: Knowing What You Want— And Getting It!* Henriette Anne Klauser, PhD, explains how simply writing down your goals in life is the first step toward achieving them. She reveals stories about ordinary people who witnessed miracles unfold in their lives after they performed the basic act of putting their dreams on paper.

4. **Abide by the Rule of Seventy-Two.** It says that when you think of or hear a great idea, you have seventy-two hours to put that idea, thought, or plan into the execution or implementation stage. If you wait longer than that, you will lose it. So when you come across an idea that is profound, you have a brief window of opportunity to execute it.

5. **Delay gratification.** As M. Scott Peck outlines in *The Road Less Traveled*, it's important to delay gratification—to put off getting something you want now for something you want even more. Peck says that delaying gratification is a form of discipline, which is vital to our growth.

6. **Distinguish between important and urgent tasks, and focus on the important ones.** Every day we're confronted with hundreds of opportunities. Many of them are urgent; they clamor to be done right away. Other opportunities may not seem urgent but are important in a fundamental and lasting way. Truly successful people know that just because something is urgent does not make it important. They have the ability to differentiate between the two, delay the urgent issues, and address the important ones. They don't fly from urgency to urgency, from challenge to challenge, at the expense of doing the important things. If you think it through, you'll realize that it makes sense to tend to the important issues before addressing the urgent issues. It's a matter of awareness.

7. **Maintain personal humility.** Personal humility and extraordinary professional will are qualities that author Jim Collins attributes to the Level 5 leader. When someone asks, "How did you get to where you are?" the humble leader does not say, "I worked twenty-four hours a day and put everything else second. Look at me." Instead, the true leader will reply, "I am successful because someone touched me. They took the time to listen to me and to redirect me. They made the effort to grow me and not just to manage me." The National High School Coaches Association is made up of coaches who do just that—they help make this a better world by mentoring youngsters at a critical point in their lives.

8. **Practice "management by walking around," or MBWA.** This concept was introduced in the book *In Search of Excellence*. If you have people

working for you, you can learn a lot by making yourself visible in the workplace. Regularly check in with your team members and engage them to find out how they're doing, what they're doing, and how they're doing it. It can help increase accountability and also shows team members that you care about their well-being.[52] If you don't have any team members, ask your customers how you're doing. Try to elicit honest feedback regarding whether or not you are living up to their expectations. Are you creating an environment in which you're underpromising and overdelivering? If so, then you're converting customers into advocates for you and your business. There's no better situation for college coaches than to have graduates nationwide who are advocates of their programs. That helps them get top-notch recruits from all over the country.

It makes sense to tend to the important issues before addressing the urgent issues.

9. **Be present in the moment.** Don't worry about the future. Wherever you are, be there. And that gets back to our number one good habit of being a good listener. If I'm preoccupied with my own issues when I have team members or customers telling me what their problems are, I'm not focused, and I'm not driven to use all of my energy to help them. We should be intensely focused on others, the way a magnifying glass starts a fire by using focused rays of the sun on a piece of paper. That's important from a leadership point of view.

10. **Be honest and therefore predictable.** Many studies have been conducted to find out what people want from their leaders. The answer, over and over again, is honesty. When you're honest, you're also predictable. Retired Major General Vincent "Vinny" Boles of the US Army said that surprise is a tool you use on your enemies. You don't want to surprise people you care about. And you won't surprise them if you're honest and predictable. They should pretty much know how you're going to react in any given situation. It's all about living in the light, not the darkness. Also, if you are a truthful person, you won't have to remember what you said, and people will want to be around you. As Quintilian, an early Roman teacher of rhetoric, said: "A liar has to have a good memory."

---

52. Thomas J. Peters and Robert H. Waterman, *In Search of Excellence: Lessons from America's Best-Run Companies* (New York: Warner Books, 1982), 122.

11. **Borrow ideas from successful people.** There are a lot of good ideas out there, and you can benefit from them if you are in the habit of being alert to them. I recently attended a study-group meeting with nine other businessmen who do just what I do. One of my study-group members, Harry Hoopis, an industry legend and a fellow member of the GAMA Hall of Fame, mentioned that he was going to hire fifty-nine college graduates that year. I asked him how many recruiters he had, and he said five. I replied that I also had five recruiters, but I was on track to hire only thirty-five recent college grads. I asked him if he was using the Internet, and he said no. I asked him to explain, and he said his recruiters were doing the same thing my recruiters were doing. I drilled down then and asked him what his recruiters were doing. He said that his five recruiters made it a practice to take a different financial advisor to lunch each day and ask him or her for the names of people they thought would do well in our business. After all, our own advisors are in a better position than anyone to know who among their former college classmates and among their circle of influence or athletic teams would succeed in our business. That was not what my recruiters were doing. While they were working hard, they were not employing this highly effective practice, but instead were attending job fairs and doing campus recruiting and Internet surfing. I took the idea back to our head of recruiting in our Phoenix office. She liked it a lot and immediately incorporated it into her best practices for her department. Rather than just assuming that Harry had better recruiters, I instead saw that he was just doing things differently. So we are now benefiting from an idea I learned from him. "Listen" was the takeaway.

> Not only is being late unprofessional; it is a sign of disrespect.

12. **Be on time.** Being on time shows people that you respect their time and your own. Not only is being late unprofessional; it is a sign of disrespect. How annoying it is to show up for a meeting and have to wait for the person you're supposed to meet? Emergencies happen, but being late should not be a chronic situation. One of my study-group members, Al Granum, an icon in our industry and a stalwart for Northwestern Mutual for more than half a century, teaches anyone who'll listen, "Never be later than five minutes early."

Here is a great story I like about being on time. Charley, a new retiree–greeter at Walmart, just couldn't seem to get to work on time. Every day he was five, ten, or fifteen minutes late, but he was a good worker, tidy, clean-shaven, sharp-minded, and a real credit to the company. He exemplified Walmart's efforts to be friendly to older people. One day, the boss called Charley into his office for a talk. "Charley, I have to tell you, I like your work ethic, and you do a bang-up job when you finally get here. But your being late so often is quite bothersome."

Charley answered, "Yes, I know, boss, and I'm working on it."

"Well good, you're a team player. That's what I like to hear."

"Yes, sir. I understand your concern, and I'll try harder."

The manager said, "I know you're retired now, but what did they say to you at your previous job if you showed up late in the morning so often?"

The old man looked down at the floor, then smiled. He chuckled quietly, then said with a grin, "They usually saluted and said, 'Good morning, Admiral. Can I get your coffee, sir?'"

13. **Start and maintain a "playbook."** *Write in it ideas that you have learned from your colleagues and other sources. Refer to it often and implement new ideas regularly (within seventy-two hours!).*

14. **Keep a consistent sleep schedule.** *Regular sleep is essential for our health and well-being and is restorative to the brain and body.*

15. **Exercise in the early morning.** *Individuals who are in excellent physical shape tend to get up early in the morning to exercise.*

16. **Engage in morning prayer or meditation.** *It sets the stage for the day and helps you get your priorities in order.*

17. **Learn to say "no."** *A habit that is harder to develop but equally important to our well-being is practicing discernment so that we say "no" to the good things and "yes" to the great things. This requires strong filters so that we can make decisions that are in our best interest.*

18. **Tend to your marriage.** *Marriage can be tough at times. It's like a garden that constantly needs to be worked. It's important that we make it a habit to check in on the emotional health of our significant other and our family.*

19. **Rest on the Sabbath.** *That is difficult to do in our society today, but it's important for revitalization.* That has been confirmed by many people who make their living coaching, like Dan Sullivan. He calls them the "off days," and he recommends that you don't even turn your computer on during those off days because that's when the rebuilding of the mind takes place. That allows you to redouble your efforts on the days you permit yourself to work.

20. **Do the right thing, even when no one is looking.** *That is one definition of integrity.* At every firm meeting we have, either the word "integrity" or

the phrase "doing the right thing when nobody's looking" comes up. In any organization, team, or family, that kind of integrity begins with leadership; the fact that you're reading this book should tell you that it begins with you!

21. **Read an all-time best-seller.** *Many high-functioning and successful people cultivate a spiritual existence. Not only can the Bible, the best-selling book of all time, offer guidance on a daily basis; it also contains many of the best leadership principles of all time.*

Facing Problems Head-On

Many people procrastinate when it comes to solving problems. A good habit to get into is to meet problems head-on and address them.

It's been said that 90 percent of problems, if left unaddressed, resolve themselves.

For example, many patients who undergo psychological counseling find that their symptoms become alleviated significantly within eight sessions. One reason for that is the old adage "time heals all wounds." Often, whatever was bothering you two months ago is not likely to be bothering you now.

Often, however, the remaining 10 percent of our problems consume 90 percent of our time and attention, and those problems need to be resolved. In his book *Adversity Quotient at Work*, Paul Stoltz notes that a good approach to problem solving is to ask, "What is the worst thing that could happen here?"[53] Then, when you determine the worst-case scenario, ask yourself if and how you could deal with it or otherwise contain it. If you realize you could actually handle that scenario, then you are on your way to solving the problem. That process takes the panic out of the equation and allows you to approach it far more calmly.

Developing Other Leaders

If you are in a position of leadership, it's important to focus on developing other leaders, and doing so requires good habits. Developing leaders requires a conscious determination to expect certain behaviors from people in the organization

---

53. Paul G. Stoltz, PhD, *Adversity Quotient @ Work: Make Everyday Challenges the Key to Your Success—Putting the Principles of AQ into Action* (New York: HarperCollins, 2000), 249.

or on an athletic team. It also requires that you constantly repeat activities that you know will work—in other words, to repeat good habits.

Great leaders are also teachers—consider the legacies of Mahatma Gandhi, Jesus Christ, Nelson Mandela, and Martin Luther King, Jr. They were all great teachers, and they were growing other leaders as they taught. Later, Jesus's apostles were leaders and teachers as well. And their legacy lives on to this very day.

Leaders are always looking for the best in others—for other people's strengths. You don't win the battle by focusing on your team's weaknesses. Great businesses are constantly focusing on their people's strengths, not on their weaknesses.

> Have your best people focus their energy and direction on the best opportunities, and have your second- or third-tier people solve the problems.

One of the best ways to succeed as an organization or team is to assign your best people to the opportunities, not to the problems. Have your best people focus their energy and direction on the best opportunities, and have your second- or third-tier people solve the problems. Solving problems brings *no* revenue to the bottom line. Having your best people focus on opportunities does! It took me a while to learn this leadership lesson. I did it adequately at times, but now I do it very consciously. You will progress and succeed by capitalizing on opportunities, not by focusing on problems.

Occasionally, I'll take out two pieces of paper. On the first piece, I write the name of the people in my Mars Group (the core group of leaders at North Star Resource Group), and on the other piece of paper, I write what I consider to be the greatest opportunity for the company in the next thirty days. Then I match the best people with the elements of that opportunity.

I want the very best people on my offense. You don't win a game by playing defense only.

On your way to finding your true north, endure the time and effort it takes to develop good habits. It will benefit you and those around you.

It's Your Turn

Exercise 7-1: Good and bad habits

Developing good habits and forgoing bad habits can help you become who and what you are meant to be.

What are some bad habits you would like to quit?

1. _____

2. _____

3. _____

4. _____

What are some good habits you would like to adopt?

1. _____

2. _____

3. _____

4. _____

Chapter

8

Mentoring: A Valuable Life-Calling Tool

At times our own light goes out and is rekindled by a spark from another person. Each of us has cause to think with deep gratitude of those who have lighted the flame within us.

Albert Schweitzer
German Theologian, Organist, Philosopher, Physician, and Medical Missionary in Africa

I grew up in a tenement at 11th and Avenue A in New York City. Many of the kids in the tenements were members of The Boys Club of New York a block south, on 10th Street, across from Tompkins Park. When no one else seemed to care, the people at the Boys Club showed their interest by taking us to watch the Yankees, Dodgers, and Giants play; to see the Ringling Brothers, Barnum, Bailey Circus; to attend the rodeo at Madison Square Garden; and to see the Bronx Zoo. They also gave us free medical and dental care. As a result of my being at the Boys Club, some of us were even on "The Howdy Doody Show" five times when TV first was seen in the late 1940s.

I will never forget a poster that was displayed near the Boys Club showing a tall man leaning over, with his hand outstretched to a little girl. It said, "A man has never stood so tall as when he stooped to help a child." Seeing that poster was a turning point in my life; the image and what it represented have remained with me to this day.

Decades later, I commissioned an artist to recreate that poster as a huge watercolor painting that now hangs in North Star's home office in Minneapolis. I want everyone around me to be reminded constantly of the importance of helping the next generation succeed, of mentoring and coaching them to new heights.

During one's lifetime, I believe it's important to both receive and give the gift of mentorship. I have been privileged to have had a quintessential professional, Maury Stewart, as a mentor in my career. Maury was recruited by and mentored by Penn Mutual Life Insurance Company General Agent Paul Jernigen, and he has been extremely successful in the insurance and financial services industry. In 2004, Maury was selected for induction into the GAMA International Hall of Fame. (GAMA International is the only association dedicated to supporting the professional development of field leaders in the insurance and financial services industry.) I was inducted into the GAMA Hall of Fame a year later. In turn, I have mentored Ed Deutschlander, who became the youngest person in the history of GAMA International to serve as its president. He attained that post before he turned forty. Now Ed is mentoring Eric Severson, Mark Bonnett, and others in our Minneapolis office. Eric is also achieving phenomenal success mentoring many young advisors in our firm. Mark, who is a senior vice president in our Phoenix office, now serves on the GAMA International Board of Directors and will be the GAMA International president in 2017–18. We have all drunk from the wells that others have dug.

> Mentors change lives forever, sometimes
> without even knowing they've done so.

Billiard Balls

Marshall Gifford, one of our top advisors in 2004, delivered a million-dollar check to one of his clients, a pregnant dentist with one child, following the death of her husband. The husband, also a dentist, died from lung cancer, despite the fact that he never smoked. At the viewing, the wife's mother approached Marshall and, with teary eyes, thanked him. She said that, in spite of all of the problems facing her daughter, the one thing she did not have to worry about was money, and for that, they were grateful. That mother did not know who Paul Jernigan, the mentor of my mentor, was. If it had not been for the mentoring chain he had established sixty-five years earlier that included Maury Stewart, Ed Deutschlander, and me, Marshall wouldn't have been in this business, and money may well have been a worry to the family. More times than not, the good that comes from helping others rarely is realized by the giving mentor, coach, or teacher. This example of the beautiful unintended consequences of helping others is similar to a game of billiards or pool, in which the cue ball sets in motion the actions of other balls in a seemingly random way with a desirable outcome."

A Mentor Is a Teacher Who Cares

As leaders, we have the opportunity to make a significant impact in the lives of the people we know. "Manager" is a title that a firm awards you. "Leader" is a title awarded to you by people who follow you. You manage things and lead people.

A mentor is a teacher who cares. I believe that all mentors are teachers, but not all teachers are mentors. A teacher doesn't necessarily care whether you fail or pass. But mentors stay with you and nurture you because they care about you so much.

A great quote that illustrates the foundational heart of mentoring is "Nobody cares how much you know until they know how much you care." Once you demonstrate the concern you have for those around you, they will be even more interested in learning the unique life lessons you can teach them.

Often, when making a presentation, I will ask my audience to take a quick mental quiz. I ask them to do the following:

1. Name the five wealthiest people in the world.
2. Name ten people who have won the Pulitzer Prize.
3. Name the last five winners of the Miss America contest.
4. Name the last five Heisman Trophy winners.
5. Name the last half dozen Academy Award winners for Best Actor.
6. Name the last decade's worth of World Series winners.
7. Name the Super Bowl winners and MVPs in 2005 and 2006.

People have a hard time with that exercise. Next, I ask them to do the following:

1. List a few teachers or coaches who aided your journey through school.
2. Name a friend who has helped you through a difficult time.
3. Name a few people who have taught you something worthwhile.
4. Think of a few people who have made you feel appreciated and special.
5. Think of someone you enjoy spending time with.
6. Name a couple of heroes whose stories have inspired you.

That's much easier, isn't it?

The point is, we don't remember the headliners of yesterday—even though they are the best in their fields. The applause dies. Awards tarnish. Achievements are forgotten. Accolades and certificates are buried with their owners. The people who make a difference in your life are not the ones with the most credentials, the most money, or the most awards. They are the coaches, teachers, and mentors who care. Mentors change lives forever, and it's usually someone other than a parent, although parents often serve this role as well.

This realization makes it easy to appreciate the work of Robert Ferraro, who founded and now serves as the CEO of the National High School Coaches Association, whose vision and insight created an organization that fosters youngsters' growth and the sharing of best practices to do so.

When I was ten years old, a neighbor named Kenny Laubach, who drove a tractor-trailer truck asked my mother if he could take me on a three-day trip. She said yes, and he drove me from Easton, Pennsylvania, to Erie, to Pittsburgh, and back to Easton. At nighttime, we slept in the cab of the truck. It was a great adventure for me. He made that experience possible for me just because he cared. I will never forget him. My takeaway was that here was someone who was neither a friend nor a relative, but simply someone who cared for a less fortunate ten-year-old neighbor boy.

In high school, I was privileged to be mentored by the late John Maitland, who was the wrestling coach and later the athletic director at Easton High School. He changed a lot of lives during his career by encouraging people. I had no intention of going to college because nobody in my family had even finished high school. Yet John continued to tell me that I was college material and that I belonged in college. He made me think outside the box—outside of history, even—and was hugely instrumental in any professional achievements I've enjoyed. I did go on to college and was blessed by being elected as captain of the wrestling team and president of the student body at Temple University. John's encouragement and a full wrestling scholarship resulted in a life far different than what it would have been had this high school coach not intervened.

When I was in high school, which is a very important age to be mentored, Tim Cummings mentored me. He was a captain of the Phillipsburg High School (New Jersey) wrestling team and football team and the only person in the school who had ever been class president for four years. To be captain of both the football team and the wrestling team and class president four times was unheard of. I was president of my eighth-grade class. As I embarked on my freshman year at Phillipsburg High School, Tim said to me something that made a significant impact on me: "It's nice to be important, but it's more important to be nice." He also said, "Jarrod, you make sure, when you're the big shot, that you pay attention to every person in that room. There are going to be eyes on you, and you make sure that you give the attention back to somebody in that room who wouldn't normally get it. And when you walk up and down the halls, make sure you don't just say hi to that other kid with the football jersey on. You say hi to everybody."

His advice opened up a whole philosophy of personal interaction that transformed the meaning of leadership in my life. Partly because of Tim's mentoring, I ended up being elected to serve as president of my class for five years in a row, and I also served as captain of the football and wrestling teams. I, in turn, shared that philosophy with my younger brother, and he grew up to be a four-time class president and captain of the wrestling team. The ripple effect of one person caring enough to pass on words of advice is profound.

The key to becoming a mentor leader is learning how to put other people first.

I was fortunate to have another mentor, too. Eyvind Boyesen was a wrestler at Lehigh University. He mentored me during high school and college and introduced me to the field of sports psychology and the capabilities within us. He gave me a book called The Way of the Peaceful Warrior *by Dan Millman. That book opened up a door to a whole new world for me. One mentor, one book, and my career path was set. That is the power of mentoring.*

Putting Others First

Tony Dungy, a former professional football player and coach in the National Football League, is a revered mentor to many in the NFL. Dungy was head coach of the Tampa Bay Buccaneers from 1996 to 2001 and of the Indianapolis Colts from 2002 to 2008.

Dungy was a remarkable leader even when he was playing college football at the University of Minnesota. Our son, Scott, played on that team with him and spoke in glowing terms about his leadership and about the care and concern he showed others. Dungy is a Christian and strives to achieve a higher purpose, and I believe that has contributed to his great success.

In his 2010 book *The Mentor Leader*, Dungy wrote, "Relationships are ultimately what matter—our relationships with God and with other people. The key to becoming a mentor leader is learning how to put other people first. You see, the question that burns in the heart of the mentor leader is simply this: What can I do to make other people better, to make them all that God created them to be?"[54]

Sharing Wisdom, Not Just Knowledge

Mentors pass on their wisdom, not just knowledge, to others. There is a difference. While knowledge is simply the accumulation of facts and experiences, wisdom implies keen discernment and judgment. Mentorship involves transferring that discernment to others, along with encouragement and guidance that takes into consideration each mentee's individual talents, skills, and abilities—those items that are at the top of the mentee's list from Chapter 1 of this book.

As mentors and coaches, we need to look for opportunities to help our mentees grow. What gifts do they have that should be encouraged? Where should we guide them to invest their ten thousand hours of purposeful practice?

> As mentors and coaches, we need to look for opportunities to help our mentees grow.

Earlier, I mentioned one of our advisors at North Star, Marshall Gifford. He specializes in meeting the insurance and financial-services needs of physicians and dentists. More than one thousand physicians and dentists are his clients, and he has three full-time team members who help him in his business. His practice has grown so much that he is now mentoring his younger brother, an attorney, to help him service his client base.

I am in awe of the unique manner in which Marshall approaches his clients. His style verges on aloofness. He presents a compelling case for the value and necessity of his products and services and then leaves it up to his clients to make the decision to buy. It's almost as if he's saying, "I don't care if you do this or not. It's not about me. If you think this is in your best interest, then you'll do it." He never

---

54. Tony Dungy, *The Mentor Leader: Secrets to Building People and Teams That Win Consistently* (Carol Stream, Illinois: Tyndale House Publishers, 2010), 5.

seems anxious about acquiring new business, and physicians and dentists seem to resonate with that approach. Credibility shines through in Marshall's style, and it makes people want to become his client. I'm sure there are cases that he has lost, based on the fact that no one style works with everyone. But apparently, it works with the majority because his closing ratio is extraordinary, exceeding 80 percent. That means four out of five people he talks to want to become his client.

In mentoring his younger brother, Marshall is passing along not just his knowledge about the products and services they're selling; he is passing along his technique, his wisdom regarding what works and does not work with his client base.

Passing It On

One of the most inspirational messages I've ever heard was a presentation made by the Reverend Robert Eugene Richards—Bob Richards. Born in 1926, Richards was known as the "vaulting vicar," the "pole-vaulting parson," and the "pole-vaulting preacher." He competed in the 1948, 1952, and 1946 Summer Olympics as a pole vaulter and was a decathlete in 1956.

He was the second man to pole-vault 15 ft. (4.6 m) and is the only two-time Olympic gold medal winner in the pole vault (1952 and 1956).

In his presentation, in which he talked about life's higher goals, he told a story that illustrates how a mentorship mentality is passed on from one generation to the next, helping young people achieve astonishing goals. Richards told about a young boy who wanted to become a champion runner. The boy asked his coach how he could accomplish that. His coach said, "Well, son, you've got to train hard, and you've got to get your knees high." With continued encouragement from his coach, that boy, Charley Paddock, went on to win gold in the 100-meter final and place second in the 200-meter event at the 1920 Summer Olympics in Antwerp, Belgium.

Paddock came back to America and began giving speeches all over the country. In one of his audiences, a spindly-legged African-American boy went up to him and said, "Gee, Mr. Paddock, I'd give anything if I could be a champion like you." Paddock said, "You can" and provided encouragement. That boy, Jesse Owens, went on to win four Olympic gold medals at the 1936 Summer Olympics in Berlin, Germany. Owens embarrassed Adolf Hitler by becoming the most successful athlete at the 1936 Games, at which Hitler had intended to showcase Aryan prowess.

Owens returned to Cleveland, Ohio. As he walked down the street, a nine-year-old African-American boy walked up to him, expressing his deep admiration. He asked Owens for his autograph and said, "Gee, Mr. Owens, I'd give anything if I could be a champion like you." Owens said, "Well, son, you can if you'll work and if you'll keep the dream in your heart." That boy, Harrison Dillard, was so skinny that everyone called him "Bones." He grew up to become the only man so far to win Olympic titles in both sprinting and hurdling. At the London Olympics in 1948, he tied Jesse Owens's Olympic record in the 100-meter dash.

There are countless examples of how one person impacts many people. At the pro level, Bill Walsh, legendary football coach of the San Francisco 49ers, has an overwhelming number of disciples in the NFL—people he has mentored. Walsh won three NFC Championship titles and three Super Bowls, and he was named the NFL's Coach of the Year in 1981 and 1984.

At the high-school level, an example of a coach who has left a great legacy is Jeff Buxton of Blair Academy, a small private school in Blairstown, New Jersey. Blair Academy won the National Prep Tournament in wrestling during every one of Coach Buxton's twenty-seven years at Blair. During that time, Blair had 145 individual National Prep Champions. Under Jeff's leadership, Blair won the USA's top in-season tournaments twenty-one times. As you can imagine, he mentored numerous athletes who have gone on to become college All-Americans, national champions, and award-winning coaches. He has since moved on from Blair but is still coaching today. In ten or twenty years, we will continue to see large numbers of young people whom he mentored grow up and fill head coaching positions. I first met Jeff when I was a young camper at Blair Academy. I am grateful to have benefited from his tutelage and am honored to be counted among the many people he has mentored.

At the local level, Thad Turner, a legendary wrestling coach at Phillipsburg High School in the 1960s, has been well known in the Lehigh Valley of Pennsylvania for many years. Nearly all of the subsequent coaches at Phillipsburg High School were coached by either Thad or his disciples. Many of my coaches in wrestling while growing up in P'burg were Turner disciples, including high school coaches Bob Jiorle and Rick Thompson. Many of Coach Turner's wrestlers have settled in towns across the Lehigh Valley and have contributed to the next generation's success in wrestling in those communities. He, too, eventually left P'burg and went to Lehigh University to coach for many years, with tremendous success. He is a major reason why the Lehigh Valley is regarded to have the best wrestling in the country.

The wisdom I learned from these phenomenal mentors is largely responsible for my success today, and it is an integral part of the philosophies that I teach to the young athletes I work with.

Mentoring from Our Messes

A lot of our wisdom is gained by making mistakes. When we think of mentoring, we typically think of passing along our successes to someone else. There is, however, another way to mentor someone that's equally, if not more, effective: We can mentor out of our "messes" and share with our mentees what we regret, what didn't work out so well for us, and where our shortcomings or challenges have been.

A lot of our wisdom is gained by making mistakes.

One of my mentors, Tim Cummings, worked hard but was not academically gifted. He knew that academic success was not likely to be his destiny, so early on, he encouraged me to get good grades. He wanted me to be not just a great athlete but a great student as well. His "mess" became his mission. Then, when top academic colleges in the country began recruiting me because of my academic record, he was so proud. I ended up attending Lafayette College, a success for Tim as well as for me.

We can provide a great service to others by sharing not just our stories of reaching the mountaintop but by sharing those times when we struggled. We can help them avoid our own costly mistakes.

The Lost Art of the Handwritten Note

I think a lot of leaders underestimate the tremendous impact they have on other people. The simplest word of encouragement can last a lifetime. And I believe that sharing encouragement in a handwritten message makes a huge impact—today more than ever because people seldom send handwritten notes anymore. Now that we have the Internet, many compliments flow back and forth among people online, but I don't believe they have the impact that a handwritten note does.

When our granddaughter, Kyla, was seven, she struggled in school. I heard from my wife that Kyla was trying really hard to do better. I wrote her a note on my company stationery that said, "Kyla, I hear that you are doing great in school and that no one in your class tries harder than you." A couple of months later, my daughter told me that Kyla pinned my note up on the wall in her bedroom. A simple act of kindness or recognition by someone who is in a position of authority or respect has far more weight than we ever think about.

I call that "the lost art of the handwritten note." It is profoundly impactful to receive one. When I receive a handwritten note, I keep it on my desk if it's work-related, or on my dresser at home if it's personal, for some time. Such notes are extremely meaningful to me.

If you are mentoring someone, consider sending them a handwritten note and offer them one of the most powerful things in the world today—encouragement. It will take you five minutes. One single dose of encouragement to a human being, especially a young person, can be so profound. Mentoring can be as simple as that.

Get "Adopted"

Mentoring is critical to the success of our advisors at North Star. We participate in the MDRT (Million Dollar Round Table) Mentoring Program, which has helped us develop eighty-two advisors who are members of the prestigious MDRT organization.

> Young men, today more than ever,
> desperately need male role models
> in their lives.

When we hire someone, we tell them, "The most important job you have is to get adopted." We want them to do so much more than we ask them to do—not because we want the extra productivity, but because we want them to get noticed. We want them to stand out from the crowd so much that one of the senior, successful, high-income earners in our company notices them. When that happens, those senior advisors will walk into my office or Ed Deutschlander's office and say, "I've been noticing that this young person is really good. I'd like to take her under my wing and have her begin to service some of my 'A' clients (as opposed to 'AA' and 'AAA' clients) and maybe think about developing a succession plan with her." Then, all of a sudden, the newer person's prospecting or business-seeking challenges are history because now she will have more work than she can handle. In fact, a variation of this model is the very one that has caused State Farm's model to become the benchmark of the industry.

It's very important for both young women and young men to have mentors. But research shows that young men, today more than ever, desperately need male role models in their lives. Staggering numbers of boys are growing up without fathers in their homes. So our young men, in particular, need male mentors to step into their lives and teach them what it's like to be a man, what it's like to treat a woman with respect, what it's like to be a successful businessperson and productive member of our society—and to teach them about God.

Do you have some extra time in your schedule to devote to a young person who could benefit from your guidance and wisdom? Many people would agree that when you adopt a young person as a mentee, you end up getting back far more than you ever gave. It is one of the best win–win scenarios.

Who Wants It More?

Mentees typically appreciate their mentors' time and interest in their success and strive to become the person the mentor believes they can be. But sometimes, we encounter situations in which we want success for the young person more than they want it for themselves.

A mentoring relationship will not be successful if the mentor wants the mentee's success more than he or she does. I've heard people say, "I've been trying to get this guy to be a success, but he doesn't want to do it." That doesn't work. They have to want the success for themselves.

I often say, "Coach, don't coax." When you want success more than the mentee does, you end up coaxing them to behave a certain way. I also believe that "When faith turns to hope, let 'em go." When your faith in somebody turns to hope, you're shoveling sand against the tide, and it's time to encourage that person to move on. It's a time saver for you and a gift to them.

Mentoring in Ten-Minute Increments

Theophrastus, a Greek botanist, humorist, and naturalist who lived several hundred years before Christ's birth, said, "Time is the most valuable thing a man can spend."

A lot of people have asked me how to find a mentor. A technique I have used personally is to identify somebody you respect and whose values you share and to mention those values in your request for the mentor's time. Tell him or her that you share those values and ask if you could have ten minutes of their time to get some advice. Give them three questions ahead of time so they can think about them, prepare for your time together, and be more efficient with those ten minutes. Make sure that you always honor that ten-minute time frame. Even if the person is willing to give you more time, don't take it.

After they have spent time with you, always send a follow-up note to thank them for their time and advice. Also, if you run across a book or CD that directly relates to the conversation you had, send it to your mentor. Let him or her know it's a small token of your appreciation. It also lets them know you're thinking of them and processing the material you discussed during your mentoring session.

People often ask if they can "shadow" me or have lunch with me. I always say no at first because I can't really afford to give up an hour and a half of my time. I'll say, "Why don't we set up a time to talk first on the phone for ten minutes?" I will ask them to e-mail to me three questions they want to ask me during that phone call. It's a filtering process. That way, I can see if they're serious. If they do all of this, I will be more inclined to give them more of my time in the future, including lunch or an internship opportunity.

Recently I sent an e-mail to a highly successful man who sold his company for more than $300 million. I sent him a text message and said, "I'm going to be in New York City on Tuesday. I would love to borrow a few minutes of your time. I'm not looking for money. I'm looking for your wisdom and experience." He texted me back right away and suggested that I send him an e-mail so that his assistant could figure out a time for us to get together. Robert Ferraro, his son, and I met with this successful businessman, and he shared with us his journey to success and his vision for the future, both full of invaluable insights of the kind that one rarely encounters and could only come from one who has been there.

During my career, I've had hundreds of requests for mentorship. The requests I have obliged were from people who communicated to me in some way that their values were similar to my own. The people I filtered out were those whom I, either correctly or incorrectly, perceived to be without gratitude. I like grateful people. I like people who thank somebody every day for what they have. I tend to avoid spending time on people who exhibit an entitlement mentality. A wonderful quote about a grateful heart is "What if we woke up today with only the things that we had thanked God for yesterday?"

A Good Mentor Is Honest

A recent study revealed that honesty is the number-one trait athletes want from their coaches. The best coaches are straightforward and truthful. You may not like what they're going to say sometimes, but you know you'll get honesty every time.

On one of the occasions when I heard noted author Jim Collins speak, he said he had been mentored by author and management consultant Peter Drucker.

When he went to Drucker for some advice, Drucker said to him, "You worry too much."

Collins asked, "What should I do?"

Drucker replied, "Be useful."

The more I've thought about that—"Be useful"—I've realized that it's a solid formula for living. Stop worrying and be useful. Drucker's advice was honest and probably stung a little, but it provided Collins with great insight and wisdom. Corrie ten Boom said, "Worry doesn't empty tomorrow of its suffering; it empties today of its strength."

> People don't want their supervisors to be nice; they want somebody who will push them to higher levels so that they can grow and become better people.

I have read that most people would return to work for a former supervisor who pushed them to higher levels and did not accept mediocrity. As the saying goes, "Kind management is cruel management." People don't want their supervisors to be nice; they want somebody who will push them to higher levels so that they can grow and become better people. They want honest feedback on how they're doing and an honest assessment of their potential.

Find a Mentor Who Shares Your Values

I believe that what your values are is not as important as having them. Most people, however, don't take the time to sit down and identify their values; this omission fosters confusion, not clarity.

If you're thinking about seeking out a mentor, as Jarrod advised, try to identify somebody you respect and whose values you share, and mention those values in your request for the mentor's time.

I recently attended a presentation delivered by Tony Hsieh, the visionary CEO of Zappos.com, an online shoe retailer that makes more than $1 billion in gross merchandise sales every year. Hsieh said that customer service is not the number-one priority at Zappos; culture is. I believe that culture is the sum total of an organization's values. As I mentioned earlier, at North Star, our values are faith, integrity, growth, gratitude, and service.

Seek Mentorship in Your Areas of Strength

As you seek out mentorship, keep in mind those top skills and traits you identified in Chapter 1. Life is too short to waste your time being mentored on the bottom or middle part of that list. Really hone in on those two or three traits that you can do that make you come alive. Then find people who are excelling in that space.

Also keep in mind that the mentoring you receive doesn't have to be face-to-face. You can go to conferences to hear people speak, and you can read their books or study their videos. We simply can't be mentored by all the people we want to, but we can be mentored indirectly by them, so it makes sense to find people who can help you sharpen your God-given strengths.

It's Your Turn

Exercise 8-1: Giving and receiving the gift of mentorship

During your lifetime, it's important to both receive and give the gift of mentorship. If you don't already have a mentor to help you excel in the areas you identified in Chapter 1 as your strongest, whom could you ask to mentor you?

1. _____
2. _____
3. _____
4. _____
5. _____

Whom could you mentor?

1. _____
2. _____
3. _____
4. _____
5. _____

Chapter

9

Be a Wisdom Seeker

By three methods we may learn wisdom: First, by reflection,
which is noblest; second, by imitation, which is easiest; and
third by experience, which is the bitterest.

Confucius
Chinese Teacher, Editor, Politician, and Philosopher

As mentioned earlier, wisdom is more than just knowledge. It is an accumulation of life experiences, insight, and perspective gained over time, while knowledge is just an accumulation of facts.

It is critical for us to understand our calling, what we're really gifted at, that sweet spot where we're supposed to spend our time. Once we know our true north, then we can seek out wisdom in that area.

The wisdom of others is all around us. In your search for your life's calling, there are several ways to discover wisdom. Finding a mentor, which we recommended in the last chapter, is one way. Here are some additional sources of wisdom.

Sources of Wisdom

Praying

The most obvious source of wisdom is our heavenly Father. James 1:5 says, "If any of you needs wisdom, you should ask God for it. He is generous and enjoys giving to all people, so He will give you wisdom."

Reading and Listening to Books

Today's readers are tomorrow's leaders. Countless experts on life, business, and sports have compiled their wisdom into books. Reading is an excellent way to discover the insight of people who have taken the time to share their life experiences. Authors strive to share their very best when writing to provide readers with clear, concise, and convincing messages.

> One of the best ways to gain wisdom
> is to listen to audio CDs during your
> windshield time.

I have found that it is worthwhile to go back and read again those books that I found useful years ago. The book doesn't change, but I've changed. Therefore, what I get out of the book is different the second or third time. There are books like *The E-Myth Revisited* that I have read three times, and each time I read them, I learn something new and profound that I didn't see the first or second time around. It was not until my third reading of Scott Peck's book *The Road Less Traveled* that I realized the entire book is encapsulated in the first three words of the book, the first paragraph, the first sentence: "Life is difficult"! It is only after coming to that realization that we can experience happiness because we are grateful when good things happen and accepting when bad things occur. Those who believe that a living is owed to them blame others when bad things happen and accept good occurrences as entitlements instead of gifts.

Many people simply don't have the time to read a lot of books. Luckily, there are several companies that specialize in publishing summaries and abstracts of executive and business books. These summaries reveal the salient points of each book so that you can glean the main points of a book without having to read it. One such company, www.getabstract.com, bills itself as "the world's largest library of business book summaries." You simply buy the abstracts online and download them. Five-page summaries reveal the most important points and can convince you that you need to read the entire work.

One of the best ways to gain wisdom is to listen to audio CDs during your windshield time. When you are driving in the car, your conscious mind is allowing you to drive, but your pre-conscious mind is activated. Your pre-conscious mind is the "back burner," where you store memories and experiences that you haven't had time to work through or resolve yet. It's possible to do some really good thinking while you're driving. And when you combine that thinking with listening to some excellent teachers and preachers on CD, it creates a great opportunity to absorb some valuable wisdom.

Studying Your Family History

To find out where you're going, one of the best exercises you can engage in is to find out where you've been. That starts with your family history. I recommend drawing out your family tree, starting with your siblings and your parents and moving on to cousins, grandparents, and great-grandparents. What were their skill sets, gifts, and careers? Did any of them have mental or physical challenges? In discovering their shortcomings as well as their triumphs, you will learn something about yourself.

Take this exercise a step further and spend some time talking with your family members so that you can learn more about your ancestors. Ask your parents to share what they know about your grandparents' most vital years, and ask your grandparents what your great-grandparents were like. In doing so, you may find that you can now see a bigger picture, with both sides of the family tree, and how all that history has formed who you are. You can gain tremendous wisdom when you draw out the family tree, talk to your family members about their history, and reflect on it.

One of the few regrets in my life came while I was helping a friend, Clarence Harrow, deliver the daily *Easton Express* so we could hit the swimming hole on the Bushkill Creek a little earlier. On his route was an old man's home in which thirty-one senior citizens lived as boarders. The matriarch of the house was a tall, eighty-eight-year-old woman with white hair down to her ankles. Coincidentally, she had the same last name as me.

Weeks later, when I again helped Clarence with his route, that woman informed me that she was my great-grandmother. Because I had met my father only three times, I had no knowledge whatsoever of his side of the family. In my many meetings with her that followed, Emma Richards taught me that her parents had migrated to America following the Civil War from the deep-shaft slate mines of Wales to the pit-slate mines of Bangor, Pennsylvania (the latter was named for Bangor, Wales). Those mines in Pennsylvania would turn a beautiful aqua blue after a rain—great for swimming.

Mrs. Richards also informed me that she was one-quarter American Indian, that she had outlived a few husbands, and that she was the spiritual and worldly leader of the boarders of the house, who simply signed over their Social Security checks to her in return for room, board, and all of their necessities (no cigarettes or alcohol allowed). While that may seem like a lot of information, it pales in comparison to what I could/should have learned from her had I invested more time in developing the relationship. My descendants are disadvantaged by the stories they will never hear. My hope is that my miscue will be a teaching point for you.

Seeking Out Competent Collaborators

Often, as we have done with this book, you can gain wisdom by collaborating with colleagues who are accomplished either in your own field or in other fields. Being open to the possibility of collaboration with others provides our work with complementary insight and perspective that we could never gain on our own. I am a member of two study groups, GAS (General Agent Symposium) and "The Group." They are populated with industry giants like Al Granum, Gary Daniels, Kelly Kidwell, Paul Vignone, R. Michael Condrey, Ron Lee, Tim Murray, Joe Mahoney, Nick Horn, Ron Long, Norm Levine, Bob Savage, Luis Chiappy, Harry Hoopis, Paul Blanco, Dave Porter, John Baier, John Langdon, Greg Knudsen, Bill Pollakov, Maury Stewart (my mentor), and many others who have been vital to the growth of North Star with their ideas, experience, and wisdom. This band of brothers has selflessly shared valuable trade secrets with fellow study-group members, thus enhancing the careers of not only one another but of all of the advisors whose lives they touch daily. More importantly, the ultimate beneficiaries are the tens of thousands of consumers who benefit from the products and services of the firms headed by these visionaries.

In the last chapter, we suggested that you seek out a mentor to help you gain wisdom. Similarly, seeking out the wisdom and complementary skills of a collaborator can help you grow and succeed in ways you never dreamed of.

Engaging in Nighttime Reflection

Often, wisdom comes to us in the middle of the night. A lot of valuable thoughts can come out of insomnia. Sometimes when our psychological defenses are down because the entire world is still, issues that are pressing on our hearts and minds bubble up, and we can make some great life decisions and solve some of the most complex problems. We can solve problems as we sleep, too. As John Steinbeck said, "It is a common experience that a problem difficult at night is resolved in the morning after the committee of sleep has worked on it."

It's a good idea to keep a pencil and tablet, or a small digital recorder, next to your bed because often those great thoughts that come to you in the middle of the night are gone the next morning. If a thought or idea is profound enough for you to think about and recognize its merits, it's worthy of being recorded so that you don't forget it.

Having a Rested and Refreshed Mind

Sometimes, though, instead of problems being solved at night, problems keep us up at night. I think we need to remind ourselves that we're not good at problem solving in the middle of the night when we're tired. We need to get a good night's sleep, have our coffee in the morning, and approach the problem and potential solutions with a fresh mind. Repeat to yourself Shakespeare's advice: "Things without redress should be without worry; when it's done, it's done."

We make great life decisions when we're well rested. If you are tired and worn out, wisdom may evade you. In fact, even the most successful people have made dumb mistakes when they were suffering from sleep deprivation. It's important to get good sleep consistently. For the same reason, it's important to take a vacation periodically so that you can step away from things, then come back and address them with fresh energy.

> The ex-conscious mind is a term I coined to describe that part of the mind where outdated material is stored.

In fact, while we're sleeping, wisdom often comes to us in the form of dreams. Many people have experienced profound moments of wisdom in the middle of the night, while they were sleeping. We process our daily activities through our dreams.

I believe that the subconscious mind has three layers. The pre-conscious mind is the back burner—that place in the mind where memories are stored that can be recalled easily but are outside of our immediate awareness. The ex-conscious mind is a term I coined to describe that part of the mind where outdated material is stored. The ex-conscious mind is a deeper level of the mind than the pre-conscious. Hopefully, as we resolve our challenges from today, they will sink down to the ex-conscious mind as resolved, positive memories. The unconscious mind is that place in the mind where memories that we can't access—such as memories of early childhood or traumatic experiences—are stored.

On a practical level, during sleep, the pre-conscious mind tries to resolve issues and push them down to the ex-conscious mind. But there can be a very spiritual component to this phenomenon, too—I believe that God can reveal insight to us in our dreams. Recall that it not only worked for Moses, but eventually led to a successful conclusion; the Israelis were freed from slavery and were allowed to return to their homeland.

Needed in America: Reverence for Older People's Wisdom

I think that wisdom, in some ways, can be gained simply by outliving others. The longer you live—if you're not prone to making the same mistakes over and over again, and if you're committed to lifelong learning—the wiser you become.

> ## I think that wisdom, in some ways, can be gained simply by outliving others.

I've traveled to Asia every year for the last fourteen years, and I'm always amazed at the reverence for old age that exists there. It's considerably less noticeable in Europe or North America. In China, for example, there is a discernible difference in the way teenagers and people in their twenties and thirties regard people who are in their seventies and eighties. They exhibit a great deal more respect than young Americans do for the fact that older people have lived a full life and now are at the peak of their wise years. In a bit of a contrast to our society and its proclivity to warehousing its senior citizens in retirement homes or worse, the Chinese have a concept called 4–2–1. That means that, because of the country's one-child policy since 1977, each child is probably going to care for two parents and four grandparents at the end of the day—a daunting thought, but one attesting to their reverence for the old. In November 2013, China revised this forty-year-old policy to allow more than one child per couple, a decision that will no doubt serve China well in years to come.

The willingness of youngsters to care for the elderly is an outgrowth of their supreme respect for the elderly.

America is in its adolescence in terms of its development as a country. One hallmark of the adolescent phase is that it's self-centered and "me"-oriented—"I've got all the answers." When we have that mindset, we fail to tap into one of our greatest resources in America—the wisdom of our elders.

The Way It Used to Be

When first becoming the leader at North Star forty-four years ago, I remember hearing a commentary on public radio while in my car. The great anthropologist Margaret Mead (1901–1978) was speaking on "the ills of society."

Mead opined that America's transition from an agrarian to an industrial culture had had profound negative consequences on our society. She stated that the agrarian society was good for families because when people lived on a farm, it was easy for them to support their parents with little effort. They were growing crops and also had eggs and meat readily available. In that environment, it was not an expensive proposition to house your parents as you raised your own family. Women were responsible for collecting eggs, cleaning out chicken coops, preparing food, and other home-centered tasks, while men would work in the fields during the day and tend to the animals. Meanwhile, the grandparents remained in the home, ideally representing and passing down to their grandchildren the wisdom of all the generations that had gone before them. The older folks had ample time to pass along their wisdom to the children and the patience to assure that the lessons took. This had a stabilizing impact on the children, who later became parents and contributing members of society.

As the industrial society emerged, there were economic complications associated with keeping parents in the home. Many people moved to towns and cities and lived in small apartments. As a result, Meade concluded, this country experienced an increase in crime and juvenile delinquency, a latch-key society resulting in a disconnect with the values of our ancestors, and a lack of respect for elders.

Not incidentally, in later life, Mead served as a mentor to many young anthropologists and sociologists.

The Cost of Lost Wisdom

Unfortunately, massive amounts of wisdom are being lost to Alzheimer's disease and other forms of dementia. In 2010, the total estimated worldwide cost of dementia was $604 billion. That estimate includes the direct costs of medical care and social care, as well as unpaid care provided by family caregivers and others.[55]

More importantly, Alzheimer's disease robs our younger generations of the sage wisdom of older people. At the peak period of people's lives, when they have the most to share in terms of real-life experiences and the knowledge they've accumulated over a period of many decades, Alzheimer's renders them unable to remember and share that wisdom with others.

---

55. "World Alzheimer Report 2010: The Global Economic Impact of Dementia," released by Alzheimer's Disease International, a London-based, nonprofit, international federation of seventy-three national Alzheimer organizations, including the US-based Alzheimer's Association, last modified September 21, 2010, accessed on November 30, 2013, http://www.alz.org/documents /national/world_alzheimer_report_2010.pdf.

Transitioning from age sixty-five to age seventy-five increases the likelihood of Alzheimer's disease from one in ten to one in seven. If added risk factors are present, the probability becomes even greater. One study showed that nearly half of all people aged eighty-five and older are afflicted with some form of dementia, and this group is at the highest risk of Alzheimer's disease. This unfortunate reality is why the Scott Richards North Star Foundation is currently sponsoring two major research grants for Alzheimer's, at the University of Minnesota and at the Mayo Clinic. One of our leaders, Shaun McDuffee, and his Lone Star Division of North Star began a four-thousand-mile walking journey across America in another fund-raising effort to stamp out this horrific disease, which affects one in three of our seniors. The website for this nonprofit effort is www.stopalzheimersnow.org. Our North Star Foundation, in partnership with the Mayo Clinic, has established an endowment at Mayo that will provide its Alzheimer's researchers $75,000 per year in perpetuity. This is part of our North Star vision—to change lives, forever.

A Psychological Perspective

Each pioneer in the field of psychology has a different recommendation for making sense of our circumstances and for optimizing our potential.

In his book *Man's Search for Meaning*, originally published in 1959 and republished several times since then, Holocaust survivor and psychiatrist Viktor Frankl described logotherapy (from the Greek word "logos," or "meaning"), a mode of therapy he invented.

In the early 1940s, Frankl labored in four different concentration camps, including Auschwitz. His parents, brother, and pregnant wife perished in the camps. As mentioned earlier, Frankl maintained that we cannot avoid suffering, but we can choose how to cope with it, find meaning in it, and move forward with renewed purpose. His theory is that our primary drive in life is the discovery and pursuit of what we personally find meaningful.

Sigmund Freud, who created the clinical practice of psychoanalysis, encouraged people to examine their childhood experiences—their past—for clues about their current state of mental health. Frankl, on the other hand, was more inclined to focus on people's current situation—the here and now—to help them optimize their potential. In his book, he explains how he worked with an American diplomat who had been in therapy in the United States for five years. The therapist had encouraged the man to "reconcile himself with his father" because the US government and his superiors were father images, "and, consequently, his dissatisfaction with his job was due to the hatred he unconsciously harbored toward his father." After a few interviews with the diplomat, Frankl determined that the man did not need psychotherapy; he simply "longed to be engaged in some other kind of work." The man changed jobs and became contented.[56]

> ## We cannot avoid suffering, but we can choose how to cope with it, find meaning in it, and move forward with renewed purpose.

The wisdom I took from Frankl's book is his conclusion that there's only one thing in this whole world that man is able to control. We can't control what happens to us. We can only control the way we react to what happens to us.

No one knows this better than my dear friend, John Michael McGrath (discussed in detail in my first book), a pilot and lieutenant commander in the US Navy who was a prisoner of war in Hanoi for six years during the Vietnam War. He is a personification of Frankl's conclusion. He survived his unbelievably difficult ordeal by controlling the way he reacted to the extreme physical torture and emotional degradation that his captors inflicted on him.

Whether we engage in psychotherapy or examine our current circumstances for clues about what will make us happy, we can learn a lot from the great men and women who spent their lives studying the human mind.

All of the great pioneering psychiatrists made significant contributions to the field, but none can be construed as being superior to all of the others; they are simply different. It is important to understand the context in which each pioneer's work emerged. There is incredible merit to what Freud did. He was working with women with deep traumatic experiences, so his work in psychoanalysis makes sense. Frankl obviously went through a traumatic experience during the war, and the "here and now" philosophy saved his life.

I think it would be helpful to study the various contributors to the field of psychology and discover which ones you resonate with most. What works for one person may not work for the next. Analyzing the "here and now" may be a perfect strategy for

---

56. Frankl, 101–102.

optimizing one person's performance, but someone else may need to look into the past to determine clues for future success.

Proceed with Caution

With the advent of the Internet, information is readily available, but we should proceed with caution. As author Nick Murray says, computers should come with warning labels that say, "Wisdom not included."

There's a saying, "Be careful whose counsel you take." You can find out everything you want about a medical condition, but who is offering up that wisdom? Many people create more stress about their medical condition by visiting websites with low credibility.

Moreover, sometimes information that is reported to be valid is later discredited. I once attended a joint meeting of two prominent medical research organizations. The researchers' consensus was that selenium was a miracle drug, as it had been shown to have a positive effect in the treatment of breast cancer, prostate cancer, lung cancer, and heart disease.

A few years later, I attended another meeting of the same group, and I asked (because I had been ingesting it religiously every day for two years) what progress had been made in further research on selenium's ability to control cancer. The physicians at the table looked at one another and said sheepishly, "We found that to be not true." Just within a two-year period, they had discovered that their original research was limited in scope. Looking at it much more closely, they found out that the so-called positive effects of selenium were unsubstantiated.

Things change. There was a time when we were told that chocolate was bad for us. Now many experts claim that dark chocolate can reduce blood pressure and that it contains antioxidants called polyphenols, which are said to reduce atherosclerosis and inhibit the oxidation of LDL ("bad") cholesterol.

And, hard to believe as it may sound, in the 1940s and early 1950s, doctors actually advertised cigarettes. On NBC's show "Mystery in the Air," announcer Michael Roy stated that three independent research organizations conducted a nationwide poll among 113,597 doctors, surgeons, and specialists in every branch of medicine. Camel was the brand of cigarettes the doctors recommended most often.[57]

---

57. Old-Time.com, "Doctors Recommend Smoking Camels," accessed on December 3, 2013, http://www.old-time.com/commercials/1940%27s/More%20Doctors%20Smoke%20Camels.html.

Passing Our Own Wisdom to Others

Just as it's important for us to seek out wisdom from others, I believe that we all have wisdom we should consider passing along to our families and others. As we age, we collect many life lessons that will never see the light of day unless we make a conscious effort to share them.

> ## As we age, we collect many life lessons that will never see the light of day unless we make a conscious effort to share them.

As a member of the Temple University Board of Trustees, I was privileged to sit next to Richard Fox, a past Temple Board Chairman. Fox is a cofounder of Planalytics, Inc., and serves as the company's chairman. He also is a founder and chairman of The Fox Companies, a major development and real-estate management company in eastern Pennsylvania. He is such an influential and successful businessman that Temple University's Richard J. Fox School of Business and Management was named after him in 1999. He is about ten years my senior and fought in World War II, and he frequently shares stories that are heartwarming and full of wisdom. I find him to be an incredibly interesting person, as well as a fine teacher.

One day, I suggested that Richard write a book. His response was, "Who, me, write a book?"

I said, "Yeah, you. You should write a book."

He said, "Oh, no. Who would want to hear what I have to say?"

"Well, I think you have had a fascinating life," I said. "I think many people would love to hear what you have to say. And what about your grandchildren and great-grandchildren? How else are they going to hear the fascinating stories you just told me?"

Happily, the last I heard, Richard Fox was writing a book!

There is an entire profession of people who make a living by capturing people's life experiences and stories on audiotape or videotape. After interviewing their subjects, these personal historians produce either videotapes or published books that contain the subject's stories, as well as photos and captions, so that future generations can enjoy their legacies. You can find a personal historian at www. personalhistorians.org, the website of the Association of Personal Historians.

About six years ago, James P. Brennan, PhD, approached me, wanting to share some office space so that he could write a book. Dr. Brennan is a past Dean of the Wescoe School for Continuing Studies at Muhlenberg College in Allentown, Pennsylvania, where he continues to teach. He also serves as the sports psychology consultant for the Villanova University men's basketball team. He has tremendous inspiration and insight to share, not only with his family but with the rest of us as well. In August 2011, Dr. Brennan self-published his book, The Art of Becoming Oneself: A Fresh Interpretation of Our Possibilities. *It is one of his greatest accomplishments.*

Imagine the wisdom we would have access to if our great-grandparents had written a book.

Imagine the wisdom we would have access to if our great-grandparents had written a book. We could pick up that book and know what they were thinking and how they survived difficult times. It would be fascinating, and it would offer valuable insight into how our families came to be. Howard Hill, my wife's father, wrote a book detailing his days growing up as a barefoot boy in Arkansas. It's titled *Out of My Mind: Stories for the Front Porch*. It is a treasure, a family history, especially since his passing.

Consider giving the gift of wisdom to those around you by recording and/or publishing your own legacy. It doesn't matter whether you are a homemaker or a company president—your stories and life lessons are unique and will be valuable to future generations.

It's Your Turn

Exercise 9-1: Finding collaborators

You can gain wisdom by collaborating with colleagues who are either in your own field or in other fields. Being open to the possibility of collaboration with others provides your work with complementary insight and perspective that you could never gain on your own. Whom could you collaborate with in a business venture, work project, or athletic training?

1. _____
2. _____
3. _____
4. _____
5. _____

Exercise 9-2: Sharing your wisdom

As we age, we collect a plethora of life lessons that will never see the light of day unless we make a conscious effort to share them. What are some of the major life lessons you want to share with your children and grandchildren? How will you share them?

1. _____
2. _____
3. _____
4. _____
5. _____

Chapter

10

Overcoming Obstacles

*I would never have amounted to anything
were it not for adversity.*

J. C. Penney
American Businessman

John Gunther, an American writer and journalist, said, "Ours is the only country deliberately founded on a good idea." Indeed, America is the only country in the history of civilization that was founded to be a republic, a democracy.

This great country of ours has been built largely by people who overcame their own generations' great obstacles. We're experiencing a tough time in American history right now, but I believe that the same fabric that was woven through the people who went ahead of us through The Great Depression and two world wars also weaves through most of us today. We, too, can have that same resolve. It's part of the American way.

In fact, George Washington, the father of our country, overcame great odds to secure America's independence from Great Britain. As commander-in-chief of the Continental Army in the American Revolutionary War (1775–1783), Washington endured unspeakable hardship as he led his soldiers to victory. He lost many battles during those years, was shot, and suffered a lack of supplies and soldiers, but his patriotic spirit and determination propelled him onward. Fortunately, after enduring years of severe hardship, he and his men were finally victorious.

To discover our life's true north—those three to five items at the top of the list we developed in Chapter 1—we must overcome the obstacles that are sure to confront us on our path to success. The following strategies can help.

Exhibiting Resilience and Persistence

The key words that come to my mind when I think about overcoming obstacles are resilience and persistence. But what do those traits look like?

Psychological resilience is very important. It is developed over time, as a person encounters and overcomes obstacles. One of the key things that I've seen with many athletes today, at both the college and high-school levels, is that they often don't have good frustration-management skills because throughout their lives, they've succeeded. They've won. They've done really well, especially those who are high-functioning in athletics and/or academics. They haven't had the tough breaks in life that help them develop resilience. Or their parents prepared the path for them, as opposed to preparing their kids for the path.

Persistence is a powerful tool in achieving success. We rarely reach our goals on the first attempt. One of my favorite quotes that I keep on my office wall is by Jacob Riis, a Danish American social reformer, journalist, and social-documentary photographer. He said, "When nothing seems to help, I go and look at a stonecutter hammering away at his rock perhaps a hundred times without as much as a crack showing in it. Yet at the hundred and first blow, it will split in two, and I know it was not that blow that did it, but all that had gone before."

Winners *will* things to happen, and this can be a learned habit.

Maintaining a Positive Mental Attitude

I think that another main ingredient in overcoming obstacles is attitude. If we acknowledge up front that life comes with obstacles and accept the fact that we're going to be confronted on a daily basis with situations that have to be overcome, we will not be floored by them. It's important to have an attitude that we're going to prevail, even if it sometimes takes us a little longer than we'd like to come up with the right idea or the right solution to a problem. Winners *will* things to happen, and this can be a learned habit.

In this regard, I think of Ed Deutschlander, my CEO-elect. It doesn't matter what circumstances he is confronted with; he will immediately come through with a positive statement, and then he will proceed to act on that positive statement. The gravity of the bad news doesn't matter. He has a way of being able to reformulate it into something both positive and productive. My mentor, Maury Stewart, shares the same trait. It is noteworthy that neither of them harbors negativity in any form.

W. Clement Stone is an example of a person who overcame great obstacles to achieve success. When Stone was three, his father died, leaving the family impoverished because of his gambling losses. When Clement was six, he began selling newspapers on Chicago's South Side, while his mother worked as a dressmaker. At thirteen, he owned his own newsstand. At the age of sixteen, Stone went to Detroit to help his mother in the insurance agency she had opened there. He went from office to office, making cold calls (he called them "gold calls") to sell casualty insurance. He devoured the Horatio Alger stories, in which poor boys overcame adversity to become successful.

In 1919, Stone built the Combined Insurance Company of America, and by 1930, he had more than one thousand agents selling insurance for him across the United States. By 1979, Stone's insurance company exceeded $1 billion in assets. Stone put into practice the principles in the book *Think and Grow Rich* by Napoleon Hill. He went on to help others overcome adversity and achieve incredible success. For example, he took Og Mandino, an alcoholic, under his wing, and Mandino later became the publisher of *Success* magazine.

Stone wrote and spoke often of the importance of PMA (positive mental attitude). He said, "There's very little difference in people, but that little difference makes a big difference. The little difference is attitude. The big difference is whether it is positive or negative."

William James, who was an active member of the faculty of Harvard University from 1872 to 1907, also believed that attitude is of paramount importance. He had six axioms about attitude:

- Attitude affects quality of life.
- Attitude is a choice.
- Attitude alters abilities.
- People with a positive attitude anticipate adversity.
- Attitude affects success.
- Actions alter attitudes. If you want to change attitudes, start with a change in behavior. My dear friend, Norm Levine, admonishes listeners to his many educational talks, "If you want to be enthusiastic, act enthusiastic." It works!

Helen Keller maintained a positive attitude throughout her life, despite being deaf, speechless, and blind from the age of nineteen months. Keller went on to become a world-famous speaker and author and is remembered as an advocate for people with disabilities. She said, "The marvelous riches of the human experience would lose something of rewarding joy if there were not limitations to overcome." What an incredible attitude! When asked if there was anything worse than blindness, she is said to have replied, "Yes—to be without vision."

Acquiring "Building Material"

In sports and in life, we must have what I call "building material." It's a combination of attitude, confidence, and a focus on the positive aspects of a situation.

Once you recognize that something worked well, keep focusing on that.

Confidence is a by-product of a positive experience. If you have a positive experience, you will become more confident. As your confidence grows, so, too, will the quality of your performance and your ability to overcome adversity. Having a positive attitude plays into that. Regardless of what happens to us—whether we experience a terrible board meeting, a bad hire, a lost football game—if we can focus our minds to discover the positive aspects of every situation and accentuate that positive, we can overcome the negative aspects of the situation. Of course, we have to acknowledge that X, Y, and Z didn't go right, but something else did. Why did that work? What was good about it? How can you expand on it?

Once you recognize that something worked well, keep focusing on that. You will develop more confidence and, subsequently, the ability to overcome the adversity that confronts you next time and the next. This accumulation of confidence is the building material that helps us overcome the obstacles that prevent us from being successful.

Turning Adversity into Advantage

When things don't go as you expect them to, ask yourself, "How can I turn this into an advantage for me?" Then, no matter what life throws at you, you can overcome that obstacle because you're finding a way to make it work for you, not against you.

If you want to overcome adversity, study success. What have successful people done? What has worked? Why did it work? How did it work? What did not work? History is replete with examples of extremely successful people who have overcome great adversity. We can learn a lot by studying their failures as well as their successes:

- Beethoven was deaf but ended up composing beautiful music.

- Henry Ford went broke five times before he experienced success.

- Richard Hooker labored for seven years to complete his humorous war novel, only to have it rejected by twenty-one publishers. The Morrow Publishing Company took a risk and published the unique novel, *M.A.S.H.* The risk paid off, and it became an Academy-Award winning film and an Emmy- and Golden-Globe-winning TV series.

- In 1960, Wilma Rudolph became the first American woman to win three Olympic gold medals in track and field at the Olympics. She was born prematurely and had polio as a young child, resulting in a twisted left leg and foot. She recovered but wore a leg brace for three years. By the time she was twelve, she had also survived scarlet fever, whooping cough, chicken pox, and measles. At age thirteen, she made the basketball and track teams at her school. In the 1960 Summer Olympics in Rome, Rudolph became the first American woman to win three gold medals in track and field during a single Olympic Games.

- When Walt Disney submitted his first drawings for publication, an editor told him he had no artistic talent.

- Robert Ripley started his career in Major League baseball. He broke his arm in his first game, and his doctor told him, "Don't attempt anything like this again." Today we remember Robert L. Ripley as the man who chronicled the world of peculiarities with the "Ripley's Believe It or Not!" newspaper panel series, radio show, and television show.

- Dr. Seuss's first book was rejected by twenty-three publishers. The twenty-fourth publisher accepted his manuscript and sold six million copies of the book.

- Hewlett Packard and Atari both rejected the Apple microcomputer, which went on to have first-year sales of $2.5 million.

- Charles Goodyear was obsessed with making rubber that was unaffected by temperature extremes, and he experimented unsuccessfully for years, only to experience bitter disappointment. He was imprisoned for debt, had family difficulties, and was ridiculed by his friends. But he persevered, and in 1839, he found that simply adding sulfur to the rubber achieved his purpose. In 1898, almost four decades after his death, the Goodyear Tire and Rubber Company was founded and named after him.

- In 1902, the editor of the *Atlantic Monthly* returned the poems of a twenty-eight-year-old poet with the following note: "Our magazine has no room for your vigorous verse." Robert Frost persevered and became one of the world's most beloved poets.

- A ten-thousand-word story about a soaring seagull was rejected by eighteen publishers. Macmillan finally agreed to publish *Jonathan Livingston Seagull*, by Richard Bach, in 1970. Within five years, it had sold more than seven million copies in the United States alone.

Abraham Lincoln is the quintessential example of a person who was faced with overwhelming adversity but overcame it and became one of the most important people in history.

- At age thirty, Steve Jobs was let go from his own company, Apple, then went on to achieve phenomenal success and revolutionize the personal-computer industry. After the devastating experience of being let go from a company he had established, he started two new companies. One of them was NeXT. Apple eventually bought NeXT, and Jobs returned to Apple. The second company he started was Pixar, which eventually became the most successful animation studio in the world. In an address to the graduating class of Stanford University in 2005, Jobs said, "I didn't see it then, but it turned out that getting let go from Apple was the best thing that could have ever happened to me. The heaviness of being successful was replaced by the lightness of being a beginner again, less sure about everything. It freed me to enter one of the most creative periods of my life."[58]

Abraham Lincoln is the quintessential example of a person who was faced with overwhelming adversity but overcame it and became one of the most important people in history. He grew up poor, and his mother died when he was nine. He failed in business twice. He was defeated in legislative, congressional, and senatorial races and also failed in an effort to become America's vice president at age forty-seven. His fiancée died, and he subsequently suffered what some refer to as a nervous breakdown and was bedridden for

---

58. John Naughton, "Steve Jobs: Stanford Commencement Address, June 2005," *The Observer*, last modified October 8, 2011, accessed on November 30, 2013, http://www.guardian.co.uk/technology/2011/oct/09/steve-jobs-stanford-commencement-address/print.

six months. After he married Mary Todd, only one of their four sons survived. But at age fifty-two, he was elected president of the United States. We will forever remember him for leading his country through a great constitutional, military, and moral crisis (the American Civil War), preserving the Union while ending slavery, and promoting economic and financial modernization.

In the sports world, there are many more great stories about overcoming obstacles:

- Anthony Robles, a young African-American from Arizona State University, won the 2010–11 NCAA individual wrestling championship in the 125–pound weight class, despite being born with only one leg. He recently launched a career as a motivational speaker so that he can encourage people with disabilities to overcome obstacles.

- Kevin Laue is a basketball player who was born with only one arm. In 2009, he received a scholarship to play Division I basketball for Manhattan College. Laue stands 6'10" and wears a size 17 shoe. He has been lauded for his "quick leaping ability" and his ability to play effectively on both offense and defense.

- Kyle Maynard was born with a disability called congenital amputation of all four of his limbs. His father, who had wrestled in high school and college, encouraged him to try wrestling. For a season and a half, the younger Maynard lost every match he wrestled—thirty-five matches in a row. Halfway through his second season, he won his first match. He continued to be a successful wrestler. During his senior year, he won thirty-six varsity matches and placed in the top twelve at the Senior Nationals, only one match away from becoming a high school All-American. His 36–1 record as a senior was good enough to earn runner-up honors in the Georgia State Championships.

- Michael Jordan was cut from his varsity basketball team as a sophomore at Laney High School in Wilmington, North Carolina. Instead of giving up, Jordan used that experience to spur himself to greater achievements, practicing hour after hour on the court. He eventually made the team and led it to the state championship. Many consider him to be the greatest player to ever play the game. No player in NBA history has ever achieved as much as he has. He is a five-time league MVP, a ten-time scoring champion, and a six-time Finals MVP with six NBA championships. Incidentally, Jordan tried unsuccessfully to switch careers from basketball to baseball. He signed a minor league contract with the Chicago White Sox and was assigned to the Birmingham Barons as an outfielder. His presence in the minors attracted large numbers of fans, but he did not excel in the sport. It may be because he did not put in those all-important ten thousand hours of practice in baseball as he did in basketball. If he had, I believe he would have excelled there as well.

As we put in ten thousand hours into a sport, occupation, or vocation, we are going to experience a lot of adversity. There are times, during that process, that we will be broken to our core. I think it is at that point, at the proverbial rock bottom, that many people finally begin to look up and resolve to do things differently or finally trust in God. From there, you start your journey anew from the deep core of who you really are. There's a promise in the Bible, in James 4:8, that says, "Draw near to God, and He will draw near to you." As soon as we make that move, God steps in, and then incredible things can happen.

Anthony Robles has said that having only one leg actually turned out to be an advantage for him. One thing, which is obvious, is that it's like boxing a left-handed boxer. The advantage belongs to the left-handed boxer, not because of the physics, but because the left-handed boxer is used to fighting right-handers, but right-handed boxers are not used to fighting left-handers.

Having a disability, challenge, or adversity in life can actually turn out to be the greatest blessing.

Robles's opponents had become accustomed to reaching for a leg and finding it. But in Robles's case, his competitors are reaching for that leg, and it's not there! They're grabbing air, and that makes them vulnerable in the same way that a missed punch opens up a boxer to a major blow. That's one of the advantages that Robles soon discovered. A second advantage is that he is not carrying the weight of a second leg. So he is wrestling a weight class or two down from someone who is of comparable size. His upper torso is enormous compared to his competitors'. Turning his disadvantage into an advantage allowed Robles to focus on what he could do instead of what he couldn't do, and that made all the difference! So there can actually be an advantage to the person with the disadvantage. But without the positive attitude that turns adversity to an advantage, the disadvantage can remain just that—a disadvantage.

What I've seen as a sports psychologist is that many individuals who grow up with a physical disability or other adversity develop a psychological mindset of resilience. Like the athletes just mentioned, they learn to focus on what they can do, not on what they cannot do. Having a disability, challenge, or adversity in life can actually turn out to be the greatest blessing.

A coach was once admonishing his team at halftime not to quit, no matter how badly they were getting beat. He said, "Did Joe DiMaggio ever quit?"

The team yelled, "No!"

"Did Michael Jordan ever quit?"

The team yelled, "No!"

"Did John Moses quit?"

They asked, "Who's John Moses?"

The coach replied, "Of course you haven't heard of him—he quit!"

Tapping into Others' Support

Support is one of the most important variables in overcoming adversity. The messages that we internalize from our parents, coaches, team members, teachers, and community leaders really matter. It doesn't take much support to encourage us enough to overcome obstacles. Even if you have just one individual who believes in you, maybe even more than you believe in yourself, that can be enough to help you overcome adversity. All you need is one person who says, "I see it in you."

It's important to develop your network of support. Sometimes we don't realize just how much support we really have around us until adversity strikes.

In Chapter 2, we mentioned Shawn Achor of Harvard, author of *The Happiness Advantage*. Shawn has said that the single greatest determinant of happiness is having a tight support group of family and friends. He notes that the people who have such a network are less inclined than other people to suffer from depression. Not only does a support network enable you to excel and overcome adversity; it also helps you to be happy.

I believe that if you want to get the best out of someone, you must look for the best that is in them. Johann Wolfgang von Goethe said, "The way you see people is the way you treat them, and the way you treat them is what they become." Gandhi refused to see bad in anybody. Khalil Gibran, the great prophet and one of my favorite philosophers, said, "Our worst fault is our preoccupation with the faults of others."

Tolerating Success

I often tell the athletes I work with, "There is more inside of you." What attracted me to the area of positive psychology when I was a student was a deep feeling inside of me that there was more inside of me, personally, than I had ever understood. There is more inside of all of us, but for some reason, as human beings, we don't quite tap into all that's within us. Simply by adopting and exhibiting a positive attitude, we can do amazing things.

For many people, the fear of success is more detrimental than the fear of failure.

So what is it that's holding us back? I have found that, for many people, the fear of success is more detrimental than the fear of failure. They are afraid to run for office, become the CEO of a company, or become an NBA player because if they won that election, became CEO, or made it into the NBA, it would change their lives forever, and they're not sure they are equipped to adapt to the life changes that accompany success. It's unfamiliar territory. As a result, they regress. They don't even reach for that next level of success. Deep down inside, everybody wants success, but in the moment of truth, on a subconscious level, many people are afraid of succeeding. And they usually don't realize that the fear of success is what's holding them back. They'll say, "I don't know why I'm not succeeding. I'm so close every time, but I just can't reach that next level." Be aware of this phenomenon, and be willing to sacrifice some familiarity for the discomfort of entering the uncharted territory that comes from a higher level of performance and success.

I have seen young athletes who perform at less-than-optimum levels because they don't want to subject themselves to higher expectations or operate in that uncomfortable area outside of their comfort zone. So they end up sabotaging their own success—they'll freeze, get hurt, or get defeated in a game or match. I often tell athletes, "Life will be as good as you can stand it to be." So the real question is, "How good can you stand it?" Some people will say, "I can stand it pretty damn good," and my response to that is, "Well, great! You're going to have an amazing life because you can tolerate success."

Reciting Affirmations or Poems

Sometimes, when faced with a difficult challenge, getting through that next moment seems like an impossible task. One way to endure difficulties is to recite a poem, affirmation, or Bible verse.

Nelson Mandela, former president of South Africa, was jailed for twenty-seven years for his work as an anti-apartheid activist. One of the coping mechanisms he used to endure his incarceration was to recite—to himself and to other prisoners—the poem "Invictus" by the English poet William Ernest Henley. Henley contracted tuberculosis of the bone when he was twelve. The disease progressed to his foot, and his leg was amputated below the knee when he was seventeen. Here is the famous poem he wrote:

Invictus

Out of the night that covers me,
Black as the pit from pole to pole,
I thank whatever gods may be
For my unconquerable soul.

In the fell clutch of circumstance
I have not winced nor cried aloud.
Under the bludgeonings of chance
My head is bloody, but unbowed.

Beyond this place of wrath and tears
Looms but the horror of the shade,
And yet the menace of the years
Finds and shall find me unafraid.

It matters not how strait the gate,
How charged with punishments the scroll,
I am the master of my fate:
I am the captain of my soul.

What is your poem? Do you have it memorized? Do you have an affirmation or Bible verse that you can repeat to yourself when you are faced with a difficult situation?

When I was growing up, a coach shared a poem with our team that helped me through many difficult times. I memorized it and still recite it to myself and share it with athletes today. It is titled "Pressure," and its author is unknown.

Pressure

How do you act when the pressure is on?
When the chance of victory is almost gone?
When fortune's stars refuse to shine?
When the ball is on your own five-yard line?

How do you act when the going gets tough?
Do your spirits lag
When the breaks are rough?
Or is there in you a flame that grows brighter
As the battle grows fiercer?

How long, how hard will you fight the foe?
That is what the world would like to know.
Cowards can fight when they are out ahead
But an uphill grind?
Shows a thoroughbred.

So if you wish for success,
Then tell me, son,
How will you act when the pressure is on?

It's one of the most powerful poems I know. Like Nelson Mandela, I often recite that poem and find inspiration in its words.

Having a Clear, Concise, Compelling Vision

When I was the student-body president at Temple in 1962, I was selected to present a Temple award to Dr. Martin Luther King, who made a presentation to the student body at our Philadelphia campus. As I stood with him on that stage at Geasy Field and got to shake his hand and speak with him, I remember thinking that his day-to-day trials and tribulations seemed insurmountable, as bigotry and prejudice were commonplace. Watching his self-assured, unflappable style, you might have thought that he hadn't a worry in the world. Three years later, an assassin's bullet ended his life. His enormous legacy is testimony to his positive attitude and his fidelity to the compelling vision in his "I Have a Dream" speech.

On August 28, 1963, the day he gave that famous speech, in which he called for racial equality and an end to discrimination, King had actually prepared another speech but threw it away moments before he made his presentation. For him to deliver such a compelling and passionate speech, it's obvious to me that he had recited those words, or at least thought them, many times before: "I have a dream that my four little children will one day live in a nation where they will not be judged by the color of their skin but by the content of their character." He had those words in his mind already. He didn't make them up in the moments before that presentation. He had a vision. He had a clear, concise, compelling sequence of words that exemplified his purpose in life. And yes, the rest is history!

We could all benefit by doing the same. If we develop a clear, concise, compelling vision that we can articulate with ease—both to ourselves and to others—it will infuse our journey to success with renewed conviction and enthusiasm.

Enthusiasm is one of the most important keys to success.

Enthusiasm is one of the most important keys to success, according to my friend Harvey Mackay. In a 2012 article titled "There's Never a Need to Curb Your Enthusiasm,"[59] Mackay says, "One of the greatest tragedies is that the curiosity, enthusiasm, and excitement about life that we are born with seem to erode as the years go by. When the challenges of daily life get in the way, it is easy to spend more energy on putting out the little fires than on sparking enthusiasm for overcoming those challenges." He goes on to quote Napoleon Hill, the famous author of *Think and Grow Rich*. "Hill says some people are born with a natural enthusiasm, and some people have to develop it. How? Simple, he says. Work at something you love."

Visualizing Success

I believe that if we constantly visualize ourselves as being successful—and remember, success is a journey, not a destination—that image of success can propel us beyond our current circumstances and help us achieve even the loftiest of goals.

As a boy, being raised by a single mother who never rose above the poverty line, I thought I was a prince. My surroundings were incongruent with that image, but I simply thought that I was the victim of deception and that I was actually a prince. I thought that when I got older, I was going to be a king. I always felt special, in spite of our modest existence. I just thought it was a passage I was going through. Some might call it denial, some hallucinating, others mental illness. But it was possibly my coping mechanism, perhaps caused by a positive mental attitude. In some ways, I still coach myself through issues today with the same technique.

---

59. Harvey Mackay, "There's Never a Need to Curb Your Enthusiasm," *Star Tribune*, October 14, 2012.

Even before a plan for college emerged, I knew I would make something of my life. I thought that someday I would work at Bethlehem Steel, and I would strive to be president of the steelworkers' union at the plant. You didn't need a college education to do that. My mother was a union member in the International Ladies' Garment Workers Union, so it would have been a natural path for me.

Optimism served as a survival mechanism for me. Anticipating and envisioning a better life helped me escape the reality of my actual one. I feel blessed to have had that vision of success because most of the kids who are in that condition think of themselves as being in a hopeless situation, with no end in sight. They don't see prosperity. They don't see independence. They don't see dignity because they don't see it in any of their elders or in their neighborhoods. But somehow, by the grace of God, I was gifted to sense all of those things.

As it turned out, my Father did turn out to be a King, albeit a heavenly one, but that's the subject of another book (*The Prince and the Cockroach*) in the making.

When I am asked what keeps me up at night, I quickly reply, "the growing disparity between the haves and the have-nots." It's a challenge we all must address. America's future depends on a resolution. The absence of hope is an incubator for bad outcomes. I saw that firsthand! Aristotle observed that members of the middle class tend to have more moderate desires, they are more open to reasonable persuasion, and they are more likely to be linked to one another by ties of civic affection. A growing, not a diminishing, middle class is the necessary gift we must leave our children!

I think that some of us know, at a very early age, that God has something greater planned for us. We don't know exactly what that will end up looking like when we're older, but we realize that God has a special mission for us in life.

Helping Others Overcome Their Obstacles

When I was thirty-seven and had achieved some success in the insurance and financial services industry, I returned to Easton and was blessed to be able to get my mother a house in Palmer Township, a lovely suburban area. Mom was fifty-three at the time, and she became a very happy person. Before that, unfortunately, she was not. They say money isn't everything, but trust me, it's a lot easier to be happy with money than without money, and she knew that. It was a tremendous blessing that I was able to be an instrument in her journey, and for that I thank the Lord.

In my experience, helping those less fortunate is more the rule than the exception to the rule today. There is a high level of compassion today that is more pervasive than I have seen at any other time in my life. I have seen many successful people turn around and help others who have been less fortunate. That spirit of giving is one of the characteristics that helps strengthen this great country of ours and our world.

It's important for all of us, once we have overcome obstacles that have gotten in the way of our success, to make sure that we remain humble, remember who helped us get where we are, then turn around and give back to others.

It's Your Turn

Exercise 10-1: Positive aspects of your life

Acknowledging what has gone well for you can help you focus on the positive aspects of your life and overcome adversity. What is going well for you in your life?

1. _____
2. _____
3. _____
4. _____
5. _____
6. _____

Exercise 10-2: Giving back

Once you have experienced success, helping others is the right thing to do. Whom can you help, and how?

Whom I Can Help	How I Can Help Them
1. _____	1. _____
2. _____	2. _____
3. _____	3. _____
4. _____	4. _____
5. _____	5. _____

Exercise 10-3: Repeating affirmations

What is an affirmation, poem, or Bible verse you recite to encourage yourself? If you do not have one, find one you like and memorize it.

_____

_____

_____

_____

_____

_____

_____

_____

Chapter

11

Adopt an Abundance Mentality

*The Abundance Mentality...results in sharing of prestige,
of recognition, of profits, of decision making. It opens
possibilities, options, alternatives, and creativity.*

Stephen Covey
Author, *The 7 Habits of Highly Successful People*

In his highly acclaimed book *The 7 Habits of Highly Effective People*, originally published in 1989, Steven Covey says the third character trait essential to habit number four, "Think Win/Win," is an *abundance mentality*, "the paradigm that there is plenty out there for everybody." He says an abundance mentality flows out of a deep inner sense of personal worth and security.[60]

Covey believes, however, that most people are deeply scripted in a *scarcity mentality*, the opposite of an abundance mentality. "They see life as having only so much, as though there were only one pie out there," Covey says. "And if someone were to get a big piece of the pie, it would mean less for everybody else. The scarcity mentality is the zero-sum paradigm of life." He goes on to say that people with a scarcity mentality have a difficult time sharing recognition, credit, power, or profit—even with those who help in the production. They also find it difficult to be genuinely happy for other people's successes. Their sense of worth comes from being compared, and they feel that someone else's success, to some degree, means their failure.[61]

We should not envy others because of their material possessions. The word "compare" should not be a part of our lexicon. We should feel happy when people

---

60. Stephen R. Covey, *The 7 Habits of Highly Effective People* (New York: Free Press, 2004), 219–220.
61. Ibid.

succeed, whether they are more successful or less fortunate than we are. I think it's important and fruitful to be selfless.

If it's all about you, then comparison is natural. But if you're grateful for what you have, then the word "compare" doesn't come into play because you're preoccupied with being grateful for what you do have versus thinking about what you don't have.

How the Theory of Alchemy Relates to Abundance

In his book *Unlimited Wealth: The Theory and Practice of Economic Alchemy*, economist, entrepreneur, and professor Paul Zane Pilzer describes his shock upon learning that the entire field of economics is based on the concept of scarcity—a finite amount of resources in the world—and the fact that the best we can hope for is a better way of dividing those resources. This realization contradicted Pilzer's belief in a true and just God, and he set out to find a theory to replace the business theories that were based on the concept of scarcity.[62]

> We live in a world of effectively unlimited resources—a world of unlimited wealth.

On his website, Pilzer says, "For the past four hundred years, virtually all practitioners of the dismal science we call economics have agreed on one basic premise: namely, that a society's wealth is determined by its supply of physical resources—its land, labor, minerals, water, and so on. And underlying this premise has been another, even more profound, assumption—one supposedly so obvious that it is rarely mentioned: namely, that the entire world contains a limited amount of these physical resources. This means, from an economic point of view, that life is what the mathematicians call a zero-sum game. After all, if there are only limited resources, one person's gain must be another person's loss; the richer one person is, the poorer his neighbors must be."[63]

But today, Pilzer says, we live in a world of effectively unlimited resources—a world of unlimited wealth. We live in what he calls a "new Alchemic world." He refers to the ancient alchemists, who sought to discover the secret of turning

---

62. Paul Zane Pilzer, *Unlimited Wealth: The Theory and Practice of Economic Alchemy* (New York: Crown Publishers, 1991).

63. Paul Zane Pilzer's website, accessed on November 30, 2013, www.paulzanepilzer.com/uw.htm.

base metals into gold; they tried to create great value where little existed before. He notes that if the ancient alchemists had succeeded in fabricating gold, gold would have become worthless, and their efforts would have been for naught. "Yet, through their attempts to make gold, they laid the foundation for modern science, which today has accomplished exactly what the alchemists hoped to achieve: the ability to create great value where little existed before. We have achieved this ability through the most common, the most powerful, and the most consistently underestimated force in our lives today—technology."[64]

In his book, Pilzer provides the example of a piece of land that is worth $1,000 because it can produce one hundred bushels of wheat. Then he notes that we can irrigate that piece of land so that it will now produce two hundred bushels of wheat and is worth $2,000. Next, we can add fertilizer, and that same one acre of land will produce four hundred bushels of wheat. Then we can employ the concept of crop rotation, and the land will produce eight hundred bushels of wheat. By applying technology, we have increased the size of the pie, thus proving the Malthusian theory wrong. The Malthusian theory or Malthusian catastrophe, as it's known, is a belief postulated by political economist Reverend Thomas Robert Malthus (1766–1834) that once population growth outpaces agricultural production, society will be forced to return to subsistence-level conditions unless catastrophes keep the population in check. An August 2007 science review in *The New York Times* contended that the Industrial Revolution enabled the modern world to break out of the Malthusian growth model.[65]

Another example Pilzer provides is that when we replace a $300 carburetor with a $25 fuel injector in an automobile, we are, in effect, doubling the automobile's mileage and therefore doubling the world's oil supply. When I was sixteen years old, there was a gas station at Walnut Street and 7th in Easton, Pennsylvania, that sold gasoline for 17 cents a gallon. If you consider the fact that cars at that time got only eight or nine miles to the gallon, compared to the thirty to fifty miles per gallon that cars get today, current gas prices don't seem so high after all. The abundance mentality again comes into play because of the ways in which technology has helped us derive more mileage from a gallon of gas. With the technological advance in fracking, today America is on the threshold of being a net exporter of oil and gas after decades of being a net importer.

---

64. Ibid.

65. Nicholas Wade, "In Dusty Archives, a Theory of Affluence," *The New York Times*, last modified August 7, 2007, accessed on November 30, 2013, http://www.nytimes.com/2007/08/07/science/07indu.html?bl&ex=1186804800&en=fbe25403514c47d5&ei=5087%0A.

I think we could all benefit from adopting an abundance mentality—a mindset that assumes there's enough wealth, fame, and success for everyone.

Some people want to keep immigrants out of the United States because they believe they are taking jobs away from American citizens. But studies have shown that immigrants actually increase the scope of jobs available. A January 2012 article in *The Washington Post* reported, "Immigrants tend to have different skills than native-born workers.... More immigrants mean that classes of jobs that might otherwise go unfilled because they don't match up with the skills of native-born workers instead get filled.... The economic evidence is clear: Immigration, in the aggregate, increases growth and, in the long run, jobs."[66]

Granted, there are individual circumstances in which a person is displaced by someone who is willing to work for less money than they are. But that's a temporary phenomenon that can be resolved by educating or training that person who has been displaced from the janitorial job he or she probably didn't want anyway.

Creating Something from Nothing

Pilzer also makes the point that technology can create a need where none existed before. He calls it "the first law of modern business"—that instead of finding a need and filling it, we should imagine a need and create it. That's what Steve Jobs did. He imagined a need for products that didn't exist and then created them.

I have always been intrigued by the idea of creating something where nothing existed. When I was attending Lafayette College, I made up my own major and called it "psychobiology"—a study of the biological aspects of psychology. My Fiji fraternity brothers joked with me, saying, "Well, that's great, Jarrod, you're a psychobiology major. What are you going to do with that—hypnotize fish?" There wasn't a market for psychobiology. But Dr. Wendy L. Hill, who is now the Provost and Dean of the Faculty at Lafayette College, supported me in my efforts and helped me navigate the uncharted waters. The major generated a lot of interest, and Lafayette Magazine *interviewed me and wrote an article about it. The major was eventually adopted by Lafayette College and has become one of the top neuroscience programs in the country. A generous*

---

66. Ezra Klein, "The Confused Argument against Immigration," *The Washington Post*, last modified January 9, 2012, accessed on November 30, 2013, http://www.washingtonpost.com/blogs/ezra -klein/post/the-confused-argument-against-immigration/2011/08/25/gIQArcOY1P_blog.html.

Lafayette alum named Walter Oechsle even stepped in and donated money to launch the new program, now called neuroscience, in a state-of-the-art facility called Oechsle Hall.

At North Star and in other companies like it, our advisors are creating wealth. They're creating something that did not exist before. If they earn $1 million in a year, they're going to put that money either into savings or spend it, either of which is good for our economy. In addition, the clients they're serving will either invest in the US economy in the form of stocks, bonds, or real estate, or they will save the cash values in their insurance contracts. Investing or spending those dollars creates jobs for other Americans. Even more important than the monetary value that's created is the quality of life that is sustained when a wage earner dies and leaves behind a life insurance policy for his or her spouse and family. When that happens, the children in those families get to live in the same homes and go to the same churches and playgrounds and stay in the same schools because somebody listened when a financial advisor recommended that they insure their human life value, for the benefit of their loved ones.

The Abundance Mentality in Athletics

In business and education, it's easy to see how the abundance mentality works. In the ideal business transaction, the goal is for both parties to be better off than they were before the transaction. In education, the more a person shares his or her knowledge, the more others learn. Competitive athletics may be one of the only endeavors in which one person's victory might be seen as another person's loss. That's really the lower end of understanding because while we may think another team or person "lost," they may have derived a tremendous lesson or strategy for improvement as a result of receiving the lower number of points in a game or match.

> ### The Olympic Creed emphasizes participation and effort—not winning.

The essence of sports isn't about the W or the L—winning or losing. It's about humans flourishing and giving all we've got—leaving it all out there on the field, court, or mat. The focus is constantly on improvement. How can we learn from that performance, and how can we improve next time? Our goal is to keep getting better and better. In sports, when you win, you're not really as good as you think you are. But the opposite is true as well—when you lose in sports, you're not really as bad as you think you are.

In fact, the Olympic Creed emphasizes participation and effort—not winning. It says, "The most important thing in the Olympic Games is not to win but to take part, just as the most important thing in life is not the triumph, but the struggle. The essential thing is not to have conquered, but to have fought well." That is the mindset of athletics that I subscribe to.

The Abundance Mindset—Another View

Another way to look at abundance is in terms of a personal quest to achieve and accumulate more. In that framework, I believe that the quest to achieve abundance can be detrimental.

One way to recognize just how much we have is to live at a subsistence level for a while.

Through scarcity, we can learn to develop an attitude of gratitude so that we can realize just how abundantly we all live. A friend of mine, Matthew Myers, is the cofounder of GiANT Partners, a company that helps companies grow through strategic planning, capital structure, leadership development, CEO coaching, and acquisitions and mergers. He uses the phrase "striving to become less." There is profound depth to that phrase. He believes the optimal high road is actually the low road and that less can actually be more. While most people strive to become greater, another approach is to reflect humility and accentuate gratitude and abundance.

In our society, many people work hard so they can achieve more power, fame, financial security, and influence, and they struggle with "affluenza"—an unhealthy desire to have more than anyone else. We're the wealthiest country in the history of the world, yet some would say we're also the most depressed country in the world.

One way to recognize just how much we have is to live at a subsistence level for a while. When I was a young adult, I used to go with my good friend, Nick D'Anna, on a backpacking trip every year. When I went out into the woods to hike for a few days, everything I needed was right there on my back. It reminded me that I didn't need much. It made me appreciate the small things. Dinner was a delicious dish of ramen noodles cooked slowly over a mountaintop fire. On those nights, I really loved those ra-men noodles!

On one trip on the Appalachian Trail in Virginia, we were high up in the mountains for quite some time and ran out of water. It was a dry summer, and we had to trek way down into the valley to get water. I became incredibly dehydrated and thirsty. At one point, I said to Nick, "If you gave me the choice of a gallon of water or a thousand dollars right now, without a doubt, I would take that gallon of water." We eventually got our water, and I got rehydrated—and appreciated it immensely.

After every backpacking trip, we would go to a nearby diner and marvel at the fact that there was a comfortable place to sit, a bathroom with flushing toilets, and as much water as we could drink. We reentered society with an abundance mental-ity—realizing just how much we had to be thankful for in our lives. I think it's important to engage in an exercise like that once in a while to remind us of just how abundantly we live.

How to Adopt an Abundance Mentality

The best way I can think of to adopt an abundance mentality is to count your blessings. Stopping to think about what you have to be grateful for makes you realize how much you really have.

Another way to adopt an abundance mentality is to realize that you probably have more than a lot of people. If you have food in the refrigerator, a roof over your head, and a car to drive, then you are wealthier than most of the people in the world. We tend to do the opposite—we compare ourselves with celebrities and other wealthy individuals and feel inferior because we don't have what they have.

I believe that, to acquire an abundance mentality, you have to really want it. Simply recognizing how unpleasant it is to have a scarcity mentality is the first step. If anything I get has to be at someone else's expense, well, that's certainly an unpleasant way to go through life. With an abundance mentality, one can attain goals without it costing anybody else anything. The more one gains, the more other people gain; it's an attitude that begins from inside and radiates outward. A rising tide lifts all boats!

Having an abundance mentality can help us navigate the path to our true north. If we abide by the principle that an abundance of success and happiness exists, it will prepare us to take advantage of those limitless opportunities when they present themselves. The sky is not the limit!

It's Your Turn

Exercise 11-1: What are you grateful for?

You more than likely have more material possessions than most people in the world. What aspects of your abundance are you grateful for? Begin each day with the thought, "If all I had today were the things I gave thanks for yesterday, how would I feel?" What would you have?

1. _____

2. _____

3. _____

4. _____

5. _____

6. _____

7. _____

Chapter

12

Create an Environment That Nurtures Success

You are a product of your environment. So choose the
environment that will best develop you toward your
objective. Analyze your life in terms of its environment. Are
the things around you helping you toward success—or are
they holding you back?

W. Clement Stone
American Businessman, Philanthropist, and Self-Help Book Author

We spend a lot of time at work, and we often devote the best part of our energy and focus to the workplace. Thus, it follows that the workplace needs to be an environment that is conducive to success in fulfilling one's life's calling.

A 2011 study revealed that many Americans are working longer hours than they used to. As company CEOs, coaches, businesspeople, and leaders, it is our responsibility to ensure that the work environment we create is conducive not only to productivity but also to our team members' physical, mental, and emotional well-being. It's been my experience that happy people are generally more productive than unhappy people.

In the book It's Your Ship, *Captain Mike Abrashoff says that, upon reviewing exit interviews of people who left the navy, he discovered that the five reasons people left were as follows. (He then learned that the reasons people leave civilian jobs are virtually the same):*

1. *Not being treated with respect or dignity*

2. *Being prevented from making an impact on the organization*

3. *Not being listened to*

4. *Not being rewarded with more responsibility*

5. *Low pay*[67]

Often, we give our best to the world, then we go home and give our worst to the people we love the most. If we are not heeding the call from the exercise in Chapter 1 to find work that energizes us—if we are not following the path that God has set out for us— then we are depleting ourselves emotionally of our energy, and by the time we go home, we're drained. Emotional energy management involves maintaining a high level of emotional energy so that we can exhibit patience and objectivity when working with other people. Low emotional energy leads to counterproductive interactions with other people and can result when we're forced to function in a less-than-optimal work environment. It is critical that all of us, whether we're CEOs, entrepreneurs, coaches, or team members, strive to create and maintain a work environment that fosters productivity, creativity, and fulfillment.

Defining Your Culture and Values

An optimal work environment starts with culture and values, the most important aspects of any organization. They set the tone for everything else. Culture must be driven from the top down, with the leader defining and demonstrating the culture and values.

> If you have a culture in which your primary mission is delivering happiness, people will enjoy going to work.

In North Star's culture (FIGGS: faith, integrity, growth, gratitude, and service), the gratitude component really stands out because we love grateful people, which is the reason we ask that question in our interviews—"What are you grateful for?" People who are grateful for their blessings in life typically have a really good attitude that is going to resonate with faith, integrity, growth, gratitude, and service.

The culture of an organization generates morale. While we don't believe in motivation, we do believe in inspiration—people being inspired to do their very best because they are surrounded by others who are doing likewise. It's contagious.

---

67. Captain D. Michael Abrashoff, *It's Your Ship: Management Techniques from the Best Damn Ship in the Navy* (New York: Warner Books, 2002), 13.

So we're constantly trying to create an environment in which people care for one another. We strive to create a sanctuary, a place of refuge.

In his book *Delivering Happiness*, Zappos CEO Tony Hsieh explains that culture is your brand, and once your culture is in place, everything else will follow. "At Zappos, our belief is that if you get the culture right, most of the other stuff—like great customer service, or building a great long-term brand, or passionate employees and customers—will happen naturally on its own. We believe that your company's culture and your company's brand are really just two sides of the same coin .... Your culture is your brand."[68]

One of our future projects at North Star, inspired by *Delivering Happiness*, is to print and distribute a book describing the culture of the company. Hsieh calls his the Zappos Culture Book. He provides it to employees, potential employees, vendors, and customers.

If you have a culture in which your primary mission is delivering happiness, people will enjoy going to work. But when people work in a hostile environment, they dread getting up in the morning and going to work. Legislation exists in America today to levy consequences against businesses that operate hostile work environments. But that's not the case in other parts of the world. In many parts of Asia, for example, you don't see as much civility in the workplace as you do here, according to newspaper accounts. I believe it will happen there eventually; happily, we're ahead of the curve and setting the bar high.

Treating Everyone with Respect

Another element of our culture is that we don't refer to our people as "employees." We consider that a harsh word. We prefer instead the phrase "team members." As Peter Drucker said, "In the final analysis, all your best employees are ultimately volunteers." I agree. Your best people can get jobs elsewhere. So they're members of your team, not employees. They are with you voluntarily! The word "employee" comes from the same Latin root as "pliable" and "compliant." It has historical implications in terms of the Industrial Revolution and in agrarian times—an employee was someone below you in the pecking order whom you told what to do. Likewise, the word "steward" comes from the Old English and referred to a sty warden, a person who took care of the pigsties. Fortunately, airlines now refer to their folks as flight attendants instead of stewards and stewardesses!

---

68. Tony Hsieh, *Delivering Happiness: A Path to Profits, Passion, and Purpose* (New York: Hachette Book Group, 2010), 152.

We believe it's important to treat every team member with respect—and again, that must start at the top of the organization. For example, our receptionist is our "Director of First Impressions." If the leadership in an organization shows great respect for everyone, no matter what their station in that company is, that becomes part of the culture.

The dignitaries I have met, as a general rule, are usually quite democratic and civil and tend to extend a welcome hand to those around them, without regard to station. In 2002, when I served as the president-elect of GAMA International, former US President George H. W. Bush was scheduled to be our keynote speaker at our Boston meeting. GAMA president Bill Pollakov asked my wife, Sue, and I to greet Mr. Bush at the curb when his limo arrived and to escort him to the elevator in the Westin Hotel. Secret Service officers were all around. They told us that under no conditions whatsoever were we to get on the elevator with Mr. Bush once we reached the hotel. Sue and I approached the car. The doors opened, and we were introduced to Mr. Bush. We escorted him to the elevator, and no less than six Secret Servicemen started to get into the elevator with him. We turned to leave, and he said, "No, no, get on. Please, get on." Then he started talking to Sue and asking her where she was from, along with other questions.

When we reached the top floor, we remained on the elevator to go back down, and Mr. Bush said, "No, no. Come on in." His suite had a main room and two side bedrooms. The Secret Servicemen walked in with us. He waved them into the side bedrooms and said, "We'll be OK. I'll call you when I need you." He engaged us in conversation for ten minutes or so in his suite, asking us about the GAMA International organization so that he could tailor his remarks to the audience. He knew nothing about us, but he was as friendly, engaging, and civil as anyone I've ever met. He is often referred to as a gentleman, and that was definitely our experience. I have to opine that the White House had to be a pleasant place when he was in office.

No Room for Toxicity

In *Built to Last*, Jim Collins and Jerry Porras discuss "cult-like cultures," which are "great places to work *only* for those who buy in to the core ideology; those who don't fit with the ideology are ejected like a virus."[69]

In other words, a healthy culture is free from toxicity, and the leader or coach is responsible for removing toxicity from the workplace or facility. I once had

---

69. Jim Collins and Jerry I. Porras, *Built to Last: Successful Habits of Visionary Companies* (New York: HarperBusiness, 2004), 89.

an advisor who constantly berated the women in our office, whether they were marketing assistants, receptionists, or his own personal assistant. He was simply mean to them. However, the guys in the office just loved him. But, for whatever reason, he did not get along with women. On a number of occasions, I called him into my office and warned him about his behavior. At times, I also counseled him, but it never worked. Finally, I let him go. He went to work with one of our competitors across the river in St. Paul. Years later, we took over that business, so as fate would have it, I got him back! Having experienced how serious I was the first time, he did change his behavior. As the saying goes, "When you've got 'em by the short hairs, their hearts and minds are sure to follow."

> ## You can't learn much about someone during a ninety-minute interview, so I often take candidates to lunch.

Our internship program allows us to get to know people before we hire them so that we can weed out people who exhibit toxic behaviors and attitudes. You can't learn much about someone during a ninety-minute interview, so I often take candidates to lunch. One thing I look for is how a person treats people who work in a service capacity. My mother worked as a bartender in New York City. When I'm in a restaurant with someone, I pay special attention to the way they treat the waiter, waitress, or bartender. You'll learn a great deal about someone under those circumstances.

Culture is simply the compendium of all the values you have. I believe that if integrity were a value at Penn State University, as they said it was, then integrity should have dictated that any and all investigations into Jerry Sandusky's alleged abuse of children occurred in a thorough way. It should have permeated the organization from top to bottom because integrity is doing the right thing when nobody is looking. The situation should have gone down differently, which is why the president of Penn State, no doubt a competent and good man, lost his job. What is not addressed and redressed becomes part of the culture. A brand or reputation may require decades to establish but can be lost in short order.

Purposeful Culture Building

I think a company's culture must be shaped intentionally. If you, as the CEO or coach, are not intentionally shaping your culture, then it will take on a life of its own, probably in a counterproductive way. I like to see coaches who have their vision and mission statements visible in the room in which athletes are training. They've got manuals on how they want to run their program. Everyone knows clearly the rules that go along with that culture. I know one coach who brings in a speaker every Friday during his team's breakfast to share an inspirational story with the team about business and life. Often it's a former athlete who played for him or a local businessperson.

If you have no values, you have a vacuum in your organization, and anything goes— you're in the Wild West.

Agreed. Your culture has to be formed purposefully, one value at a time. The values a company has are not as important as having them. If you have no values, you have a vacuum in your organization, and anything goes—you're in the Wild West. They're not just words; they're standards of behavior that provide the guidelines for how your company operates and how people will treat one another.

It can take time to build a culture and communicate it to all of your team members. In the sports world, when you're bringing in a new coach, it's customary to give him or her five years to succeed. If they don't succeed in five years, then they may be let go. It takes that long to get your first and second waves of recruits on board and trained and to get your program under way. By the third, fourth, or fifth year, you've created a new culture.

Assessing Your Culture

Today a variety of assessments are available to help business leaders assess and improve their corporate culture. For example, David Olson,[70] president of Walton Consulting Inc. in Allentown, Pennsylvania, has done a nice job of working with companies to measure and develop their corporate culture. Olson says a company's culture is ultimately defined by the behaviors of its team members. Beliefs affect attitudes, and attitudes affect behaviors. But a company's leaders have the ability to shape team members' beliefs.

Olson uses an opinion survey called The Culture Compass™ to measure team members' beliefs. The company keeps survey participants' answers anonymous and confidential. After the surveys are completed, the company analyzes the answers and

---

70. Walton Consulting Inc.'s website, "Biography of David W. Olson," accessed on November 30, 2013, http://www.waltonconsulting.com/index.php/the-walton-team/david-w-olson.

provides a comprehensive quantitative and qualitative report, an executive sum-mary, and recommendations for immediate and long-term implementation, based on the survey's findings.

A Higher Moral Purpose

In addition to culture, another key ingredient of successful firms is the high-er moral purpose. That is, your vision has to encompass something more than money. At North Star, our vision is "Changing Lives Forever." Tony Hsieh's is "Delivering Happiness." The vision of MaryKay Cosmetics is "Unlimited Op-portunities for Women." The vision at the Mayo Clinic is "The best interest of the patient is the only interest to be considered." The vision of Southwest Air-lines is to "democratize flying."

The vision of my company, Mind of the Athlete, is "Improving the Emotional Health of Athletes." Great companies have a vision that is dedicated to a greater good.

Southwest Airlines is a perfect example of that—they have democratized flying so that it's possible for poor people to fly as readily as rich people. Having such a noble purpose energizes Southwest's people and creates a higher moral purpose to running the airline. Southwest Airlines has made a profit for more than thirty years in a row, a feat that is remarkable in the airline business.

When you have a higher moral purpose, profits are important, but even more important than profits are the good you do and the legacy you will leave.

I've seen instances in which a company changes what type of products it sells or its mode of service, but the culture never changes; the values never change. That's because the higher moral purpose does not change. If shoes were not nec-essary tomorrow, it wouldn't matter what Zappos's product would be; delivering happiness would still be its higher purpose. The theme of successful companies, according to Collins's and Porras's book *Built to Last*, is "preserve the core, stimu-late progress."

Creating a Sanctuary

I believe it is important for leaders to create a sanctuary at work. A sanctuary is a place of refuge. In my opinion, the tougher the business, the more the leader has to create a sanctuary-like environment so that people who face rejection or other difficulties in their work feel nurtured. At companies like North Star, our advisors are being rejected 90 percent of the time—according to Al Granum's 10:3:1 ratio, ten client approaches will result in three meetings and one new client. Creating a nurturing environment is a stated goal at North Star.

During those times when we face hardship or when we are in an environment that is unpleasant, we can actually create a sanctuary in our minds. One thing you can do is visualize the most beautiful place in the world and imagine yourself being there. Whether or not you have actually visited that place is unimportant. As a kid, I dreamed of going to the Caribbean. I would read books about the Caribbean and look at pictures. As an adult, I was finally able to go there. So now, for me, Caneel Bay on St. John Island is the most beautiful place in the world that I can think of. When I need a mental break, I picture myself being on its pristine beaches or in the crystal-clear, warm, blue water.

Churches have always provided a place of refuge and retreat for me. I think that the inside of a Catholic church or cathedral is incredibly peaceful. When I lived in Chicago, there were two churches near my school in the city, and I would go inside them to just sit and pray. There's something mystical and peaceful about a sanctuary in the middle of a concrete jungle. I think it's important to have those quiet places. It's where I go to connect with God. Some people like to go to a mountaintop, a lake, a cabin, or a beach to connect with God. Identify the places that are a refuge for you, and go to them whenever you can—either physically or mentally.

Establishing a Pleasant Physical Environment

To create that sanctuary environment, it's important to ensure that the physical attributes of your work space are pleasant to all five senses. Whatever people see, feel, touch, smell, and hear in your office should make them feel comfortable. Ultimately, what we're talking about is the vibe in your office. People can feel the vibe. You might not be able to articulate it, but the vibe matters. The vibe is a combination of what people see, feel, touch, smell, and hear when they enter your space.

I have oversized chairs in my office that are made of soft, supple leather. They feel comfortable and soothing. My office is filled with natural light, which is superior to fluorescent overhead lighting. Bright, natural sunlight significantly improves our mood. To create a homey, soothing scent, I burn candles that smell like French vanilla or oatmeal cookies. I also play soft piano music with no lyrics to create a soothing ambiance. In my candy dishes are mints, lollipops, and chocolates. I want to make sure that all five of people's senses are attended to when they enter my office.

Managers at high-end hotels are masters at creating an optimal environment. They design their rooms with soothing colors and decorations, play soft music, and place a chocolate on your pillow when they turn your bed down at night. (Ritz Carltons truly do this best).

The music should be appropriate for the venue. There are different styles of music for different intensity levels of performance. At a football game, you want to have a different kind of music playing in the stadium than when you're going to go out for a fancy dinner. When I was working on my doctorate, I would study to relaxing music by performers like pianist Danny Wright. My roommate would study to heavy metal. We were both in the same program, but our brains operated differently, and that's OK. One size doesn't fit all. You need to find the type of music that stimulates your brain and makes it easiest for you to concentrate. Or perhaps silence is appropriate.

Whatever people see, feel, touch, smell, and hear in your office should make them feel comfortable.

Human beings are composed mostly of water, so we tend to gravitate to water. Many people like to vacation near an ocean, river, or lake. To work best, I chose an office with a water view—it has large windows that overlook a scenic confluence of two rivers. It is incredibly relaxing to look at water, especially moving water. It's peaceful. Many office buildings and malls feature decorative water fountains for that reason.

Most of us work in offices that have no fresh air, so it's important to have live plants in your work space. Plants give off oxygen and clean the air. I have a dozen plants in my office. If you have ever walked into a large greenhouse, you can just feel that oxygen in the air.

We spend a third of our lives in bed, and sleep is a top factor in optimal performance, so it's critical to have a well-made, comfortable mattress at home. Never skimp on your mattress! Put some time and energy into designing your bedroom. Make it comfortable, with nice linens and pillows. That is often an overlooked area.

Colors affect our mood to a great extent. Much research has been done to determine which colors are best for a certain type of business. For example, light blue walls in a hospital will create a soothing atmosphere for patients and family members. Many fast-food companies have red in their color scheme. Psychologists have found that the color red stimulates appetite (possibly a primitive-brain association with freshly killed meat), encourages strong emotions, and—important for fast-food places—encourages fast turnover of patrons.

Another critical aspect of an optimal work environment is the people around you. To the extent possible, surround yourself with people who have a positive attitude. Also, a support network is one of the biggest determinants of a person's success, so spend as much time as you can with people who support you in your endeavors. We discuss the importance of a support system in greater detail in Chapter 13.

Removing Distractions

Some of the most innovative workplaces in the world attract and retain top talent because they remove the distractions that deter people from focusing on their work. The best example I've ever seen of this is the Chick-fil-A headquarters in Atlanta.

A few years ago, I had the good fortune to spend some time with S. Truett Cathy, the company's founder, chairman, and CEO. He is one of the most remarkable men I've ever met. He is credited with introducing the chicken-sandwich concept to the quick-service industry. He opened his first restaurant in 1946 and founded Chick-fil-A, Inc., in the early 1960s, on biblical principles. Since then, Chick-fil-A has steadily grown to become the second largest quick-service chicken-restaurant chain in the United States, with more than 1,500 locations in thirty-nine states and Washington, DC. In 2010, annual sales exceeded $3.5 billion.

> Is your office a sanctuary? If not, transform it into an environment that nurtures success.

At the Chick-fil-A headquarters, the company provides free lunch for everybody who works there. (Incidentally, they refer to their people as "team members," too.) They have a gym with personal trainers and encourage their team members to work out or lift weights whenever they want to. They also provide a car-washing service, a laundry service, a nurse, and child care so that team members can take their young children to work and see them during the day. The company eliminates all the distractions that might occupy a team member's mind, thus creating an optimal environment for people to succeed. You don't have to worry about the things that most people worry about because they're taken care of for you right there. If you get a job there, you won't want to leave. Where else are you going to go that would be better than that? They create a positive vibe there. In fact, when you walk in the door, the first thing you see is a life-size statue of Jesus washing Peter's feet, which sends a message that the company is there to serve its team members. Service is part of their culture.

Another company that is pleasant to visit is ESPN. A few years ago, I visited ESPN's headquarters in Bristol, Connecticut, with my friend Larry Holmes, the former heavyweight boxing champion of the world. Everyone eats in the cafeteria with everyone else, whether you're a famous athlete, an intern, or the janitor. The vibe is democratic and inclusive.

Is your office a sanctuary? If not, transform it into an environment that nurtures success. Your team members will be happier and more productive. You will be, too.

It's Your Turn

Exercise 12-1: Creating a sanctuary-like environment

What changes can you make to your work environment to make it more like a sanctuary, a place of refuge?

1. _____
2. _____
3. _____
4. _____
5. _____
6. _____

Exercise 12-2: A higher moral purpose

What is your or your firm's higher moral purpose?

_____

_____

_____

_____

_____

_____

Chapter

13

Finding Support throughout Your Journey

Success depends on the support of other people. The only hurdle between you and what you want to be is in the support of other people.

David Joseph Schwartz
American Author and Motivation Expert

In *StrengthsFinder 2.0*, Tom Rath provides a strategy for finding your strengths. First, you complete an online assessment, after which you'll receive a comprehensive Strengths Discovery and Action-Planning Guide based on your results. The guide uses more than five thousand "Strengths Insights" to discover what makes you unique. They are designed to help you understand how each of your top five "themes" play out in your life. You also receive ten "Ideas for Action" for each of those top five themes, for a total of fifty specific actions you can take to help you align your job and goals with your natural talents.[71] It is a comprehensive and complicated process, but a worthwhile one. For those with time, it is worth experiencing.

We believe you can discover your strengths much more quickly by completing the exercise in Chapter 1 of this book. To reiterate: Just list twenty-one tasks or job functions that have been a part of your life and your work, and rank them in the order of the ones you like to do the most down to the ones you like to do the least. Then look for a job description that will make use of your strengths and passions—the items at the top of your list. If one doesn't exist, think about how you can create a job description or opportunity that will allow you to take advantage of those strengths.

---

71. Rath, v–vi.

Addressing students at the University of Nebraska, Warren Buffett, one of the world's wealthiest people, said, "If there is any difference between you and me, it may simply be that I get up every day and have a chance to do what I love to do. If you want to learn anything from me, this is the best advice I can give you."[72]

We have given you a formula to enumerate and prioritize what you love to do. It's a shortcut to finding your strengths so that you have an opportunity to end up like Warren Buffett, getting up every day and doing the things you love to do.

The Power of Positive Reinforcement

Chances are, you have probably done those activities at the top of your list in the past, and you have probably received praise and accolades for them. Parents, teachers, coaches, or other people have probably said, "Look how good you are at that. Look how well you do this." That positive reinforcement is likely a primary reason why those particular passions or strengths are at the top of your list. Likewise, activities that you have not been praised for, or those that people have said you are not good at, are probably at the bottom of your list.

Nobody gets to the top of the mountain alone.

Nobody gets to the top of the mountain alone. I don't know a single person who has ever discovered his or her unique talents and achieved self-actualization without significant support from others. Whether it's a spouse, family member, friend, teacher, coach, or mentor, someone is behind our success.

All of us have innate interests that God has predestined us to have, but if we don't have people around us to support us in that activity—or if we have people criticizing us—then that passion, skill set, and interest may go dormant. I once knew of a young man who was curious about how things worked and loved fixing things. But his father would always tell him, "You're no good at fixing anything. You're not mechanically inclined. You don't know how to do that." So the kid never fixed anything, never built anything, and never felt comfortable with tools. Later in life, he discovered that he loved working with tools. He was quite handy, and he could build amazing things. He managed to find and nurture his strength, despite growing up in an unsupportive environment. But imagine what he could have accomplished if his father had encouraged and praised him with this interest when he was young.

---

72. Marcus Buckingham and Donald O. Clifton, *Now, Discover Your Strengths* (New York: The Free Press, 2001), 19.

In the book Outliers, *Malcolm Gladwell explains that a disproportionate number of hockey players in the National Hockey League were born in the first quarter of the year—in fact, 40 percent of hockey players in elite groups, including the NHL, were born in January, February, or March. When they start playing hockey as kids, the players born in those months have an advantage over their peers because they are a few months older, they are more developed, and they receive more playing time and more encouragement from their coaches.[73]*

Having had two sons who played hockey all the way up through high school, I understand the game well. The best coaches want to work with the A squads, which are the elite traveling teams. Just making the A squad in itself gives players positive reinforcement. Traveling teams can play as many as 120 games in a year, whereas the B or C squads play perhaps 40 games. So the players on the A squad are accumulating their ten thousand hours in the sport. They get more practice time and play time, better coaching, and positive reinforcement, all of which help them become even better players.

When I was in graduate school, I learned about a study that had been conducted among third-graders by a teacher, Ms. Jane Elliott, in Iowa beginning in 1968, the day after Martin Luther King, Jr., was murdered. She gave her third-grade students a first-hand experience in the meaning of discrimination.[74] In 1970, William Peters made a documentary titled Eye of the Storm *for ABC News; it was later included in the documentary* A Class Divided *(1985), which featured a class reunion among the same students in 1984.*

One day, the teacher told the third-grade class that blue-eyed students were better and smarter than brown-eyed kids and allowed them extra privileges. As a result, two boys got into a fight during recess. The next day, the teacher told the students she had lied and that brown-eyed students were actually better and smarter than blue-eyed students. Finally, she explained that no one is better than anyone else based on their eye color or skin color.[75] It was a cruel thing to do to kids, but the experiment proved that positive reinforcement brings positive results and negative reinforcement brings negative results.

Dick McCloskey, another inductee into the GAMA Hall of Fame, shared a story about a water-polo coach in California who coached both of Dick's sons. Dick's son's team had won every high-school water-polo championship throughout

73. Gladwell, 23.

74. PBS website, "A Class Divided," accessed on November 30, 2013, http://www.pbs.org/wgbh /pages/frontline/shows/divided/etc/view.html.

75. The YouTube video was available in 2012 at http://www.youtube.com/watch?v=8bWITZZN3DY but was later removed because of a copyright-infringement claim by WGBH Educational Foundation.

their high-school career. Dick studied the coach's style. He noticed that it didn't matter what one of the water-polo team members did in the water. When the kid came out of the water, the coach would put his arm around the boy and give him positive reinforcement, even if he had screwed up badly. He would give his team members only positive feedback. He never got mad at any of them, never criticized any of them, never told any of them what they did wrong—at least not in public. His team was undefeated, probably in great part because of that strategy. Praise in public, criticize in private.

When a parent or coach says to a child, "Hey, I really liked the way you handled that situation over there; that was fantastic," it's more likely that the kid is going to handle a situation like that again. But a lot of times in life, unfortunately, people instead point out one another's faults. I believe that approach isn't nearly as effective as pointing out the positive aspects of someone's performance. Of course you have to offer some constructive criticism at times so that people can improve. But there's a time and place for that. I believe it is most effective when done in private, as part of a teaching moment.

Asian families are known to be extremely supportive and encouraging of their children. In *Delivering Happiness*, the Zappos story, Tony Hsieh says that when Asian parents get together, they don't talk about who has a Bentley and who has a Rolls Royce. They talk about the academic achievements of their children. That's what gives them bragging rights and stature.

"The kids would watch TV while the adults were in a separate room socializing and bragging to each other about their kids' accomplishments," he says. "That was just part of the Asian culture: The accomplishments of the children were the trophies that many parents defined their own success and status by. We were the ultimate scorecard." He goes on to say that there were three categories of accomplishments that mattered to Asian parents: academic accomplishments, career accomplishments, and musical-instrument mastery. "My parents, just like the other Asian parents, were pretty strict in raising me so that we could win in all three categories."[76]

Sources of Support

The first and most obvious source of support is from our heavenly Father. Throughout the Bible are verses that remind us to lean on Him when we need encouragement. For example, James 5:13 says, "Is anyone among you suffering? Let him pray."

---

76. Hsieh, 8.

Your parents, grandparents, siblings, and other family members can be a huge source of support because they have known you for your entire life and typically want only the best for you. They want to see you succeed. Unfortunately, there are instances in which people derive little or no support from their family members. Those people must seek support outside the home.

It's important to choose a life partner who complements you and enables you to focus on doing the things you love.

Another powerful source of support is your spouse. It's important to choose a life partner who complements you and enables you to focus on doing the things you love.

You also need to identify people in the workplace who believe in you. If you're not happy in your job, but somebody else in your company or in another company believes you have talent, go work for them instead. Put yourself in an environment in which somebody really believes in you and your skills. It gives us a powerful boost to be around someone who says, "I see something special in you, and I believe in you."

Other sources of support include online communities, professional associations, religious organizations, community programs, and personal coaches.

With the right support, the sky is not the limit in terms of your potential success.

Ask for Support, and You'll Probably Get It

The number one factor in longevity of an athlete's career is support. Not only do athletes need encouragement; they also need people to invest time and resources in them. They need someone to travel with them, buy them equipment and uniforms, and pay for their meals on the road. In the business world, people need encouragement, as well as business advice or an investment in their start-up companies. The first step in garnering support is to define what that support looks like. It comes in a lot of different forms. What do you need?

My brother-in-law, Mike Irons, once told me, "The answer is always no unless you ask." He is absolutely right. Go ask people for their support. Ask them for what you need from them. You might be surprised to find that people will readily say, "Of course I can give you that ride. Of course I can mentor you. Of course I can sponsor you." If you don't have the support you need in your life, whom have you asked?

Three frogs are sitting on a lily pad. One decides to jump off. How many are left? Three. *Deciding* to do something doesn't change anything. You have to act. You have to put your decision in motion. Many times, in anticipation of receiving a "no," we don't ask when, in fact, the answer would have been "yes." If you've thought about asking someone for help but haven't put that thought into action, it's not going to help you.

> ## Let the mentor see that you have a bigger plan in mind—to pass his or her knowledge on to others, not just to better yourself.

Whom we ask matters, too. We're going to garner more support from people who are passionate about the activity we're engaged in if, at some point in their lives, they've had a deeply emotional experience around it, either positive or negative. For example, cancer has affected many people in our society. As a result, if you're participating in a Relay for Life or other event that raises money for cancer research, you'll probably find a lot of people to support you in that fund-raising effort because they've had a personal experience related to the cause.

In Chapter 8, we discussed the value of mentoring. I think successful athletes or businesspeople will be more inclined to mentor you if they believe there will be a ripple effect associated with the mentorship they provide. I recommend saying something like, "I'm really interested in helping other people grow professionally, and I can do that more effectively if I can learn from the very best. Will you mentor me?" Let the mentor see that you have a bigger plan in mind—to pass his or her knowledge on to others, not just to better yourself.

Jesus's apostles carried His message of salvation to the world. The time He spent with them had an extraordinary ripple effect that has continued for two thousand years.

Why We Don't Ask for Support

Asking for support certainly sounds easy. But few people do so. Why is that? Pride is a primary reason. Pride can be a big weakness, and we have to be careful with that. Proverbs 16:18 says, "Pride goes before destruction, and a haughty spirit before stumbling."

Lack of humility is a huge stumbling block. The people who tend to garner the most support are those who are humble. Consider Tim Tebow, the Heisman Trophy-winning

NFL quarterback—he is extremely successful, and he has a huge support network and fan base. Why? He is the first guy to compliment everybody else, and he doesn't praise himself. He is a great leader. In his "Bleacher Report" blog, sportswriter Dilan Ames wrote: "Stats don't win games; Tebow wins games. Stats are only important to a certain extent; players should be measured by their impact on the team rather than their individual numbers. Granted, 'impact' often translates to touchdowns or interceptions, but the impact Tebow has is different than most."[77]

Tim Tebow has the two elements that Jim Collins says are innate among the Level 5, or top CEOs, he studied: personal humility and professional will.[78] Unfortunately, he has a lot of detractors who detest the fact that he genuflects and prays when something good happens to him on the football field. I read recently that pride is the reason many people in the intelligentsia and the press have such a difficult time accepting Tebow's public profession of faith. To admit the existence of an Almighty Being would require that they cede control and execute the will of that Almighty Being. Their pride causes them to have difficulty with this outcome.

Does Support from Others Dwindle as We Age?

Does it ever seem to you that as we age, we tend to become closer to our children and grandchildren and rely less on friends and acquaintances? It's not a withdrawal—we're not withdrawing from those outside our families—rather, it's a refocusing of attention to that critical support group, our family. This enables us to continue to increase the support we are able to give to our loved ones. And the closer the support group, the more attention we give them. This is partly because our friends die off as we get older and partly because our familial relationships simply become even more important to us.

I personally believe that as we begin to lose friends and family members, the more acceptable the concept of death becomes because there's a little less to live for. I believe it's God's way of preparing us for death. If you're thirty years old and are about to die, leaving behind young children, close friends, and all the people you went to college and high school with, it's more distressing than to die at the age of eighty, when many of the people you love have already passed on and are waiting for you above. It's been said that everyone wants to go to heaven—just

---

77. Dilan Ames, Bleacher Report blog, "Tearing Down Tebowmania: Why Do People Hate Tim Tebow?" last modified May 10, 3013, accessed November 30, 2013, http://bleacherreport.com/articles/1635274-tearing-down-tebowmania-why-do-people-hate-tim-tebow.

78. Collins, 13.

not today. Knowing that your loved ones are waiting for you alleviates the fear associated with dying.

Sometimes we need support from others because we feel that they can replace elements of our personalities that we've lost during traumatic experiences. In The Divine Matrix, *Gregg Braden explains that when we enter survival mode to endure such experiences, we compromise huge parts of who we are, and that leaves an emptiness that is waiting to be filled.*

"When we find someone who has the very things that we've given away, it feels good to be near him or her," Braden writes. "When we find our 'missing' pieces in others, we'll be powerfully and irresistibly drawn to them. We may even believe that we 'need' them in our lives, until we remember that what we're so attracted to in them is something that we still have within us…it's simply sleeping." He goes on to say that once we realize that we still possess those characteristics and traits, we begin to reincorporate them into our lives and are no longer drawn to the person who mirrored those traits for us.[79]

Seeking help from others is a healthy strategy unless we find that we are leaning on them for an inordinate amount of support. If that happens, we need to pull back and look within ourselves and to God for strength and wisdom.

Providing Support to Others

Throughout our careers and lives, as we seek support from other people, the right thing to do is to pay it forward and help people we come into contact with. At its deepest level, support is really love. When we support one another, we are essentially loving them.

In the Bible, 2 Corinthians 1:4 says, "[God] comforts us in all our troubles so that we can comfort those in any trouble with the comfort we ourselves have received from God."

Athletes are masters at supporting one another—they constantly pat one another and exchange high fives to offer encouragement to their teammates and celebrate victories both large and small.

---

79. Gregg Braden, *The Divine Matrix: Bridging Time, Space, Miracles, and Belief* (New York: Hay House, 2007), 181.

We all can offer support to other people in myriad ways, and most support costs nothing. Here are some ways we can offer support to those around us:

- Acknowledge what's important to them.
- Show interest in their activities.
- Provide verbal praise that singles out specific contributions they're making.
- Send them a handwritten note of encouragement or appreciation.
- Provide written praise about them to their supervisor at work.
- Offer to help them on a project at home or work.
- Listen when they need to vent.
- Spend time mentoring them.
- Remind them of their strengths and talents.
- And remember, compliments are verbal sunshine.

It does not take much to encourage someone. Offering any amount of support to another person can have a huge impact!

It's Your Turn

Exercise 13-1: Asking for support

Chances are, if you ask someone for support, they will provide it. If they do not, then you did no harm by asking. If you don't ask for support, though, you can almost guarantee that you won't get it. What kind of support can you ask for, and whom should you ask? Once you write this information down, go ask them and see what happens.

What Type of Support I Need:	Whom I Will Ask:
1. _____	1. _____
2. _____	2. _____
3. _____	3. _____

Chapter

14

Dream Really Big

*If one advances confidently in the direction of his dreams,
and endeavors to live the life which he had imagined, he will
meet with a success unexpected in common hours.*

Henry David Thoreau
American Author, Poet, and Philosopher

Socrates said, "Man is a goal-seeking animal." The opposite of having goals is aimlessness. It's lethargy. And lethargy isn't a great legacy. Our civilization and everything we have today are the result of somebody having a dream and fulfilling that dream by setting a goal and achieving it. Yes, we're drinking water from wells dug by those who have gone before.

People who dream big and say that nothing is impossible are the ones who have made the biggest contributions to society. The companies that stand the test of time and prosper, some of the largest of the Fortune 100 companies, have had founders who simply had no fences around their thought process or how big things could become. (Tom Watson at IBM is one of them.) The people who have always impressed me are those who conceptualize their business as it will look in five or ten years, and then behave exactly according to their dream to create that outcome. Behaving like the CEO of a $10 million-a-year firm when one starts out seems to elevate one's attitude, persona, and will.

Dreams become a self-fulfilling prophecy, to a certain degree. We see a dream in our mind's eye before it exists, then we work to make the dream come to fruition. This is the reason I am often impressed with artists. An artist can see something in his mind's eye and then create it. It's the same concept with a business, but the process takes years instead of weeks or months.

Set Goals to Achieve Your Dream

As mentioned earlier, in the insurance and financial services business, goals rule the day, and they have to be accompanied by accountability and consequences.

We have also found that people who communicate their dreams and goals to others are far more likely to reach them than those who keep the dreams and goals to themselves. Doing so builds accountability and consequences into the goal-setting process. As the Olympic gold medalist Bob Richards said, "Goals will pull you through."

> I always suggest that people write a letter to themselves about their vision and dreams—where they want to go and what they want to do.

At the end of each year, many of the advisors at North Star write down their goals for the next year, seal them in an envelope, and give the envelope to someone they really respect. A year later, that mentor opens the envelope and compares it with the goal setter's actual progress. It's important to share your goal with someone you respect, such as a parent, coach, or mentor, because it will be uncomfortable for you if you don't hit the goal, and that discomfort is likely to motivate you to do better. If you share it with a stranger, there are no consequences because he probably doesn't care if you reach your goal or not. I think the critical elements of goal setting are as follows:

1. You must write the goal down.

2. You must understand the "why" of that goal—its importance to you, its worthiness.

3. You must engage someone whom you respect to hold you accountable for reaching the goal.

4. You must follow through!

It's gratifying when people in the organization come and ask if I'll hold their envelope for them until the end of the year. They're timid about doing it, but of course I'm overjoyed to do it because the one thing I know is that they will hit that goal! Having the courage to bring the CEO that envelope demonstrates their solid commitment to their goal, and that's impressive. Bet on those people; they won't let you down.

I recommend a similar exercise involving written goals. I always suggest that people write a letter to themselves about their vision and dreams—where they want to go and what they want to do. This is a practical exercise that I recommend in a lot of my speeches. Tony D'Angelo, a phenomenal speaker who leads a company called Collegiate EmPowerment, taught me this technique, and I have found it to be highly effective in helping people clarify and reach their goals.

Write an inspirational letter to yourself about what you plan to do in the next year or two and what your vision is for your life. Seal that letter in an envelope and address it to yourself. Sign your name across the back so you'll know that nobody has ever opened it. Then give your letter to someone you respect, such as your coach or athletic director. At an appropriate time—maybe three, six, or nine months later—that person will mail the letter to you. Then one day, long after you've probably forgotten about it, you'll get a letter in your mailbox, and you will recognize your own handwriting. You'll open up the letter, and there will be your goals and vision. Then you can assess how you are doing in your quest to achieve that goal by the end of the year. If you're well on your way, it's encouraging to know you're doing what you said you would do. If you're not making the kind of progress you had hoped, it will, hopefully, motivate you to renew your commitment to your goal and vision. I've mailed a lot of self-written letters to athletes to help them achieve their goals.

In the August before my senior year, I had to write a caption for my high-school yearbook that indicated what I wanted to do with my life. I wrote: "Become a doctor." I was seventeen years old at the time and reluctant to put such a big dream out there in public. If I didn't achieve it, I would be embarrassed. But if I did announce that goal in public, I would be even more likely to achieve it. And, ten years later, I did.

Segment Your Goals into Tiers

I believe there are three levels of goals we can set:

1. **Big, Hairy, Audacious Goals (BHAGs).** This type of goal, described in the Collins and Porras book *Built to Last*, is the goal that is so high that it's almost unrealistic. You're shooting for the heavens. It's been said, "Shoot for the sky, you'll hit the fence; shoot for the fence, you'll hit the ground."

2. **Realistic goals.** This is the type of goal you can realistically achieve.

3. **The level below which I will not fall.** This is the absolute minimum performance you will allow from yourself. In my case, in wrestling, I once sparred with a guy named Davey Adams when attending Charlie Speidell's wrestling clinic as a sophomore in high school. Davey pinned me. After that, I vowed to never be pinned again, whether on the practice mat or in a

match. And I got through my career without ever being pinned again, even in practice. That was the level below which I would not fall. That lesson is not ignored when coaching others.

To apply these tiers, let's say an advisor at North Star is shooting for a goal of earning $1 million in new revenue this year (a BHAG goal), but $500,000 might be her realistic goal, and $250,000 might be the level below which she will not fall.

I agree that we should think in tiers when dreaming big. While working with high-school athletes who are applying to college, I advise them to apply to seven schools they would like to attend. Two of those schools should be absolute reaches. It's unlikely they would get into those schools, but there is a slight chance, so go ahead and put Harvard on the list if that's one of them. Three of the choices should be schools to which the student is pretty likely to get accepted, but it's not certain. The last two should be schools that are certain to accept the student. That provides the student with a comfort zone as well as an opportunity to shoot for the stars.

Visualize Something That Doesn't Exist Yet

Recently, I was a speaker at the same Allianz meeting as Aron Ralston, the author of the book *127 Hours*.[80] (A movie based on the book was released in 2010.) Ralston was hiking in Utah when an eight-hundred-pound boulder tumbled loose, pinning his right hand and wrist against a canyon wall. For six days, with little water, food, or warm clothing, Ralston tried to free his hand from the boulder.

Finally, as he contemplated giving up and letting himself die, he had somewhat of an out-of-body experience in which he saw himself walking down the canyon. He came to a door, and inside it was a little blond boy playing. He recognized the boy as his future son. He was single at the time and did not have a girlfriend. Realizing that he had a wonderful wife and son in his future gave him renewed resolve to get out of his situation alive. He set his goal to survive, and he did so. It's an amazing story of survival, and it illustrates the power of a goal. Before he envisioned his future son, he did not have the compelling goal of surviving. If you have read his book, you know that the incredible story ended when Ralston used his pocket knife to cut off his own arm, freeing him to live on, and to love.

---

80. Aron Ralston, *127 Hours: Between a Rock and a Hard Place* (New York: Simon & Schuster, Inc., 2004), 274.

Ask "Why Not Me?"

One way to dream big and achieve that dream is to adopt the attitude of "Why not me?" Someone could convince you that someone else will get the job you applied for, or someone else will win the competition you entered or the game you're playing. Instead of listening to them, instead ask, "Why not me?" Someone has to get that job. Someone has to win that contest or game. A positive attitude like that helps ordinary people do extraordinary things.

The Bible contains many stories of God using ordinary people to do something extraordinary. He selected people who were clearly flawed in some way, like Moses, who was not very good at speaking, yet God selected him to be the leader of a great many people. And he chose Mary, a young unmarried woman, to give birth to Jesus.

One way to dream big and achieve that dream is to adopt the attitude of "Why not me?"

Mother Teresa, who made a tremendous impact on the lives of poor, sick, dying, and orphaned people of India and other countries, said, "We can't do great things. We can only do small things with great love." One of my mantras for myself has been to do small things with great love.

Along this same line of thought, motivational speaker Mark Sanborn wrote a fantastic book called The Fred Factor.[81] *It's the story of a postman named Fred who did small things, but he was exceptional because he did them with great love. We all can do that. You could be checking out in the grocery aisle, and if the person in front of you is a little short on cash and you hand him some bills to make up the difference, you have made that person's day and maybe even changed his outlook on life. You have done an ordinary thing with great love.*

Waiting in line in a Scottsdale pharmacy with my friend Lewis Katz, we overheard the woman in front of us tell the pharmacist, "Three hundred dollars? I don't have three hundred dollars." Lewis opened his wallet and threw that amount on the counter, saying, "Well, I have three hundred dollars. Give the lady her drugs." Jaws dropped in the store, not the least of which belonged to the pharmacist. An act of love, you bet—it's one I'll not soon forget. Lewis's driving

---

81. Mark Sanborn, *The Fred Factor: How Passion in Your Work and Life Can Turn the Ordinary into the Extraordinary* (New York: Doubleday, 2004), Kindle edition.

goal is to alleviate pain in this world; that's what drove his generous outburst. His love for the less fortunate is an inspiration to all around him.

Don't Wait for Someone Else

Sometimes we don't realize we can accomplish something until someone else paves the way and accomplishes it first.

> Set your sights high, and don't listen
> to naysayers who claim something
> cannot be done.

For example, even the most informed observers believed it was impossible for a human to run a mile in four minutes or less. English runner Roger Bannister set the sub-four-minute mile as his goal, and at a meet in 1954, he ran the mile in 3 minutes, 59.4 seconds. According to organized sporting authorities, he is the first man to run a sub-four-minute mile. Two months later, his record was beaten, and others continued to run sub-four-minute miles after that. In the past fifty years, the mile record has been bettered by almost 17 seconds. The record for the fastest men's mile is held by Hicham El Guerrouj of Morocco, who set the world mark at that distance with 3 minutes, 43.13 seconds in Rome in 1999. No woman has yet run a sub-four-minute mile, but stay tuned.

Similarly, in the 1800s, some believed that a man would die if he ran faster than 18 miles per hour. Today men have been clocked running at 27 mph. These arbitrary limitations that we place on ourselves or that others place on us are just waiting for somebody to conquer them. So don't limit your dreams to what has already been accomplished. Set your sights high, and don't listen to naysayers who claim something cannot be done. "Don't impose your puny human limits on creation." The sky is not the limit.

Look at Cael Sanderson, the wrestling coach at Penn State University. How did he go through four years of wrestling at Iowa State University, never lose once, win 159 times, and take four consecutive NCAA Division I titles? Only twelve opponents came within ten points of his total score! Before winning an Olympic Gold Medal, he became the only wrestler in NCAA Division I history to be undefeated, with more than one hundred wins in official matches. It's incredible. It defies logic. It would be interesting to know whether or not he set specific goals to achieve those accomplishments, or if they just happened to him. Because he has since coached three straight NCAA Division Wrestling Championships at Penn State, my guess would be that he set specific goals.

Make Big Dreams Manageable

When you dream big, the question is, how do you get there? I always suggest that people focus on the small technical aspects of the activity they're involved in. Try to do your best one moment at a time, one game at a time, one competition at a time. The only way to make the big dreams come true is to roll up your sleeves, get to work, and focus on all of the technical aspects that you can control.

As mentioned earlier, in our industry, we make big dreams manageable through quarterly goals. The CEOs of all publicly traded companies get visited quarterly by the rating agencies and the Wall Street analysts, and they must give an accounting of what has happened in the past ninety days, along with much other information. The price of their company stock is at stake, and the ratings the agencies give their companies affect their borrowing costs.

We do the same with our advisors. We have them set annual goals and then break those into quarterly periods. The best advisors then break the quarterly periods into weekly and even daily time frames. They will ask themselves, "Did I win or lose today?" There are certain quantifiable tasks that we all have to do to measure whether or not each day is a victory or a defeat. If you can measure it, you can manage it! One of our top advisors, Jeff Jarnes, has used intricate bar graphs to propel himself and his productivity to record-smashing results throughout the years.

In *The E-Myth Revisited*, Michael Gerber says that building a prototype of your business requires innovation, quantification, and orchestration. First you have to come up with new ideas. Then you have to quantify your efforts so that you will know whether or not you're winning or losing. Finally, you have to orchestrate whatever it is you want to happen.[82]

So if your goal is to create a $10 million-a-year company, you've got to break that down. If you create $2.5 million in revenue the first year, it will take you four years. You'll reach $5 million the second year, $7.5 million the third year, and $10 million the fourth year, assuming your growth rate is lineal and you achieve the same $2.5 million per year.

---

82. Gerber, 118.

If you don't achieve one of your interim goals, such as your quarterly goal, then you have to make a choice—you have to either decrease your goal or increase your activity. If you keep doing the same level of activity you've been doing, you will keep getting the same results you've been getting. If you're willing to accept those results, then you can lower the goal. If you're not willing to accept those results, then you have to take that activity, measure what it would have taken to hit the quarterly goal, and increase the next quarterly goal not only by that amount, but enough to catch up on what you didn't do in the first quarter. If you are religious about complying with your own formulas, at the end of four years, you're going to have a $10 million-a-year company.

At North Star, our goal for 2011 was to move from being a $40 million-a-year company to a $50 million company. We broke that down into interim goals. We also launched an initiative called READ—Revenue Enhancement and Diversification. We ventured into other areas we hadn't been in before and redoubled our effort in other ventures. Then we put our best people in charge of those areas. At every weekly meeting of our Servant Leadership Steering Committee, the person responsible for each goal gave a report on where they were in terms of the total goal, where they were year-to-date, and whether they were ahead or behind schedule in terms of achieving that goal. In 2012, North Star became a $50 million-a-year company.

You can break your goals down into manageable chunks in any endeavor, including sports. You must be able to quantify progress. Once you do so, you can measure your performance against a set of standards, and you will know whether you're winning or losing long before the end of your specified time period.

The game a team plays on Saturday is really nothing but a computer, an adding machine that adds up all that happened before the game. Wins occur because of the quality of the strategizing and practicing a team engages in before the game on Saturday.

In business, at the end of the year, if the CEO didn't achieve what the expected output was supposed to be, the company begins looking for a new CEO. If you are a stockholder in that firm, you deserve nothing less.

Back in 1969, when I assumed the leadership of North Star, I wanted North Star to be the number one office in the country for our largest manufacturer, Securian. At that time, eighty or ninety different organizations were competing for that honor. It took me until 1988 to achieve that goal. In 2013, we won for the twenty-third year in a row. Now, not only have we bested everybody for twenty-three consecutive years, but being number one for twenty-three years is a new record; no one has ever led that manufacturer for that amount of time. Dream big; it all begins with a big dream.

Choose Goals That Are Congruent with Your Talents

In Chapter 1, we asked you to write down twenty-one activities that are associated with your vocation and personal life and to rank them in terms of the ones you enjoy the most down to the ones you enjoy the least. It is highly likely that those activities at the top of your list—the ones you enjoy the most—are activities you excel in. But that may not always be the case. For that reason, it is important for you to consider more than one of the activities as your life's calling. If one turns out to be incongruent with your talents, consider pursuing the next activity on the list.

> Be flexible, and keep an open mind.
> Anything can happen!

Remember the three components of a BHAG that Jim Collins said must be present for a goal to be achievable: You have to be passionate about it, it has to be something someone will pay you to do, and it has to be something you can be the best in the world at. If none of those components exist, you need to rethink your goal.

For example, as I noted earlier, I am extremely passionate about sailing, and I think that if I really applied myself, I could be the best sailor in the world. But no one's going to pay me for it! So sailing as a vocation would not be a wise choice for me.

Sometimes we discover talents and passions we didn't realize existed. I believe that God has a way of converging events and situations in our lives to create unique opportunities we never would have imagined. Many people will say, later in life, "Now I can see how it all came together, but I didn't see what was happening at the time."

Be passionate about many things. Be flexible, and keep an open mind. Anything can happen! The late North Carolina State University coach Jim Valvano told his players before the NCAA championship game with Houston to "stay in the game." Houston was a heavy favorite over North Carolina State that year, and the latter was not given much of a chance by the odds-makers, so

Valvano realistically admonished his players to just "stay in the game so that if a miracle happens, it will help." What he meant was that if you were behind by fifty points and a miracle occurred, it would not help. Well, that day, a miracle did happen, and North Carolina won the national championship 54–52 with a basket by Lorenzo Charles at the buzzer.

Make It a Team Effort

When we think of dreaming big, we often think of it as a solitary effort. I suggest finding another person with whom you can do what I call "vision casting," or envisioning significant achievements. We could all benefit from having someone in our lives with whom we can dream big and say things like, "I know this sounds absurd, but I believe that in five years, my company will double in size." Or "Let's just imagine what it would be like if this idea really took off." This person to vision-cast with could be a spouse, a friend, a business partner, or a mentor.

I suggest finding another person with whom you can do what I call "vision casting," or envisioning significant achievements.

Earlier I mentioned Tony D'Angelo. Periodically, Tony and I go for a walk along the Delaware River in Easton, Pennsylvania. We'll vision-cast and talk about what's coming up in the next year. We will ask each other, "What would you like to see happen in the next year or two?" It's nice to have a person to discuss dreams with. I think it's important to get those dreams out of our heads and share them with someone else. That's what makes it so impressive when the dream actually comes true, and somebody comes back later and says, "I remember when you and I talked about that!"

I always wanted a beautiful old stone farmhouse when I was a kid, but I lived in Phillipsburg, New Jersey, where there were no stone farmhouses. When I was in high school, I told myself—and other people—"I'm going to own a beautiful old stone farmhouse in Bucks County, Pennsylvania, someday." Then one day, as a house-hunting adult, I drove through Northampton County, about ten miles away from Bucks County, and saw a beautiful old stone farmhouse. Something about the vibe, the look, the feel of it resonated with my soul, and I said, "This is where I'm meant to live." In 2002, my wife, Abby, and I bought that stone farmhouse and moved into it. We have been lovingly restoring it and will likely live there forever. Several people have said to me, "I remember when you used to talk about that in high school."

Enjoy the Journey

I want North Star to be the largest financial planning firm in the world, as ranked by GAMA International. We've been in the top three for five years in a row, and we've been as high as number two and as low as number three, but we've never been number one. Every year, that's our goal. We are an independent firm, owned by no other company, so we are the largest *independently owned* financial planning firm in the world, but that's not good enough. When you accomplish a goal, you should be reaching for the next one. Maximizing the talents we've been blessed with is the expectation we should strive for.

I have highly worthy "opponents." They are amazing recruiters and marketers. Sometimes I think it's more fun to fight for the victory than to achieve the victory. In fact, after some victories, there's a huge letdown. When that happens, you have to go back and give thanks for the fun journey you've experienced in the years leading up to the achievement of that goal. In my case, the two organizations that are larger than North Star are led by two good friends and fellow study-group members, Dave Porter and Paul Blanco, both of them formidable competitors. Each of them could have written most of what I have included in this work.

As the old adage says, "Life is a journey, not a destination." If you're going to dream big, you need to enjoy the journey you'll take getting there. For example, many people want to become the president of the United States of America. I think that's a great dream, and it's a big dream. But between here and there, you really ought to like politics and being a mayor or a congressman. You'll really need to enjoy the political process because you're not going to enjoy life so much if you're happy only when you get to that goal. The happiness comes from the journey, not the destination.

When going to Temple University, I had two goals. The first was to be president of the student body because I had served in that position in high school. I achieved that goal. My second goal was to be president of the United States. Obviously, I did not make it. The more I thought about what the president of the United States goes through to get to be the president—eating the rubber-chicken dinners, smiling when you don't feel like it, and spending a lot of time away from your family—it quickly lost its appeal. As I matured, I also realized that the accuracy in politics tends to be soft. It's not the kind of truth most of us believe in. Most politicians, in my opinion, who always tell the truth will be politicians for a short period of time. With Congress currently enjoying a 9 percent approval rating from Americans, the sacrifices are not appreciated. Abe Lincoln and Harry Truman, I believe, were both truthful and heroic and were exceptions to the rule.

History has rightfully been kind to them. For anyone with clear values, a life of service as a public servant is challenging.

Take It One Step at a Time

Rome, one of the greatest empires in the history of the world, was built one brick at a time. If you ask anyone who has ever had a big dream come true, they will tell you that they did it by putting one foot in front of the other. There is no magic potion to achieving your dreams. The old Chinese proverb says, "A journey of a thousand miles begins with a single step."

There is no magic potion to achieving your dreams.

Did you hear about the goal setter who was told to slow down because Rome wasn't built in one day? His response was, "Yeah, but I wasn't on that job." That's the attitude we need. That guy is a big thinker with a great attitude!

The other story I like is about the guy who applied for a job as a woodcutter in Alaska. No jobs were available. The foreman said, "We have enough people."

The woodcutter replied, "But if you knew my credentials, you would hire me."

"Well, why don't you tell me something about yourself?"

"OK. Have you ever heard of the Sahara Forest?"

The foreman said, "You mean the Sahara *Desert?*"

"Well," the woodcutter said, "That's what they call it *now!*"

The big thinkers are also the people who don't often lose. In Chapter 10, "Overcoming Obstacles," we listed many people who achieved big dreams against all odds. They are the real visionaries and dream makers who were determined to win. They sought to achieve BHAGs—unrealistic goals—and succeeded.

A strategy that is similar to writing your goals down is to use creative visualization. A great creative visualization exercise is to create a collage of the visual manifestation of your goals. You can use photos you've taken and images you've cut out of magazines. The images might include a new home, a successful business owner, and a happy couple. Then arrange the images in a pleasing layout—or you can create the collage electronically. Then focus on the images and imagine yourself in them.

In high school, I had a goal of playing football for Boston College. So I did a creative daily visualization exercise—I taped a picture of the Boston College stadium above my bed on the ceiling of my bedroom. Every day, I asked myself upon waking and seeing it, "What can I do to get closer to that stadium and go play there?" The summer before my senior year in high school in Phillipsburg, New Jersey, I was at Boston College's football camp, and the BC head coach, Tom Coughlin, yelled to me during the camp, "Hey, P-burg! Come on over here."

So I went over to talk to the coach. He said to me, "How would you like to come play for me next year at Boston College?"

I couldn't believe it! I replied, "Coach, that has been my dream."

"Great. Well, listen, I was watching you out there playing, and I'd love to have you come be a part of my team."

It was an honor to be recruited to BC and get accepted academically. But life took me in a different direction, and I ended up going to Lafayette College and playing football there. While I did not play at BC, the daily visualization was a huge success.

Trust God to Help You Succeed

We both believe that the number one source for the inspiration, talent, and resources we all need to achieve our goals comes from God. He will allow you to soar even higher than you imagined if you remain open to His guidance.

One day, while driving home from a meeting with my friend, Brad Weiss, a grand vision for the company titled Mind of the Athlete entered my mind. The company would allow me to help athletes improve their emotional health and physical performance. It would be a revolutionary sports psychology company. God gave me this vision, and not only did He give me the idea for the company—He also gave me a vision for how the company would grow after one year, two years, five years, and ten years. I told my wife, "I can't get this out of my head. I'm all fired up about it. It's bigger and better than I ever possibly imagined." That was in the genesis phase of the company I now operate.

So dream big. Put it on your ceiling. Put it in your yearbook. Tell a friend about an old stone farmhouse. Put it out there. Keep doing more of the same. Share your goals with your spouse, friends, and colleagues.

It's Your Turn

Exercise 14-1: Setting personal goals

When you write down your goals and share them with others, you will be more likely to achieve them. What short- and long-term goals would you like to achieve?

1. _____
2. _____
3. _____
4. _____

Exercise 14-2: Vision casting

When we think of dreaming big, we often think of it as a solitary effort, unless the dream involves a sports team. If your goal does not involve a sports team, find another person with whom you can do "vision casting," or envisioning significant achievements. We could all benefit from having someone in our lives with whom we can dream big and say things like, "Let's imagine what it would be like if we had a million dollars. Let's just imagine what it would be like if this idea really took off." It could be a spouse, a friend, a business partner, or a mentor. With whom can you vision-cast?

1. _____
2. _____
3. _____
4. _____
5. _____

Chapter

15

Communication: Ensuring Mutual Understanding

The single biggest problem in communication is the illusion that it has taken place.

George Bernard Shaw
Irish Playwright

The word "communication" comes from the Latin word *communis*, which means "shared, or held in common." According to John C. Maxwell, the author of *Everyone Communicates, Few Connect*, we are bombarded with 35,000 messages a day, and most people speak about 16,000 words a day.[83] But communication is not simply speaking or sending and receiving messages. It is creating a shared meaning and ensuring mutual understanding.

That means all parties involved in the communication need to understand what is being said and what is expected of them as a result of the communication. Too often, our communication with others is ineffective, and we or the other parties are left wondering what needs to be done next—and trying to read between the lines. Author and management consultant Peter Drucker said, "The most important thing in communication is to hear what isn't being said."

Effective communication will be an important tool as you seek the true north for your life's path, enlist the help of mentors and coaches, and progress through your career. To execute effective communication requires that we enter into each communication with an open mind, without preconceived

---

83. John C. Maxwell, *Everyone Communicates, Few Connect: What the Most Effective People Do Differently* (Nashville: Thomas Nelson, Inc., 2010), 1.

notions or assumptions; that we ask the right questions; and that we share all the pertinent details about the situation at hand.

Our legal system is thriving largely because of poor communication. Attorneys make a lot of money figuring out what was really said and what wasn't. When it comes to communication, the first thing any attorney will tell you to do is to get things in writing. Admittedly, I believe in the old-school cowboy handshake, the belief that "my word is my bond." But that does not necessarily work well today. We are wise to get things in writing.

Assumptions Contaminate Our Communication

A guy walks into a doctor's office. The receptionist asks, "What is the nature of your visit today?"

The guy answers, "I have shingles."

She instructs him to sit down and gives him some paperwork to fill out. After he completes the forms, she takes him into an examination room.

The nurse asks, "What do you have?"

"Shingles."

"OK, take off your clothes," the nurse says. "The doctor will be in shortly."

A few minutes later, the doctor walks in and says, "Where are your shingles?"

"They're in the truck," the guy answers. "Where do you want me to put them?"

Obviously, some wrong assumptions were being made there. Assumptions are at the root cause of many miscommunications, and I recently had a personal experience with this.

A year ago, I had two conversations with the leader of one of our distant state offices. His issue, by his own admission, is that he is not a good delegator. The more we communicated and the more questions I asked, I was able to find out what the source of his delegation difficulty was. Unfortunately, because of poor communication during our initial meeting, this diagnosis was made not at our first meeting, but a week later. The real issue is that he had a few "C" players instead of people he trusts. It doesn't excuse him from his delegation needs, and he readily admitted that. But even if he were a good delegator, he would have difficulty trusting the people around him to carry out the duties he might assign to them. It was little wonder he felt that he had to do everything himself to get it done right.

Once we came to that conclusion, the manager asked me, "Should I get rid of them all?"

I advised him not to overreact by letting everybody go but rather to look for positions they could be "recycled" into. In situations like this, it is extremely helpful to have people complete the exercise from Chapter 1 of this book. Have them write down twenty-one activities and tasks associated with the industry or position they work in, then have them put those items in order of the things they like doing the most all the way down to the things they like doing the least. That simple exercise, again, will probably reveal their calling, talents, and passions. That simple exercise may be the process that saves their job, and that's always a good thing if done correctly.

That same leader learned that his office manager has poor attention to detail. That's a conundrum. How can you have an office manager who's not detail-oriented? You can't. But we looked for a position that would make use of her strong suits. We believe in moving people into the positions where they have a better chance at excelling. In this case, her experience in our industry and strong marketing skills made her a good fit to support a newer advisor who needed a kick-start in building a clientele. "Forget the paper and recycle people" is not only the noble purpose here; it is also cost-effective.

Assumptions are at the root cause of many miscommunications.

When my leader and I began these conversations, we were not communicating effectively. Looking back on it allowed me to realize that the barrier we had to good communication was the fact that I was making assumptions. I went into the conversation assuming that my manager's inability to delegate was the problem. I also assumed that he was surrounded by people who were capable of performing whatever task he might delegate to them. They were both incorrect assumptions on my part, and it caused us extra time and frustration.

Other Reasons We Miscommunicate

Addressing his players one day, baseball manager Casey Stengel (1890–1975) said, "Now, all you fellows line up alphabetically by height."

Miscommunications occur every day, although some aren't funny—they cause personal conflicts and cost companies a great deal of money in lost productivity. Whether we're speaking or sending an e-mail, we often fail to provide enough information to someone else, or what we say is misinterpreted. Language and cultural barriers are sometimes to blame.

Knowing when to be silent is just as important as knowing when to speak up.

A good deal of the time, misunderstandings occur because the speaker talks too fast and fails to take the time to ensure the listener is keeping up with him or her. It takes patience to be a good communicator. It takes a good listener paying attention to body language to be a good communicator. Crossed arms are one telltale sign that I am not communicating—or worse, that my message is not resonating.

Frequently, preconceived notions cause misunderstandings. There are few things that cause as much unhappiness as when you're in a conversation in which another person tries to anticipate what you're saying, and they get it wrong. They're filling in words that are not what you're trying to say. It can be quite frustrating. If communication is the goal, care must be taken to exercise patience with that person and respectfully correct the erroneous fill-ins.

Another challenge inherent in communication is the reality that the five hundred most commonly used words in the English language have more than fourteen thousand definitions. No wonder our communication often creates confusion and misunderstanding.

And sometimes we say things that we realize later we should have kept to ourselves. Saying the wrong thing, or even saying the right thing in the wrong way, can damage relationships and even cost someone their job. Calvin Coolidge said, "I've never been hurt by anything I didn't say." This has been true for centuries; Publilius Syrus, a Roman author who lived in the first century before Christ, said, "I have often regretted my speech, but never my silence." Knowing when to be silent is just as important as knowing when to speak up.

The Dynamics of Communication

Dynamics play a significant role in communication, and they can be quite complex. Often, while we know that we are well versed in our area of expertise, we still freeze up when we get in the presence of a certain person. The reason this happens can lie in the dynamics of our past relationships. For example, if you grew up with a parent who was an authoritarian, and he or she had an extremely direct communication style and was unwilling to listen to you, you may have fallen into the role of a respectful, obedient child. Now let's say you grow up and get a job, and your supervisor is an authoritarian. You may slip into that respectful, obedient role again because it's familiar and you don't want to anger your supervisor. But if you allow that to happen, you will not be able to express or assert yourself, and that does not bode well for your career success. It happens often, both in business and in sports. When the right dynamics exist between a team member and a supervisor, or between a player and a coach, it can make all the difference in the success of the organization or team and the individuals.

I recommend paying attention to your dynamics and trying to break out of that role if you find yourself in it again. This is where psychological insight and self-awareness come into play. Psychological insight is that ability to know yourself, to know what is going on in your mind. Again, self-awareness, as we discussed in Chapter 6, is being aware of what's going on around you, and how it resonates with you. Psychological insight plus self-awareness equals better judgment. Good counseling can help you get there. The more self-aware you are, the better you'll know how your communication is impacting the people around you.

Why It's Difficult for Some People to Say "No"

One of the most important words we can use in our communication is "no," yet many people have difficulty telling people "no" when they need to set boundaries. We are often hesitant to say the word "no" to certain people because, again, we may be slipping into a familiar role from the past or because we don't want to disappoint another person. Disappointment is a powerful motivator, so we might take on more than we should because we don't want to disappoint someone. Saying the word "no" also can be difficult when you reach a level of the organizational hierarchy where people aren't used to hearing it.

Again, you need to have insight and awareness to ensure that you are able to state your opinion and ask for what you need. I call it "finding your voice"—developing the ability to express your feelings in an assertive manner directly to a person in a stressful situation. Most of us tend to be either passive or aggressive, and neither strategy will work out well in the long haul. But if you can express your opinions and needs assertively, that is the sign of a good communicator.

I encourage people to state their feelings, not their thoughts. People can argue against your thoughts, but they can't argue against your feelings. This sets up an interesting dynamic that forces the other person to do one of two things—they're either going to dismiss your feelings or value them. If the person is more validating, you're going to have some good communication with him or her. You'll be able to work through any situation together. But if the person is dismissive of your feelings and says, "Aw, suck it up. Don't worry about it. I don't want to hear about it. You're going to be fine," that's a definite sign that the person probably doesn't have your best interest in mind.

Stating your feelings is a wonderful way to find out where you stand when you have a difficult subject to discuss. You may not get the reaction you hoped for, but you'll at least feel better because you got it off your chest.

Reading Nonverbal Cues

In communication, there is the 70–25–5 rule—that means that 70 percent of our communication is nonverbal, 25 percent of communication is our tone of voice, and 5 percent is composed of our words. We spend so much time focusing on our words, but they represent only a fraction of our message. Because our nonverbal cues and tone of voice play such a significant role in our communication, what we're really expressing are vibes. Distinguished writer Maya Angelou has said, "I've learned that people will forget what you said, people will forget what you did, but people will never forget how you made them feel." That's because 95 percent of our communication is made up of nonverbal vibes.

The people at Entrepreneur.com asked body-language experts to translate some common gestures into business vernacular. We have paraphrased their seven nonverbal cues as follows:[84]

1. A closed-off posture such as crossed arms implies resistance.

2. A brief touch to the hand captures people's attention and forms a quick connection. But be careful about touching team members' hands; the action could come across as condescending or inappropriate.

3. A nose rub is often linked with deception.

---

84. Jennifer Wang, "Seven Nonverbal Cues and What They (Probably) Mean," last modified April 10, 2009, accessed November 30, 2013, Entrepreneur.com, http://www.entrepreneur.com /article/201202.

4. When someone puts up a physical barrier between themselves and you (a desk, for example, or even a handful of papers), it can mean they are trying to gain distance from you.

5. A hand placed under the chin can indicate that a decision is being made.

6. Feet pointed toward the door means the person has tuned out and is ready to leave.

7. A back-of-the-neck scratch can mean the person has questions and concerns.

You can also watch for eye cues. If people look up to the right when they're communicating, it could mean they are searching for ideas. If they look up to the left, it could mean they are trying to consolidate past ideas. Casting the eyes downward is a nonverbal cue that is associated with shame and lying. I had a recent encounter with a car dealer's service department manager. He kept looking down when he was speaking to me, and I knew he was lying to me. He knew that I knew he was lying, and his face turned red.

The most powerful universal nonverbal communication in the world is a smile.

The universal symbol of power, control, and strength is to tap your fingertips together. Donald Trump does this on his show "The Apprentice." Sometimes a new book will come out from a motivational speaker, and on the cover photo, he will have his hands in that position. I coach people to tap their fingertips together when they are in difficult meetings or situations, to assert their power and control. I also have recommended to a number of coaches that they make that sign on the sidelines when they're trying to convey to an athlete on the field or court that they need to assert their control and power. When the coach sees the athlete losing it a little out there, he will tap his fingertips together. It tells the athlete, "You're in control. You have the power. You can do this."

I once heard a speaker on nonverbal communication finish his presentation by saying that the most powerful universal nonverbal communication in the world is a smile. Even if you don't know another person's language, you can communicate respect and kindness to him or her with a smile.

Reading Your Audience

When you're speaking, it's important to pay close attention to those you're speaking with, to see if they seem to understand what you're trying to convey. If you sense that the other party doesn't understand you, provide clarification or state what you're saying in another way.

When giving a presentation, I will have three or four times as many PowerPoint slides as needed. When giving the presentation, I try to read the audience. If they seem to have a great deal of interest in what is being said, then I'll continue focusing on the topic at hand. But if I'm losing them, I will shift gears into a different set of slides and move into a much different presentation than the one I was giving, while staying within the topic. As an aside, for those of you who present to groups often, I've learned through trial and error to assemble about 550 slides in my PowerPoint arsenal. When learning who the audience is and their needs, it is quite simple for me to organize an hour or longer presentation by simply reviewing the slides, writing down the ones needed, and e-mailing the numbers to Jacci, my assistant, who then assembles them out of Dropbox into a finished presentation.

Reading your audience's nonverbal cues is critical.

I recently made a presentation in Thailand to an audience of about five hundred managers. It takes about two hours to deliver a one-hour presentation there because after every two or three sentences, the interpreter translates my English into Thai. During our break, I asked the translator to ask the audience in Thai what topics they wanted me to spend the rest of our time on. They answered that they wanted to focus on leadership—not the management topic I had been asked to speak about. But because I had an abundant number of slides, I was able to make a fluid transition into the topic of leadership and provide them with information they wanted. Reading your audience's nonverbal cues is critical.

Incidentally, strategically placed pauses can enhance a presentation. Mark Twain said, "The right word may be effective, but no word was ever as effective as a rightly timed pause." Musicians know that music is in the space between the notes.

I believe that e-mail communication often leads to misunderstandings because there are no nonverbal cues or tonality of voice for us to "read." We have only the words in front of us, and they tell only 5 percent of the story. My two cardinal rules on tough e-mails are as follows: (1) Never write anything that we don't want on the front page of *The Wall Street Journal* the next day, and (2) keep the e-mail in the out box for twenty-four hours before hitting "send." E-mails often result in lost lawsuits and jail sentences, as well as hurt feelings.

Engaging in Positive Self-Talk

In addition to the communications we engage in with others, we are constantly having communications with ourselves. We're talking to ourselves about what we think the other person is saying, what we might say next, and our reaction to what's being said. Experts believe we typically "say" two hundred to twelve hundred words per minute to ourselves. Our self-talk matters a lot, yet we often ignore it when we think about communication.

Our self-talk should be positive. According to a Psychology Today *blog, negative self-talk usually leads to anxiety and depression and may have other unfortunate results. "Self-fulfilling prophecies are quite common: You start believing your own propaganda and bring about what you fear," Dr. Clifford Lazarus writes. "Happily, the converse is also true. Positive self-talk will tend to achieve desirable outcomes and generate good feelings."[85]*

Do you really believe you can do the top three things you know you are called to do, are meant to do, love to do, and aspire to do? How do you communicate that confidence to the world? If you can convince yourself that you excel in certain areas and that you will accomplish goals you've established for yourself, it will radiate outward from your own mind to other people. And when people know you're passionate about those three activities, they'll hear it in the tone of your voice because you've been saying it to yourself for a long time already. If you believe in yourself first, others will believe in you.

My father-in-law is one of the top antique iron dealers in the world. When Martha Stewart aired an episode of her show that featured ironing, she called him. Coincidentally, his name is Dave Irons. He has written four books on the topic. When Dave Irons talks about irons, he comes alive. He's gifted in this area and passionate about it, and he communicates that passion to the world. When someone needs an expert on this topic, he's the guy they call.

This is what we all should aspire to—to find that one thing that we are so good at and so passionate about that the entire world knows about it and considers us the expert in that area.

---

85. Clifford N. Lazarus, PhD, "What to Say when You Talk to Yourself," Psychologytoday.com, last modified July 15, 2010. accessed on November 30, 2013, http://www.psychologytoday.com /blog/think-well/201007/what-say-when-you-talk-yourself.

Things Change

There is a fundamental reality about communication—things change. What we discussed and agreed on may have been accurate last week, but maybe something happened recently, and things have changed. Often things change and we don't tell other people about it because we want to try to avoid tension and/or because we don't want to disappoint other people. A lot of problems can occur, however, if we fail to communicate how the parameters of a situation have changed and how that change can affect our outcome.

Many of us tend to have an approach–avoidance response when it comes to change—we try to avoid change rather than approach it.

American journalist and author Sidney J. Harris said, "Our dilemma is that we hate change and love it at the same time; what we want is for things to remain the same but get better." If you hate change, you'll hate irrelevance even more!

When a situation changes, we must be assertive about communicating it to those around us.

How to End a Meeting

Good communication, frequently, is all about asking the right questions.

Many of us spend a lot of time in meetings. The way most people end a meeting is by asking, "Are there any questions?" That may help you and your team get closer to your collective goal, but it isn't the best question to ask at the end of a meeting. The reaction to that question is usually silence. To make sure that your meeting mattered, that it counted for something, and that you're going to be prepared for the next meeting, go around the room and ask each person this question instead: "So what do you have to do between now and next week?" That way, everybody receives their marching orders. Think of how much more efficient your organization or team becomes when each person has said, in public, "I understand what I have to do." Now everybody in the room understands what they have to do, and we're all on trial with a deadline between now and next week to get certain things done.

Parents often say to children, "Now tell me what I just told you. Repeat back what Daddy just said" to see if they really got it or not. Half the time, you find out they didn't—probably because we miscommunicated it to them. There are effective and nonthreatening ways of doing that between adults as well. You can say, "Just for my benefit, help me out. Tell me what you think it is that I'm trying to get at, what I'm trying to accomplish." When they verbalize it back to you, it will be readily apparent whether or not effective communication has taken place. It's a simple thing to do, and we don't do it enough.

Another oversight we commit as parents is to judge a child's understanding about a question we ask by their answer. They may have understood you better than their answer indicates, but their limited verbal skills simply didn't allow them to communicate that effectively.

You can also offer that kind of confirmation to make sure you're on the same page as your coworker or supervisor. You can say, "Let me make sure I understand you correctly. What you want me to do is...."

Whenever we communicate, we have to ask ourselves how our message might be perceived, whether it could be misunderstood, and what we can do to make that communication clear and effective so that everyone involved understands what is happening, what has changed, and what is expected of them. Ensuring mutual understanding is healthy for individuals, sports teams, and organizations, and it saves time, effort, and frustration. It also facilitates every interaction you have with other people on your journey to your true north.

It's Your Turn

Exercise 15-1: Positive affirmations

Negative self-talk usually leads to anxiety and depression and can have other unfortunate results. Positive self-talk can arm you with confidence and help you demonstrate to others that you believe in your own abilities. What are some positive affirmations you can tell yourself to boost your self-confidence?

1. _____

2. _____

3. _____

4. _____

5. _____

Exercise 15-2: Smile more

It is the single most effective nonverbal communication known to man.

Chapter

16

Embracing Change

Enjoying success requires the ability to adapt. Only by being open to change will you have a true opportunity to get the most from your talent.

Nolan Ryan
CEO, Texas Rangers

Does the following news editorial resonate with you?

"The world is too big for us, too much going on. Too many crimes, too much violence and excitement. Try as you will, you will get behind in the race, in spite of yourself. It's an incessant strain to keep pace. And still you lose ground. Science empties its discoveries on you so fast that you stagger beneath it in hopeless bewilderment. The political world is news seen so rapidly, you are out of breath trying to keep pace with who's in and who's out. Everything is high pressure. Human nature can't endure much more."

That editorial appeared in the *Atlantic Journal* on June 16, 1833. Even 181 years ago, change was happening at such an accelerated pace that people had a hard time keeping up. And that was before the Internet and most of today's modern conveniences had been invented. Today, most of us are exposed to even more stress from our fast-paced lives.

Jack Welch, former chairman and CEO of General Electric, once stated: "The change in the 1990s will make the '80s look like a picnic, a walk in the park. Simply doing what worked in the '80s will be too slow." His comments also preceded the Internet and social media.

Considering the impact of the Internet, it's profound how fast-paced our lives have become. If you are unable to adapt to change in today's sophisticated technological environment, you will not do well (and may be miserable) in a profession that requires you to be conversant with and able to use cutting-edge technology.

<blockquote>
To benefit from change,
we must embrace it.
</blockquote>

Accepting the Inevitability of Change

Change happens all around us, in every aspect of business and life. It is inevitable. To benefit from change, we must embrace it. A quote I like says "Change is inevitable; personal growth is your choice."

In the *Minneapolis Star Tribune* in just one day in the year 2000, articles on the following topics appeared:

- Chase buys J. P. Morgan.
- Merrill Lynch won't survive.
- Twenty million people earn major income at home.
- Bill Gates says no current Microsoft product will exist in ten years.
- Seven new people get on the Internet each second.
- Thirty-five percent of Fortune 100 companies have changed since 1995.
- California is the first state in which white people are a minority.

To further demonstrate how much times have changed, consider the top problems teachers reported having with students in 1940 and then fifty years later, in 1990:

Top problems reported by teachers in 1940:

- Talking out of turn
- Making noise
- Running in the halls
- Cutting in line
- Dress-code violations
- Lingering
- Chewing gum

Top problems reported by teachers in 1990:

- Drug abuse
- Alcohol abuse
- Pregnancy
- Suicide
- Rape
- Robbery
- Assault

Also, consider the number of years it took for each of the following types of media to reach an audience of fifty million people:

Radio: 38 years

Television: 13 years

Internet: 4 years

Facebook: 2 years

It's also estimated that fewer than one hundred of today's Standard & Poor (S&P) 500 companies existed in 1957.

Dr. George Odiorne, the father of Management by Objectives (MBO), said, "Things that do not change remain the same." Things can't get better without change—in sports, in business, or in your personal life.

Change is at the root of any sport. We all compete, but we continue to strive to get better, and to get better requires change. It requires new learning, new drills, new experiences. In any sport, that's the common denominator—wanting to change for the better. Yet overall there is a tendency for us to resist change. Frankly, it's sheer madness to think that the weapons or tools that have worked in the past will be as effective in the future in a completely new world. Staying in your comfort zone gives you the false illusion that you are safe when just the opposite is true. The more things around you change, the greater the need for you to make the necessary adjustments to ensure both your safety and your success.

Kerry McCoy, a two-time Olympic wrestling coach and the current head wrestling coach at the University of Maryland, has a huge sign in his wrestling room that says, "If nothing changes, nothing changes." He's famous for saying that again and again to his athletes to try to get them to improve their skills. That's a wonderful, positive way of making the point that you've got to change to make things better. Change isn't all bad.

Accepting What We Cannot Change

Just as we must accept that change is inevitable, we must accept the reality that we cannot change some things. A Chinese proverb says, "What you cannot change, accept." I think that is a helpful mantra to adopt and one that soothes frustrations.

Ann Landers said, "Maturity is the ability to live in peace with that which we cannot change." The serenity prayer, used by Alcoholics Anonymous and similar groups, is also about accepting what we cannot change. It is attributed to American theologian Reinhold Niebuhr, and it says, "God, grant me the serenity to accept the things I cannot change, the courage to change the things I can, and the wisdom to know the difference."

The serenity prayer is so profound and powerful that in the world of mental health, it is a compelling tool in the treatment of addiction, which is one of the most complex conditions known to mankind. It helps people with addictions find peace of mind in the middle of the storm, when change and unpredictability seem to be rampant and emotions can be labile. That prayer is commonly accepted and recited because it helps people relinquish control, which is one of the foundational pieces of managing change better.

The Role of Faith in Accepting Change

Faith is a factor in managing change well.

After football player Tim Tebow was traded to the New York Jets, someone asked him if he thought he would be the starting quarterback for the Jets. His response was, "I don't know what my future holds, but I do know Who holds it." That was a brilliant response because not only did he avoid a quarterback controversy and remain cool under fire, he also shared how his faith in God helps him manage change.

When we're anxious, we are exhibiting our fear of the unknown.

For many of us, change brings up a lot of negative emotions. Change makes us anxious, and a definition of anxiety is "fear of the unknown." So when we're anxious, we are exhibiting our fear of the unknown. That's a normal, natural response. But we can manage change better if we take the Tim Tebow approach and say, "I don't know what the future holds, but I have an underlying trust in God that He will provide what I need." God has your best interest in mind. And therefore, no matter what's going to come, even though it is currently unknown, we can be assured that it is likely to be good.

Being Open to New Experiences

Another key component to managing change well is an important concept called "openness to experience," which is one of the commonly listed "Big Five" characteristic traits. The "Big Five" model is a theory that describes personality using five basic traits: openness to experience, conscientiousness, extroversion, agreeableness, and neuroticism. You can remember these five traits easily by remembering that they form the acronym OCEAN, and you can learn more about them simply by searching for "Big Five personality traits" on the Internet.

People who have the "openness to experience" trait tend to be more creative, more open to new and different ideas, and more in touch with their feelings. People who score lower on openness to experience tend to be more closed off. They are generally more resistant to change. While there is no right or wrong way to be, it is helpful to understand where one stands on that continuum.

Why We Resist Change

Many people find change to be disconcerting and unsettling, and they try to resist it. That reluctance to change with the times is exemplified in the popular quote "Change is good. You go first."

In psychology, when we attempt to understand why people resist change, we can trace that reluctance back many centuries, when people lived in villages and tribes. The men often would go out to hunt during the day, and the women would stay back in the village, taking care of the children and cooking. When the men left, the women became somewhat vulnerable. If a woman spotted something out on the horizon that looked different, out of the ordinary, that change represented a potential threat. Perhaps it was a storm cloud moving in, or a predator or enemy. She needed to communicate that threat to everybody around her quickly. That is, in part, why women became more verbally communicative than men.

Similarly, ages ago, if a child had an infection of some kind and his parent noticed some slight change, it was a very real threat—there was a possibility that the child could die or that the infection could spread among the village or tribe. Many people could die. As a result, change became highly associated with a threat to survival, which meant we had to have a swift reaction to it.

As a result, we have been hardwired for a long time to pay attention to negative stimuli—anything that appears different than the status quo. Today, we can manage many of those threats more easily because of our modern conveniences—if a storm moves in, big deal. Just about all of us have a roof over our head and climate-controlled rooms, so we'll be fine. Yet change is so innate in us that some people get upset when the weather changes.

Our perceptions are based on our personal experiences.

All of us grew up in different environments, so the changes in our environment that we perceive as threats are going to vary. My reaction to a particular change may vary greatly from someone else's. For example, I live with my family in an old stone farmhouse. When we hear that an old barn is going to be torn down to make way for growth and development, that change is hard for me to accept because I value the antiquity of old places in American history. I live in a community where this type of situation occurs too often. But somebody else may be happy to see that old barn being torn down so that a new business can be built to help create new jobs.

Our perceptions are based on our personal experiences, our childhoods, what we find interesting, and what we value, and these factors determine how we view every change that occurs.

Wisdom, Resilience, and Institutional Memory

It appears to be true that the older we get, the more set in our ways we become. I have found that one must fight harder to welcome change more than before. The older we become, something physiologically, chemically, or psychologically happens that causes us to be less aggressive about accepting and embracing change.

From a psychological standpoint, I'm not sure if we fully know a solid rationale for why we resist change more as we age. But I do know that a positive spin on aging is the wisdom that comes with it. When we think of somebody who is growing old, we recognize that they're growing wiser and that they have demonstrated resilience over many decades of change.

Derek Isaacowitz, PhD, is an associate professor in the Department of Psychology and Volen National Center for Complex Systems at Brandeis University. His research focuses on emotion in adulthood and old age. He heads the university's

Emotion Laboratory, which investigates how people of different ages manage their emotions and what role attention plays in emotion regulation and maintenance of well-being. He says we gain resilience as we grow older. In this quote, Dr. Isaacowitz refers to a study he conducted at Brandeis. The results were published in the journal Psychology and Aging: *"The study suggests that the way individuals in late life process information enables them to stay on an even emotional keel and feel good. By focusing more on positive things and avoiding negative ones, older adults are able to maintain emotional resilience, which becomes acutely important in the face of dwindling time."*[86]

Just as older people are resilient, children are a great example of resilience. You can take a child to play on a jungle gym on a new playground, and she will likely make friends quickly. They adapt. We could learn a lesson from children about losing the fear associated with new situations.

In Chapter 1, one of the four tasks I listed that I enjoy most is institutional memory. That fits in with wisdom because institutional memory causes me, after fifty-plus years in business, to say, "We tried that. It did not work. Let's not make the same mistake a second time." Therein lies the wisdom. But on the other hand, saying "Let's not try that again" may appear to be a resistance to change.

As an example, I mentioned earlier that we recycle people at North Star. If someone does not succeed in the task we hired him or her for, we try to keep that person in the organization if he or she is a good person who shares our values, loves our culture, is well-liked, has high energy, and is ethical. Forget the paper, recycle people; they're far more important.

Frequently, we have taken a salesperson who is marginal—not earning enough money—and turned her into a recruiter. We have been successful at that. We turn marginal salespeople into recruiters because they love the business. They just don't have the skills to get their earnings up fast enough to be successful in a sales position. Not only is this the right thing to do for the individual, but it serves as a true morale booster for the firm when others realize the extent to which the organization will go to keep its team members. Discharging good people simply because they can't succeed at the position for which they've been hired is illogical when they may well be successful at another position in your organization. Recycling people is an ideal solution for the individual as well as the firm.

---

86. "Dwindling Time Fuels Happier Outlook," News Medical, last updated April 13, 2006, accessed on November 30, 2013, http://www.news-medical.net/news/2006/04/13/17339.aspx.

But when we've tried to recycle *half* a person, we have failed. In other words, when we ask someone to be a recruiter 50 percent of the time and a salesperson 50 percent of the time, it has failed—not most of the time, but every time. And we've tried it many times because it seems logical. The reason it fails is that humans tend to gravitate to the least threatening or least painful activity. The recruiting activity—bringing other young people into the business—is more pleasurable to them than selling life insurance and financial services and enduring the consequent rejection, so they end up spending 100 percent of their time in recruiting and none of their time in sales.

As a result, we know not to try this again. That's my institutional memory. People have come to me to discuss a marginal salesperson and have said, "Hey, let's make him a half-time recruiter." That's when I say, "No, no, no, no, no, no. We've tried that many times, and it has never worked, not once. Period."

You have to walk a thin line in terms of institutional memory so that you are not perceived as being resistant to change. Furthermore, it is not dependent on IQ because it is nothing more than one's ability to recall those things that historically have not worked.

Institutional memory requires discernment. Wisdom gained over time gives you incredible discernment when you are presented with a direction that somebody else thinks might be positive but you know is negative. They might see you as being resistant to it, but what you're really doing is exercising great discernment. That's an important piece because if we think about the positive side of change as being in the realm of resilience, the ability to weather change well, then discernment is a key variable that one develops with life experience.

Another key variable in the ability to manage change well is selflessness. Selflessness is often said to be "thinking of yourself less, not thinking less of yourself." We must ask ourselves how what we are doing may affect others—the greater good. Being able to think about someone other than yourself in the process of change is a hallmark of resilience. It also fits nicely with the concept of servant leadership.

Preserving Core Values in the Face of Change

In the book *Built to Last*, authors Collins and Porras show a circle. On the left side of the circle, it says "Preserve the core." On the right side, it says "Stimulate progress." The best companies do both. Your values don't change; the culture and the values of your company are sacred. But there might be things outside of the values that need to be stimulated, improved, or changed. We need to keep those two thoughts always in mind and use them as a filter to determine what is good change and what is not good change.

Believing prevailing assumptions can prevent our personal and professional growth.

Jesus was a man who shook up the culture and realigned core values—in other words, a radical change agent.

For instance, in the Old Testament, the admonition was "an eye for an eye, a tooth for a tooth." Then Jesus came along and told people to "turn the other cheek" if someone treated them poorly. That was a radical change, but Jesus was remaining true to His Father, preserving the core while effecting change. It is noteworthy to acknowledge that the "eye for an eye" remedy in the Old Testament was to redress the practice of that day, which involved an overreaction to an injury by making the reaction far worse than the actual injury. Doing no more than what was done to you was considered progress; an eye for an eye and a tooth for a tooth was a civil response in a day when overreaction was the rule of the day.

I go to the best-selling book of all time, the Bible (sales of more than 150 million per year) to establish my core values and try to understand change. In that book, I find the ability to manage change.

Every day for the past twenty-plus years, since 1992, I have read at least one chapter in the Bible. I have never missed a day because it is a habit; as we mentioned earlier, it is not a big deal when it's a habit. The messages in it set the tone for the day for me in terms of proportionality, humility, gratitude, and priorities.

After the terrorist attacks on 9/11/01, church attendance increased, and people were trying to manage that change by finding or forming spiritual communities. A lot of people turn to God when they need resilience.

The Need to Challenge Assumptions

In the book *Mastering Change: The Key to Business Success*, author Leon Martel describes three common traps that keep us from recognizing and using change to our advantage:

1. Believing that yesterday's solutions will solve today's problems

2. Assuming that present trends will continue

3. Neglecting the opportunities offered by future change

Believing prevailing assumptions can prevent our personal and professional growth. It's been said that if you don't like change, you'll hate being irrelevant even more!

Many people told Tony Hsieh of Zappos he would never be able to sell shoes on the Internet because people need to try shoes on before they buy them. He moved forward with his idea, though, and my guess is that today Zappos sells more shoes than anybody in the world. He is successful because he challenged assumptions. One of Zappos's core values, by the way, is to "embrace and drive change." Because Zappos was sold to Amazon.com for $850 million, it appears that Hsieh was right!

Like Hsieh, we have to continually test assumptions, even if they have served us well in the past. There may be an even better future ahead of us. Maybe those assumptions were created decades ago. Times have changed, and dramatically. We have to test those assumptions in terms of the world we're in today versus the world that existed when those assumptions were created.

I started my career in the insurance industry as a change agent, and I challenged some assumptions. In 1969, our agents were selling securities when the insurance industry would not permit it. At that time, you were not allowed to mix risk products like life insurance with non-guaranteed products like stocks and bonds. As a result, the life insurance industry ostracized me.

I was on the Board of Directors at the Minneapolis GAMA (it formerly stood for "General Agents and Managers") organization. I received a phone call one day in 1972 from one of the other board members, who informed me that the Board of Directors had asked me to tender my resignation because they learned that our agents were selling stocks and bonds. I did resign because if I didn't, they would have voted me off the board anyway. And it was the right thing to do. Groucho Marx's comment came to mind: "I refuse to join any club that would have me as a member."

To show you how drastically things can change, in 2003, GAMA International, the parent organization of GAMA Minneapolis, asked me to be its president. I didn't change; the industry changed. In the 1980s, more and more companies began selling stocks and bonds, and by the 1990s, almost every company in the industry began doing so. In fact, today the only major life-insurance company I know of that doesn't sell securities is the highly successful Knights of Columbus, a purpose-driven firm that has preserved its core mission of caring for widows and orphans.

In 1969, almost everyone thought
I was insane when I made a resolution
to hire only college graduates, right
off college campuses.

In 1968, I created what I thought was the original pinwheel with the client oc-
cupying the center, surrounded by circles representing each of the services we
provided. Years later, I learned that my good friend, Norm Levine, had invented
the same model thirteen years earlier, in 1955. It was of little wonder that Norm
went on to be president of MDRT, GAMA International, and the National
Association of Insurance and Financial Advisors, as well as the author of eleven
books about our industry. Humility is a good characteristic, and a dose of it now
and then is a healthy thing.

In 1969, almost everyone thought I was insane when I made a resolution to hire
only college graduates, right off college campuses. People said, "Nobody's going
to pay all that money to go to college just to sell life insurance, which they don't
need a degree for." But I challenged that assumption, and now I think almost
every company requires financial planners to have degrees. It paid off to be on
the leading edge, not at the tail end, of change.

And today, we are still at the leading edge of change, which is what drives our
company. We strive to always stimulate progress and always look for new revenue sources. We have the premier disability-income website in the world, and
its consumer-driven comparison focus is unique in our industry. The fact that
North Star, as a distribution point, is absolutely independent from a financial or
governance point of view is ahead of the industry. We have preferred providers
and partners leading to a successful business model. While we are an outlier, I'm
certain that others will one day emulate the model. As Cicero said, "I criticize by
creation, not by finding fault."

What Will Never Change: Maury's Nine Timeless Anchors

Throughout my career, my mentor has been Maurice L. "Maury" Stewart, CLU,
ChFC, CLF. He has dedicated his leadership and passion for life insurance to
The Penn Mutual Life Insurance Company and our industry for more than sixty
years. There is little doubt that this 2004 GAMA International Hall of Famer
has mentored more leaders and advisors in his career than anyone else.

Growing up in rural Iowa during World War II, Maury lost his mother at an early age and was forced to take over his family's eight-hundred-acre farm when he was only thirteen years old.

In 1948, Maury enlisted in the Army Air Force, and just three years later, he joined the war effort in Korea. Taking great pride in defending his country's freedom, Maury flew more than fifty bombing missions. He married in 1952 and decided to start his career as an agent for Penn Mutual in Topeka, Kansas. After Maury took over the Philadelphia office in 1960, it became the top agency for Penn Mutual for twelve consecutive years under his leadership.

Once you're on the path you're meant to be on, it will be easier for you to embrace change.

Maury knows a lot about change in our industry. He has taught all of us that there are nine things that will never change. I call them "Maury's Nine Timeless Anchors." Whether you're in the financial services industry or some other industry, they can help you be successful. By focusing on them, you will always be relevant and prepared.

1. **A positive mental attitude is a must.** The people with a positive mental attitude will survive and be prosperous in the future, just as they have over the past fifty years.

2. **BHAGs (Big, Hairy, Audacious Goals) fuel your ambition.** People who think big will do better than people who think small.

3. **Activity solves all problems.** You've got to execute. You have to *do* things—the bigger the better.

4. **Integrity wins the day.** Ethics is jacks or better. ("Jacks or Better" is the name of a poker game in which one of the players has to hold two jacks for the hand to be played out. Otherwise, all players throw in their hands, and a new deal is required. "Ethics is jacks or better" means that there is no game without ethics and that ethics are a condition for the game going forward.)

5. **Practice makes perfect.** Drill, drill, drill. Rehearse. Memorize your scripts.

6. **It is critical to inspect what you expect and to expect only what you inspect.** We discussed this concept in Chapter 4. Trust but verify.

7. **Practice empowerment, not power.** Forget the paper—recycle people. Manage things, lead people. Trust people. Don't use your power to tell them what to do.

8. **You must have purpose in your mission.**

9. **The miracle of life insurance is the game changer.** Widows, widowers, kids, jobs, and businesses matter, and protecting them is a noble thing to do.

That list is my way of "preserving the core." Those things are non-negotiable because I know they've stood the test of time for more than fifty years and will be around for the next fifty. Maury is an ardent advocate for The American College, which together with Penn Mutual has funded a lecture series in his honor. In 2012, GAMA International published a Master Firm Builder book about Maury's legacy—*The Miracle Business: A Lifetime of Lessons on Leadership*. The book embodies his noble and timeless beliefs and is laden with his wisdom.

Mahatma Gandhi said, "Be the change you want to see in the world." I believe that's what we all should do. Challenge the status quo. Shake up the system a little bit. Hire in a different way. Look for a candidate in a way that may be slightly different. Find your spot, your calling in the world, even though others may not understand why you've chosen a certain path. Once you're on the path you're meant to be on, it will be easier for you to embrace change. In fact, you may welcome it. For those who embrace change and make the best of it, the sky is not the limit!

It's Your Turn

Exercise 16-1: Embracing change

Change is inevitable, and to be successful at following our calling in life requires that we accept and embrace change. What are some changes you have embraced while striving to be successful?

1. _____

2. _____

3. _____

4. _____

5. _____

6. _____

7. _____

Chapter

17

Discipline Leads to Happiness

The ability to discipline yourself to delay gratification in the short term in order to enjoy greater rewards in the long term is the indispensable prerequisite for success.

Brian Tracy
Author, Speaker, Entrepreneur, Business Coach

In Chapter 7, we discussed habits and how, once you develop a habit, you no longer need self-discipline to accomplish tasks like exercising regularly. Developing good habits is critical to your success because habits form your character. Once you form a habit, that task becomes second nature to you. You don't have to think about it or struggle to perform it. Until you reach that point, though, you will need self-discipline to accomplish the tasks you've identified as critical to accomplishing your goals.

It has been my personal experience that acquiring discipline leads to happiness. If happiness is the goal, then discipline is the bridge to get there.

There are multiple forms of discipline—physical, mental, spiritual, and financial. We need to strive to exercise discipline in all areas of our lives. A person who is quite disciplined in one area of her life but not in others is likely to have her overall success undermined by the underdiscplined area.

A Key Aspect of Discipline: Delaying Gratification

In his famous "marshmallow test" in the late 1960s, Stanford psychology professor Walter Mischel, who has taught at Columbia University since 1983, presented a number of children with a choice—they could eat one marshmallow right away, or they could wait for a few minutes and have two. Dr. Mischel conducted additional research more than a decade later and discovered that the children who ate a marshmallow right away were more likely to have behavioral problems, both in school and at home; to get lower SAT scores; to struggle in stressful situations; to have a difficult time paying attention; and to have trouble maintaining friendships. The children who could wait fifteen minutes before eating any marshmallows had SAT scores that were, on average, 210 points higher than those of the kids who could wait only thirty seconds.[87]

That often-cited study demonstrated that self-discipline is a key factor in both academic and personal success.

In *The Road Less Traveled*, psychiatrist M. Scott Peck says, "Discipline is the basic set of tools we require to solve life's problems. Without discipline we can solve nothing .... With total discipline we can solve all problems."[88]

Some degree of pain is necessary for us to develop discipline.

Peck explains that a key part of discipline is delaying gratification, which "is a process of scheduling the pain and pleasure of life in such as a way as to enhance the pleasure by meeting and experiencing the pain first and getting it over with. It is the only decent way to live."[89]

The pain–pleasure principle is a common topic in psychology that drives human behavior. We are innately hardwired to avoid pain and gravitate to pleasure, and that creates some challenges. We don't want to suffer. Some might say that our strong desire to avoid pain is one cause of some of the challenges we face in American culture. Today in America, children have so much. You can go to any yard sale and, for $25, load your car up with toys, whereas decades ago, children didn't have as much, and in many parts of the world today, people don't have that ability to bring joy to their children for so little money. The disciplines of the past are somewhat compromised because in America today, we are surrounded by all types of pleasure, both sensory and material, and because of our affluence, we are more able to avoid the pain associated with doing without. I would argue that some degree of pain is necessary for us to develop discipline.

---

87. Jonah Lehrer, "Don't: The Secret of Self-Control," *The New Yorker*, last updated May 18, 2009, accessed on November 30, 2013, http://www.newyorker.com/reporting/2009/05/18/090518fa _fact_lehrer#ixzz1wUW8zYmd.

88. M. Scott Peck, MD, *The Road Less Traveled: A New Psychology of Love, Traditional Values, and Spiritual Growth* (New York: Touchstone, 1978), 15–16.

89. Ibid., 19.

When he was the coach of Notre Dame, Lou Holtz talked to his entering freshmen about delaying gratification. He said this to them—and I'm paraphrasing: "It's easy to tell the individuals who are going to be All-American and those who aren't going to make it here at Notre Dame. Every day it comes down to one simple decision. After practice, when you're tired, you're going to go back to your dorm room. There's a desk and a bed. Those individuals who choose the bed and lie down for a while and say, 'I'll get to my studies later' often don't have the success here that they had hoped they would. But those who have the discipline to sit down at their desk and get their schoolwork done and only then lie in bed, those are the ones who have tremendous success. Those are our All-Americans here at Notre Dame."

Discipline Requires Making a Choice

Discipline comes down to a choice. As mentioned earlier, choice is giving up something you want for something else you want more. An athlete would probably like to sleep in every morning, but if he wants to improve his physical conditioning, he may have to get up before school and go for a run, on a regular basis. It all comes down to which he wants more—the extra time sleeping or a better athletic record. Discipline requires being conscientious about what you're choosing.

If we think back on our wrestling careers, we did a lot of drills, push-ups, weight lifting, and running that most people would simply not want to do. In fact, we didn't want to do it, either. The discipline of staying in shape is necessary to have a successful wrestling record. Author John Irving, who also was a wrestler, said this about discipline: "I became involved with wrestling at the age of fourteen.... I competed until I was thirty-four, kind of old for a contact sport. I coached the sport until I was forty-seven. I think the discipline of wrestling has given me the discipline I have to write."

I am a little bit biased about the sport of wrestling because, like gymnastics, wrestling requires a high level of discipline. When you are an athlete in school, there are three main realms of your life: academics, athletics, and socializing. You can be good at only two of them. Coaches, teachers, and parents hope, of course, that young people will choose academics and athletics and have the discipline to say, "I'm not going to stay out late on a Saturday night. I'm going to go to bed early so I can get up on Sunday and go to church, study, and feel energized." It's difficult to excel if you don't have discipline.

Discipline can be intermittent or occasional. When someone wants to lose ten pounds, they need to develop the discipline to exercise and avoid certain foods for a certain period of time. They have to make better choices until they reach their goal. An accountant may need to discipline herself to get up early and stay up late for the first few months of the year so that she can make sure all her clients' taxes are completed by April 15th. I think it can be difficult to muster the discipline necessary to accomplish a short-term goal. But again, if you engage in an activity enough that it becomes a habit, you won't need discipline to do it regularly.

There are many times in my life when the nature of running my company, Mind of the Athlete, requires me to get up and do work early in the morning. Then, when my wife and children wake up, I stop what I'm doing. Every time I do that, it reminds me of being a high-school athlete and getting up at five o'clock in the morning to go for that run in the dark or to go over to the high school to lift weights. At that time, I was a hungry athlete, and now I'm a hungry business owner. I know I need to put in a little bit more time than others, and I'll do that by having the discipline to get up early.

There are many occasions in business, especially when traveling in China, when people will be celebrating by opening champagne in the morning. I have had a rule since high school, following an unpleasant experience with alcohol, that I never, ever, under any conditions, touch alcohol before noon. Period. And on a daily basis, I don't drink before five o'clock. But the pressure to have that champagne or Bloody Mary on a company outing is great enough that I have had to tell a white lie and say, "It's a religious thing." Frankly it is, in much the same way one gives up pleasures for Lent. That's the only way I have found to stay with the habit of refraining from alcohol in the daytime without a major disagreement, or at least an argument with hosts. That requires discipline, and I'll go to whatever honest lengths it takes to exercise that discipline. It is not a challenge to a habit I am confronted with regularly, thank the Lord.

I have to do the same thing with desserts. For Lent in 2011, I decided that, because I hadn't given anything up for Lent in a few years, I would give up something I really liked. I narrowed it down to either red wine or all desserts and sugar. It took some time to figure out which one to give up because I enjoy them both. Finally, I thought, *What would God want me to do?* Before I reached a decision, a divine (and convenient) revelation occurred to me—I thought, *What would the Mayo Clinic tell me to do?* Of course they would say the red wine is healthier than the sugar. So, as you might imagine, I gave up desserts and sugar instead of red wine. As an afterthought, I realized that Jesus, in the Gospels, occasionally used wine, and I am unaware of His using refined sugar.

At the end of the forty-day Lent period, I realized I didn't miss sugar or desserts. I haven't had a dessert since then. Shedding the extra pounds put me back at my college wrestling weight. Now it's a commitment. It's a form of fasting. People give up certain foods for Lent, but it doesn't have to be confined to that particular period of time. That discipline is so familiar to me now that it has become a habit I don't have to think about.

Why Some of Us Avoid Discipline

Discipline is developed, to a great extent, during our childhoods. Parenting plays a significant role in helping children learn discipline. Effective parents teach children to get their homework done before they go outside to play and to eat their vegetables before they can have dessert—those are small disciplines, but they are important. Mentors, coaches, and the church family—they all matter in establishing discipline. It's easier to establish discipline earlier in life than it is to try to develop it later on.

One reason we might shy away from
discipline is because it can come
with a heavy hand.

One reason we might shy away from discipline is because it can come with a heavy hand. Maybe a coach abuses his power with discipline, or maybe a parent has high discipline and lacks warmth. We need to look back to our childhoods to see what messages about discipline were instilled in us. If there were negative messages, we will have to work to overcome them. Hopefully you received reinforcement of discipline in a positive manner. Discipline (including self-discipline) should be administered in a loving way.

French author Francois Mouriac addressed that topic when he said, "Where does discipline end? Where does cruelty begin? Somewhere between these, thousands of children inhabit a voiceless hell."

Discipline in Training

In a previous book, *Twenty-Five Secrets to Sustainable Success*, I discussed our training philosophy at North Star; we are merciless with new college grads hired to the company. Until we determine that they have discipline, we provide it just as the Marine Corps does. We call it "Cop, Coach, Consultant," and North Star is the cop in phase one.

In keeping with our decades-old strategy of hiring college grads only, we continue to find that these young people are similar to a liquid that takes the form of whatever vessel they are poured into. Pour it into a cup, looks like a cup, into a flask, looks like a flask, into a pitcher, looks like a pitcher. We have not found the same with forty-somethings, but the discipline that lies at the heart of our system is easily assimilated by twenty-somethings. When the newcomer displays discipline, we no longer need to play the cop role but move to the coach phase. Finally, after advisors reach a certain predetermined level of success (MDRT), we move into a consulting role. People frequently ask us why new graduates are willing to accept the discipline enforced upon them. We answer that they know we care. People don't care what you know until they know that you care. They'll take a bullet for you if they know you love them. Furthermore, the cop, coach, consultant scenario is explained to them in detail during the selection phase. It actually serves as a recruiting tool because the twenty-two-year-old views it as part of a training program, and the many college athletes we hire are quite used to the discipline of sports.

<blockquote>
People don't care what you know
until they know that you care.
</blockquote>

The Connection between Goals and Discipline

American author and writer Jim Rohn said, "Discipline is the bridge between goals and accomplishment." Once you have established a worthy goal, then it's the discipline you have that enables you to achieve that goal, whether it's in athletics, education, or your profession. Meeting goals requires a sacrifice of some kind, whether it's four years in medical school plus a residency and fellowship, training to become an Olympic gold medalist, winning a state championship, or running a successful business.

In *The Leader Who Had No Title*, author Robin Sharma contends that leadership is the single most important discipline and that anyone can be a leader, regardless of their station in life.[90] Setting and then reconnecting with your goals on a regular basis is a powerful discipline that can lead to success. "Your goals create a fantastic amount of focus in your career and in your life," Sharma says. "Goals generate hope and positive energy.... Goals ensure that you live life deliberately and productively versus reactively and accidentally."[91]

---

90. Robin Sharma, *The Leader Who Had No Title: A Modern Fable on Real Success in Business and in Life* (New York: Free Press, 2010), 27.

91. Ibid., 181.

What Our First President Said About Discipline

I am a big fan of George Washington and Revolutionary War history. In May 2012, I led ten men on a George Washington leadership retreat. We walked the steps of George Washington for two days. We visited the Princeton Theological Seminary in Princeton, New Jersey, and the staff there shared with us part of their private collection of Washington-related items. We got to see original documents, one of which was a copy of a letter Washington wrote to a young man he was mentoring. I read, in Washington's own writing, these compelling words that he wrote to the young man about discipline: "Rise early, that by habit it may become familiar, agreeable, healthy, and profitable. It may for a while be irksome to do this, but that will wear off. In the process, you'll produce the rich harvest forever thereafter, whether in public or private walk of life." That is profound wisdom from the founder of this great country about the discipline of simply rising early.

George Washington also said, about the discipline that is instilled in soldiers, "Nothing can be more hurtful to the service than the neglect of discipline because that discipline, more than numbers, gives one army the superiority over another." And he said, "Discipline is the soul of an army. It makes small numbers formidable, procures success to the weak and esteem to all."

Along those same lines, retired US Marine Corps gunnery sergeant, drill instructor, and actor R. Lee Ermey said, "Without discipline, there is no Marine Corps."

A lot of times we think, Oh, no! I don't want discipline. It's important for us to frame it in a positive context. Discipline is a good thing. I have seen a lot of young men and women go into our armed forces and emerge much better people after having gone through some discipline and training. It does wonders for them. A lot of times we look at discipline as a negative, but I think the military is one good example of how discipline teaches people to take control of their lives.

Discipline in the Book of Proverbs

The book of Proverbs in the Bible is replete with wisdom about discipline. It provides great words to live by, transcending time, culture, and religion. Here are just some of the verses from Proverbs that compel us to discipline ourselves and our children:

- "The fear of the Lord is the beginning of knowledge, but fools despise wisdom and discipline." Proverbs 1:7

- "For whom the Lord loves he reproves, even as a father corrects the son in whom he delights." Proverbs 3:12
- "He will die for lack of discipline, led astray by his own great folly." Proverbs 5:23
- "Whoever loves discipline loves knowledge, but he who hates reproof is stupid." Proverbs 12:1
- "A wise son accepts his father's discipline, but a scoffer does not listen to rebuke." Proverbs 13:1
- "He who withholds his rod hates his son, but he who loves him disciplines him diligently." Proverbs 13:24
- "Train up a child in the way he should go. Even when he is old he will not depart from it." Proverbs 22:6
- "Foolishness is bound up in the heart of a child; the rod of discipline will remove it far from him." Proverbs 22:15
- "Do not hold back discipline from the child. Although you strike him with the rod, he will not die. You shall strike him with the rod and rescue his soul from Sheol." Proverbs 23:13–14
- "Correct your son, and he will give you comfort; he will also delight your soul." Proverbs 29:17

Remember, discipline comes down to a choice, and choice is giving up something you want for something else you want more.

As you set out on the path to find your true north by discovering what your strengths and passions are, you'll need to say no to a lot of endeavors in life that will not bear the kind of fruit that brings you closer to your goals. It takes discipline to say no to relationships, jobs, recreational activities, or other situations that don't fit into our overall plan, once we discover our life's calling. Remember, discipline comes down to a choice, and choice is giving up something you want for something else you want more. Make your choices carefully each day, and you will experience more happiness, as well as academic, personal, financial, and professional success.

It's Your Turn

Exercise 17-1: Self-discipline

Self-discipline involves choice, and choice is giving up something you want for something else you want more. Identify something you want but are willing to give up for something you want more.

What I Want But Am Willing to Give Up:	What I Want More:
1. _____	1. _____
2. _____	2. _____
3. _____	3. _____
4. _____	4. _____

Chapter

18

Winning Breeds Confidence

Without a humble but reasonable confidence in your own
powers, you cannot be successful or happy.

Norman Vincent Peale
Author, *The Power of Positive Thinking*

Once you complete the exercise in Chapter 1 of this book to discover the things you enjoy most and are best at, you will gain confidence because you will have begun the process of using your God-given talents to excel in life.

You learn confidence by being good at what you do and by winning. The theme of this book is to do those things you love to do, simply because if you love doing them, you'll do them better than people who don't have that passion. This will help you win, and winning breeds confidence. Do the things that will continue to lead to success, and marginalize those things you're not good at or hate doing. As stated earlier, even your first hire should be tested in this way, even if it is an unpaid intern. Effectively leveraging your time is productive at any stage of your business or professional career and should begin as soon as possible.

When we lack self-confidence, it may be because we're striving in areas that are out of sync with our calling. Many individuals pursue a path because it's what someone else, perhaps a parent, told them to do, then they discover that they are not good at it and don't love it. Eventually, they end up doing their own thing and find out that they're gifted in an area that was not originally valued by their family. There are so many stories like that.

Also, sometimes we downplay areas of our life in which we are having a lot of success because someone close to us may not value it. That's a dangerous trap. We should embrace whatever we're good at.

213

After you complete the exercise in Chapter 1 and begin to get in sync with your calling, you will develop a greater emotional intelligence and a deepening spiritual intelligence, as well as a higher intellectual intelligence. As you execute those top few tasks well and enjoy them, your confidence will grow in a healthy way as you follow that calling. It's like canoeing down a river and catching an exciting ride—you're moving along at a good pace, having a great run.

Confidence Begins at an Early Age

I have read that by the time we reach age two, 50 percent of what we ever believed about ourselves has been formed. By the age of six, 60 percent has been formed; by age eight, 80 percent; and by age fourteen, our self-perception is 99 percent developed. It is easy to see why encouragement from parents is critical, especially during the early years. It follows what the Jesuits taught us following the unfortunate inquisition, "Give me the boy until he's seven; I'll give you back the man, and you won't change him."

Operation Head Start for children is effective.

While people often can't remember the memories of their early childhood, we do know they're the most vital.

We know that in the first six years of life, more neuronal, or nerve-based, connections are made in the brain than at any other time in our lives. And while people often can't remember the memories of their early childhood, we do know they're the most vital. The foundation for abstract concepts like trust and confidence is established in the brain in those first six years. Positive reinforcement from parents and others is vital during that time. I believe that the more parents can be home with a child when he or she is a toddler, the more confident the child will become.

Focus on the Small Technical Aspects of Your Performance

Confidence is the by-product of positive experiences. To grow your confidence, you need building materials, which are the specific, positive aspects of any performance—not the final outcome. No matter what our endeavor in life is, it is important for us to mentally reflect, analyze, process, break down, and study any positive aspect of what we've done. It's very common for high performers to focus on the negative aspects of their performance, but that does not grow confidence.

As a sophomore in high school, I wrestled a state champion in an important match as an uncontested sophomore. I got in deep on my opponent's leg and drove him out of bounds. The crowd cheered, thinking I was going to give him a run for his money. But about a minute later, he pinned me, and the match was over. I was devastated. But later that evening, my coach said to me, "Jarrod, if you can get in that deep on a state champion's leg, then you can get in that deep on everybody else you wrestle for the rest of the year." He took the negative experience of losing and gave me the confidence to know that at least I could shoot for a take-down and get in on anybody, which enabled me to be an even better wrestler who was skilled at taking opponents down.

There is always a positive aspect of your performance that you can focus on.

I received a picture from an Olympian from Canada, Matt Gentry, whom I've served. In the photo, he's holding a beautiful medal and wearing a Mind of the Athlete bracelet that says "Clearer mind, better performance."™ *In a tournament just prior to the Olympics, he had just defeated the defending Olympic champion, so he was feeling confident. In helping him before the Olympics in London, I continued to remind him that as his confidence grew, it was important to keep his mind focused on the small technical aspects of his performance that got him to where he was.*

It happens all the time in football. Every year in college football, there's a number-one team that gets beaten. We put the team that beats the number-one team on a pedestal, but then that team becomes vulnerable and often gets beaten in the next game. Part of it is that the players get overconfident. They focus on the outcome instead of on the things they did to beat the stronger team.

There is a story that I love because it demonstrates the importance of finding something positive about your performance, regardless of the outcome. A little boy named Pete is a T-ball player. Practicing one day, he throws the ball into the air, tries to hit it, and misses. He throws the ball into the air a second time and again misses. He throws the ball up a third time and misses once again. He puts the ball down, wipes his brow, and says, "Boy, what a pitcher!"

That is the epitome of confidence.

Kenny Rogers's "Baseball Song" tells that story. At the end of the song, the boy says, "I am the greatest, that is a fact, but even I didn't know I could pitch like that."

Recognize Your Uniqueness

Finding the tasks you enjoy the most, the goal of Chapter 1, will help you discover who you are. Your life calling is unique to you. The more you try to be like someone else instead of being the unique person God created you to be, the more you are destined to be number two or worse. If you try to be someone else, that other person is the original, and you're a copy. The quest is to find out who you are and to be uniquely you.

Holocaust survivor and psychiatrist Victor Frankl said, "Everyone has their own specific vocation or mission in life.... Therein, we cannot be replaced, nor our lives repeated. Thus, everyone's task is as unique as their specific opportunity to implement it."

We humans have a tendency to compare ourselves to others instead of recognizing that each one of us is God's unique creation. Society tends to encourage competition in many ways, and that fuels our propensity to compare ourselves to others. But each one of us is a masterwork, an original, a Rembrandt. There's only one. It doesn't matter if you can't run as fast as someone else or if you are not as good-looking. Those are irrelevant issues if we focus on being ourselves and on using our God-given talents to be the best we can be. Confidence emerges from the recognition of our singularity and the fact that no matter what disabilities we may have, we are still original creations by God, a God who doesn't make mistakes.

The popular singer John Denver once gave a commencement speech at his former high school and offered this encouragement to the graduating seniors: "The best thing you have to offer the world is yourself. You don't have to copy anyone else. If you do, you're second best."

Geneticists have discovered that the possibility of there ever being anyone like you is ten to the two-billionth power. Those are the odds of your parents having another child like you, but not an identical twin. The combination of characteristics that constitutes each one of us will never be duplicated, but you will never achieve above the value you attribute to yourself. Embrace your own identity and make the most of the talents God gave you.

The Crab Barrel

The confidence you have in yourself is, in good part, a result of the people you have in your life. If you spend time with people who belittle you, that will not result in a high level of self-confidence. It's critical that you choose the people you spend time with carefully. Choose to be around people who reinforce you and build you up, people who don't tear you down. Even when we're not succeeding, we need people who continue to encourage us and lead us on the road to confidence in ourselves.

The easiest way to destroy another person's confidence is to sprinkle a little doubt over them.

As a youngster, I'd pass a Polish delicatessen on 11th Street between Avenue A and Avenue B in Manhattan, inhaling the garlic odors emanating from the pickle barrel in the store. Beside the pickle barrel was a second barrel containing live crabs. However, only one of the barrels had a lid on it, and it wasn't the crab barrel. The pickle barrel had a lid to keep the garlic odors inside to flavor the pickles. The crab barrel didn't need a lid because as crabs neared the lip of the barrel to try to escape, the other crabs would pull them back in. It didn't escape me that some people are a lot like those crabs, and they're the ones to avoid.

Today, the term "crab mentality" is used to describe a mindset of "If I can't have it, neither can you." The metaphor refers to a container full of crabs like the one I saw in Manhattan. Individually, they could escape easily, but instead, they grab at each other in a useless competition that prevents any of them from escaping and leads to their collective demise. Often, members of a group, whether in business or athletics, have a crab mentality. They try to keep others from succeeding because of their own feelings of envy, conspiracy, or competition.

Similarly, in wrestling, there is a move called the "crab ride." A wrestler uses this move to keep his opponent down on the mat and prevent him from escaping. Getting out of a good crab ride requires patience, leverage, and quickness. Sometimes people attempt to sabotage other people's success without realizing it; other times, it is intentional. To build others' confidence requires that we avoid the crab mentality.

Confidence is fragile. The easiest way to destroy another person's confidence is to sprinkle a little doubt over them. It can show up in a lot of different ways. For example, if you say to your spouse, "Are you going to wear that?" or if you say to a colleague as you enter a meeting, "Are you really prepared for this?" those questions are going to make them doubt themselves and erode their confidence. Planting that kind of doubt in someone's mind can be really crushing. You can tear a person down or build a person up in one moment. Our goal should be to build one another up and to remove others' self-doubt.

I like the saying "Confidence is what's left when doubt is removed."

Use Visualization to Increase Confidence

I developed a CD called "Visualization for Relaxation and Positive Thinking." It's one of the most popular sports psychology techniques I use with athletes. The CD contains guided imagery set to music. In the CD, I ask you to imagine yourself in the most beautiful place in the entire world that you can think of, and then we do a life review. I ask you to think about how far you have come from your humble beginnings and to think about obstacles in your life that you have overcome. Then I ask you to think about all the positive aspects of your life—all the people who have helped you, all the places you've been, all the gifts you have—as well as your hopes and dreams and how blessed you are.

The purpose of this exercise is to relax you deeply and increase your confidence. (For a free copy of this recording, simply request it via the Mind of the Athlete contact page at www.mindoftheathlete.com/contact. Enter your e-mail address and a note requesting the CD. We will send it to you electronically via an attachment.)

Thinking about how far you have come is tremendous fuel that many athletes thrive on.

Visualization is a topic I am extremely interested in—in fact, I wrote my master's thesis on it after someone introduced me to it. I have spent a lot of time researching this powerful technique, and I have seen it increase people's confidence dramatically. You can do your own guided imagery and sit quietly while listening to soft music. I think it will be a gift for you.

Think of confidence as fuel. You can use confidence to fuel your success when you're tired, overextended, or drained. Thinking about how far you have come is tremendous fuel that many athletes thrive on. When I work with athletes at a camp, I will have them do this visualization exercise to help increase their confidence. Sports camps are draining and tiring, and this is a great source of fuel for them because it makes them think back on their success and recognize how hard they're working. The key is to translate your confidence into fuel.

Follow the Energy

In Chapter 3, we talked about how important it is to follow the energy. Knowing what energizes you and following that path can boost your confidence. The people you enjoy being with, the things you enjoy doing, the places you enjoy going—what energizes you today? Those aspects of your life are important because they are in sync with your natural giftedness. If you are following the energy, it is a sign that you're following the right path, which, in turn, will increase your confidence.

Save Greeting Cards People Send You

A technique that boosts my confidence is to save greeting cards that people, especially my wife and children, have given or sent to me. I display those cards on my desk at work or on my dresser at home. I'll often go back and reread them; they're touching and encouraging. Save the cards and positive letters you receive and look back at them. Leave them on your desk for a month or two, then slip them between pages of books that you consult, and let them remind you how much others care about you and respect you. It will build your confidence.

Videotape Your Performances

In the sports world, I often tell the athletes I work with, "Don't wait until the end of the season to make a highlight video of yourself. Make it now. Then you can watch it and realize that you are better in your sport than you thought you were. You'll realize you may have been too hard on yourself previously. Review your performances." This is important because to increase confidence, you need to keep in your mind the images of what you're doing well. Video is an ideal medium for seeing ourselves.

I know of some teams that will create highlight videos of every single game. The coach will show them to the team to let them see what they do well and what the coach wants to see more of. It dramatically increases the players' confidence.

Even at home, video imagery can remind us of the beauty in our lives and how fortunate we are. Often at Christmas time, I'll go through all of our pictures from the year, put together a montage of photos that is set to music, and give it to my wife as a gift. It's something she really cherishes.

Adopt a Quiet Confidence

Some people can be confident to the point of being arrogant. I think our society prefers quiet confidence as opposed to someone who comes across as cocky. Most of us admire people like Abe Lincoln and legendary coach Tony Dungy—people who get things done with a quiet confidence.

Confidence is a continuum. It is somewhat paradoxical in that the individuals who seem to have the healthiest confidence exhibit a great deal of humility—their quiet confidence is at one end of the spectrum; at the other end is a more boastful confidence, or even arrogance.

I believe that, in many cases, that arrogant type of confidence is grounded in insecurity. Many people are, by society's standards, quite successful, but you can tell that they are deeply insecure. They seem confident, but we can sense a narcissism that is built on a weak foundation. Some people have had tremendous success just because they're ridiculously driven with a singular focus, but that's different from following your calling, which tends to produce a demeanor that's much more grounded, charitable, and giving. People who have a quiet confidence seem to have an abundance mentality. They're eager to give, share, and help because they know that the source of their confidence is based on divinity, not on their striving.

People who have a quiet confidence seem to have an abundance mentality.

A Quiet Confidence Comes from the Lord

Having faith in God will produce a quiet confidence. Jeremiah 17:7 says, "But blessed is the one who trusts in the Lord, whose confidence is in him." Isaiah 32:17 says, "The fruit of that righteousness will be peace; its effect will be quietness and confidence forever."

In my opinion, Jesus Christ was the most confident individual who ever lived, and He had a quiet confidence. His faith was complete. His belief in his Father and His destiny gave Him the confidence to say, for example, "Get behind me, Satan." There was no doubt in His words when He said it.

Your relationship with the Lord is the greatest source of confidence you can find. Whatever is in second place is so far back, it borders on being irrelevant.

It's Your Turn

Exercise 18-1: The technical aspects of your performance

In your career or on your team, what are some positive aspects of your performance in the past few months? List anything you can think of.

1. _____   5. _____
2. _____   6. _____
3. _____   7. _____
4. _____   8. _____

Exercise 18-2: What energizes you?

List the people you enjoy being with, the things you enjoy doing, the places you enjoy going—they are what energizes you today. Those aspects of your life are important because they are in sync with your natural giftedness. If you are following the energy, it is a sign that you're following the right path, which, in turn, will increase your confidence.

1. _____   4. _____
2. _____   5. _____
3. _____   6. _____

Exercise 18-3: The crab barrel

Remember the crab barrel. If someone is pulling you down just as you are about to succeed, what will you do about it? When? Is there anyone in your circle who denigrates you regularly? If they are in your inner circle, should they remain there?

_____
_____
_____
_____
_____
_____

Chapter

19

Build Relationships Based on Trust

Coming together is the beginning. Keeping together is progress. Working together is success.

Henry Ford
Industrialist and Founder of Ford Motor Company

Surrounding yourself with people who want you to succeed is critical to your ability to thrive in the vocation you have identified as your true north. We seldom accomplish anything alone. In business, sports, and life in general, we work together with others to achieve our goals. Some people play an indirect role in our success, whether it's through support or encouragement, while others play a more direct role in helping us develop our talents in the areas in which we excel.

Knowing how to build strong, lasting relationships helps you thrive on a team, and being a team player is a characteristic that is valued in the business world, the sports world, and society.

Start with Shared Values

There is a hard way to build a team, and there is an easy way. An easy way is to build a team composed of people who share similar values. So often, I see that teams are ineffectual because the values of some team members differ from the values of other team members. It's a lot easier getting to "yes" when everyone on a team shares similar values.

Your values should never change. Your strategies, techniques, and even your mission can change. But your values never do. As mentioned earlier, our values at North Star Resource Group form the acronym FIGGS—faith, integrity, growth, gratitude, and service. If all of the people on a team share those values, getting to yes is easy. In addition to our fidelity to hiring recent college grads who will be molded easily into our values and culture, we focus on gratitude.

Recently, a consultant we hired asked me, "How do you look for people who fit into your culture and exhibit faith, integrity, growth, gratitude, and service?"

I told him what I first mentioned in Chapter 3 of this book: We try to detect gratitude. When I take somebody to lunch or dinner, I observe closely how he or she treats the waiter or waitress. That tells me just about everything I need to know about their gratitude. If a person is rude, that tells me one thing. If they're complimentary or kind throughout the entire meal, that tells me something, too. You may fool me in a half-hour interview. But during a meal that lasts an hour and a half, I'm going to be watching how you're treating other people.

The Value of Relationship-Building Skills

According to the Report of the New Commission of the Skills of the American Workforce, employers now value applied skills such as collaboration, teamwork, and relationship building more than they do basic knowledge and skills such as reading comprehension and mathematics. The Information Age has made it more important than ever for students to develop those skills. A deficiency in relationship-building, teamwork, and conflict-resolution skills is apparent in many arenas. It costs businesses immeasurably in terms of market position, the inability to respond to changing customer needs, failure to identify new market opportunities, a lack of focus in training or cross-functional decision making, increased time required for management's intervention on issues related to process and staff performance, poor responsiveness, and time inefficiencies.[92]

Being a team player is one of the most valuable skills you can have. It makes you pleasant to be around as well.

Your Inner Circle

It is important to seek out people you trust. I think relationships thrive and prosper when you have an environment of trust that underlies those relationships.

---

92. Yihancheng, "DU Sport Psych," the official blog of the Sport & Performance graduate psychology program, University of Denver, "Relationship: The Reflection of Relationship Building," accessed on December 1, 2013, http://dusportpsych.wordpress.com/2011/09/26/relationship-the-reflection-of-relationship-building/.

In the insurance and financial-services industry, getting referrals helps advisors build their businesses, and trust is implied when a referral is made. If one of your clients refers you to a colleague who needs your services, in a professional capacity, that new client is going to trust you even before he or she meets you because of the degree of trust the original client has in you. The new client will be operating from an assumption that you are trustworthy because of the referral. The trust from the third party then becomes yours to lose. In other words, that new client is going to trust you until you show that you're not trustworthy. I think a relationship based on trust clearly has greater sustainability than one that is not based on trust.

> ## A relationship based on trust clearly has greater sustainability than one that is not based on trust.

Bernard Madoff built his Ponzi scheme on referrals and trust. Stealing upwards of $60 billion over decades is proof of the trust inherent in the referral process. However, Madoff proved not to be trustworthy, in spite of the fact that he was trusted by those who were unfortunately fleeced.

It's important to identify whom you trust. Who is on your personal Board of Directors? Whom do you open up to, and with whom do you share your dreams and desires? Write down on a piece of paper your key advisors, the people whose counsel you accept when it comes to money, health, your car, family issues, spirituality, etc. After you identify these people who are in your inner circle, nurture your relationships with them because those are the relationships that matter the most.

It is those people from whom you should seek wisdom. Today, we have a plethora of information available from the Internet, but it's only information; it's not wisdom. The people in your inner circle have your best interest at heart and can help guide you with wisdom as you discover your true north.

A Story about Building Relationships and Influence

These are some of the things we can do to build strong relationships based on trust:

- Maintain a positive attitude.
- Use uplifting language to build others up.

- Share.
- Give others credit.
- Use other people's names frequently.
- Communicate effectively and listen.
- Be willing to disagree without being disagreeable.
- Support others.
- Resolve differences amicably.
- Abide by the Golden Rule.
- Be yourself.
- Be trustworthy.

I have a story from the insurance and financial-services industry that shows how important these characteristics are in building relationships—and in influencing others. AXA Financial wouldn't release the speech, but my colleagues at AXA have told me that this is, in fact, what happened.

About fifteen years ago, Equitable of New York was one of the premiere life-insurance companies in this country, well over one hundred years old and one of the top three or four companies in America. They experienced some financial difficulties and were bought out by AXA of France. All policyholders were unaffected and were treated fairly. The Equitable of New York advisors across the country were fanatically loyal to Equitable and, in fact, still are today. When the company changed hands, many agents and leaders across America were concerned that their company's name would be changed to AXA.

After AXA bought Equitable, they demutualized the company, turned it into a stock company, and made it possible for the Equitable agents and managers to acquire stock under favorable conditions—either through stock options or reduced pricing. It was a tremendous financial success and continues to be successful to this day. But still, at the time, the field people did not want their company's name changed from Equitable of New York to AXA.

An AXA vice president called in hundreds of field people from around the country who were with Equitable of New York and gave what I consider to be the second-best sales presentation I've ever heard—the first one being Mark Antony's often-quoted Act III speech in Shakespeare's *Julius Caesar*, the famous funeral oration that begins "Friends, Romans, and countrymen, lend me your ears." In that speech, Antony persuades the people of Rome to follow him instead of Brutus, the leader of the conspirators who killed Caesar. Mark Antony addressed a hostile crowd who believed in Brutus and turned them 180 degrees with his talk. It is my opinion that this AXA presentation is number two only to that sale of Mark Antony's.

Essentially, the AXA vice president said something like this: "I know all of you have great concern about changing our name. That's not a problem. We're not hardened to the fact that it has to be called AXA. With the unfavorable press that Equitable has received because of the financial challenges, surely you agree that keeping the name Equitable will make all of your jobs more difficult. We can get a committee together and hire some outstanding consulting firms to come up with a new name, even though that would take years and could cost millions of dollars, which we're willing to spend. Of course, it's going to be your money, too, because all of you will be stockholders in the new company. It will require a name change, but we'll have to come up with a name that is satisfactory to all of you. On the other hand, if you want to save that money, you might want to consider what the advantages are in terms of using the name AXA. It is an internationally recognized name. You can go to almost any country in the world, and they know who and what AXA is and how financially strong it is. It's a well-regarded, well-respected, well-rated company that would add validity to your sales presentations and to the willingness of the American public to buy your products. What's interesting about the name is that it's spelled the same backward and forward, so it's easy to remember. It's your call. We're not going to do anything to upset you. You are instrumental and vital to the success of this venture. Please think about it and get back to me."

> He established trust among his charges.
> That's how he was able to get to
> "yes" so quickly.

After that presentation, the agents and leaders overwhelmingly agreed with the name AXA. Today it is called AXA Equitable. But for fifteen years or so, the name was AXA alone. Today it is a company led by many of the finest leaders in our industry, including Bucky Wright, Luis Chiappy, Mark Rooney, and Chris Noonan.

That vice president had all the characteristics of an effective team player. He was brilliant, agreeable, respectful, and willing to resolve differences. And he established trust among his charges. That's how he was able to get to "yes" so quickly.

Emotional Connectedness

Relationships are largely built on some type of emotional connectedness, and that's something that many people lack in this technologically driven world. A lot of young people have many Facebook friends but few friends with whom they have a deep emotional connectedness. Connectedness is something we need to cultivate because it matters in building relationships.

The most important factor in therapeutic success is the relationship between the counselor and the patient or client.

According to research, the most important factor in therapeutic success is the relationship between the counselor and the patient or client. It doesn't matter what the counselor is wearing, and it doesn't matter whether she is in a beautiful, well-appointed office or in a small, ordinary office with no windows. It's the relationship that matters the most. That critical relationship based on trust, the level of emotional connectedness, can determine whether or not the subject is able to improve and heal his or her emotional wounds.

Wine expert Gary Vaynerchuk grew up in a family that owned a liquor store. From a young age, he started reading The Wine Spectator *and wine books. With a wealth of knowledge and an entrepreneurial spirit, Vaynerchuk spent every weekend of his college years at his parents' wine store. In 1997, he launched www.winelibrary.com and helped grow his family business from $3 million to $45 million by 2005.*

In 2006, he launched Wine Library TV, which revolutionized the wine world. His wine reviews soon attracted more than one hundred thousand viewers each day, and his die-hard fans nicknamed themselves "Vayniacs." On Vaynerchuk's website are videos in which he talks about how those who have the most success are the ones who have deep personal relationships.[93]

In a 2011 article, he said, "I always say that our success wasn't due to my hundreds of online videos about wine that went viral, but to the hours I spent talking to people online afterward, making connections and building relationships. I could have talked

---

93. Gary Vaynerchuk's website, accessed on December 1, 2013, http://video.garyvaynerchuk.com /keynotes.

to a million people a day about wine, but if I or my employees had come off as phonies or schmoozers, my company would not be what it is today."[94]

Relationship before Opportunity

Jeremie Kubicek wrote the book Leadership Is Dead: How Influence Is Revising It. *In the book, he shares one of his favorite philosophies, which is "relationship before opportunity."*[95] *I think that's a great way to move through life and business because putting relationships first cultivates emotional connectedness. He says, "Focus on others first, and strong relationships will follow."*[96] *So you should pursue the opportunities that come from your relationships, but don't establish relationships simply for the sake of profiting from them.*

Perhaps the best example I've ever seen of building relationships while following one's calling was my grandfather, Art Tron. He operated a restaurant on the main street in Phillipsburg, New Jersey, in the 1970s and '80s, and it was called Tron's Villa Marie. It was a small restaurant but had great success in an era when the Italian culture was a big part of that community. He also built tremendous relationships. He lived in humble conditions above the restaurant, so for him it wasn't about money or success. But when he died, hundreds of people attended his funeral, and there was an article about it on the front page of the local Express-Times *newspaper. He really modeled to me the value of quality relationships; he put relationship before opportunity.*

Relationship Building in Sports

In the sports world, what I observe about athletic success is that the teams that have the healthiest emotional connection with each other tend to have the most wins. There's no better example of this than the NCAA basketball tournament. You may be on a great basketball team, but by the end of the year, if you can't stand the other guys on the team, you're not going to do well in the tournament. Many teams that do really well at the end of the year do so because the guys actually like each other. They have good relationships. Now, where did that come from? I think one key variable is that their coach intentionally encouraged and developed those relationships. Some teams do team-building exercises outside of their sport so that they can get to know each other on a more personal

---

94. Gary Vaynerchuk, "Building a Business in the 'Thank You Economy,'" last modified March 15, 2011, accessed December 1, 2013, http://www.entrepreneur.com/article/219296.

95. Jeremie Kubicek, *Leadership Is Dead: How Influence Is Reviving It* (New York: Howard Books, 2011), 141.

96. Ibid., 143.

level. When that occurs, and people build a deep emotional connection with one another, it's amazing how it translates into success.

Basketball great Michael Jordan described how critical teamwork is in his 1994 book I Can't Accept Not Trying. *He wrote, "There are plenty of teams in every sport that have great players and never win titles. Most of the time, those players aren't willing to sacrifice for the greater good of the team. The funny thing is, in the end, their unwillingness to sacrifice only makes individual goals more difficult to achieve. One thing I believe to the fullest is that if you think and achieve as a team, the individual accolades will take care of themselves. Talent wins games, but teamwork and intelligence win championships."*[97]

The teams that have the healthiest emotional connection with each other tend to have the most wins.

In the 2012 NCAA basketball tournament, Lehigh University upset Duke University. Lehigh's coach, Brett Reed, is a fantastic guy and a good friend of mine. Both before and after that game, he talked about how important it is for his team members to trust one another. He models that by encouraging meaningful relationships among his players.

The Lehigh wrestling coach, Pat Santoro, who has one of the top teams in the nation, also does a great job of developing relationships among his athletes. Pat places great emphasis on trust and loyalty. People appreciate it and respect him for that. So two of Lehigh's top programs have coaches who have great success, and that I really admire. In large part, their success is the result of strong relationship building.

I think each coach recruits to his or her individual value system. They seek out excellent athletes who fit the culture of the program they're creating. As an example, consider John Wooden, who won ten NCAA national championships in a twelve-year period—seven in a row—as head coach at UCLA, an unprecedented accomplishment. Within that period, his teams won a record eighty-eight consecutive games.

Wooden believed in sticking to his standards. He had a rule that he articulated often to his players—they had to have short hair and no facial hair. One day Bill Walton, one of the greatest college players in history, showed up in Wooden's

---

97. Michael Jordan, Mark Vancil, and Sandro Miller, *I Can't Accept Not Trying: Michael Jordan on the Pursuit of Excellence* (San Francisco: Harper, 1994).

office with long hair and a beard. Walton had been named National Player of the Year as a sophomore and thought that would give him some leverage with his coach.

Wooden said to Walton, "Your hair's too long, and you have a beard. That's against the rules. You can't play with hair like that."

Walton replied, "You can't make me cut my hair, Coach."

"No, Bill, I can't. Is long hair important to you?"

"Yes, Coach. It is."

"Well, that's good," Wooden said. "I admire a man who sticks up for his principles."

"Thanks, Coach."

"We're going to miss you, Bill."

Walton cut his hair, shaved his beard, and went on to win two more Player of the Year awards and one more championship playing for Wooden at UCLA.[98]

Wooden recruited to his own value system and ensured that no one wavered from those values.

Stepping into Roles

In our families, we all take on roles growing up. The first-born might be an overachiever, and the second-born might be a bit of a rules follower. Another child might become the one who accommodates everyone else's needs. Other roles include the comedian and the black sheep. Where we have teams—and a family is one type of team—inevitably we look to see who is taking which role, and then we step into a role that's available. The role we step into, however, may not be our natural, innate calling. It might not be our highest level of giftedness. It just means that that's the role that was available, or we opted for it.

---

98. Wally Bock's Three-Star Leadership Blog, "In Memoriam, John Wooden," accessed on December 1, 2013, http://blog.threestarleadership.com/2010/06/06/in-memoriam-john-wooden.aspx.

Often athletes who are in their junior or senior year will come into their own because they are finally able to step into the role that is most in sync with their innate giftedness. Maybe they become the team leader because the former team leader has now graduated and moved on. Or maybe they become the caregiver because the caregiver has left. Sometimes we have to go through a maturation process on teams before we are able to step into the role that's most in sync with our giftedness. Once we're in that spot, we tend to thrive, our relationships grow and develop even more, and we begin to achieve greater success.

Stepping into roles is largely a subconscious process. When I work with athletes, I try to make them aware of it, and once they realize it's happening, they get it. It happens in business, too. Every new employee of a company steps into a role, perhaps without realizing it. Being aware of this phenomenon can help you step into the role that makes the best use of your talents and abilities. Look around. See who is fulfilling which role, and be mindful of stepping into the role that will best help you develop your giftedness, follow your calling, and find your sweet spot, despite what other people are doing. When you do so, other people will see that you are being true to yourself and that you fit the role well.

Treasure Your Relationships

I often think of the saying, "People come into your life for a reason, for a season, or for a lifetime." Often, it's apparent to us why someone has come into our lives, and it's easy to see why we were meant to spend time together. But some people—maybe a childhood friend or a high-school buddy—are in our lives for only a season. Very few friends stay for a lifetime. We should really treasure those long-term relationships and recognize how special they are.

I believe that as we age, we have fewer opportunities to form deep relationships. Form relationships early in your life, and get to know as many worthy people as possible, as early as possible, because those opportunities are going to cross your path less frequently as you age. I've observed that the earlier people retire, the more they miss out on opportunities to form friendships because they are no longer in a work environment, which is often conducive to forming friendships.

Building relationships based on trust takes time and effort, but it's worth it in the end. Relationships at home, at work, and in sports enrich our lives and provide us with a constant source of companionship, support, and guidance as we discover the true north for our life's path.

It's Your Turn

Exercise 19-1: Your inner circle

Identify the people who are in your inner circle, those you trust the most. They are the people from whom you should seek wisdom and guidance as you find and fulfill your life's calling.

1. _____ 5. _____

2. _____ 6. _____

3. _____ 7. _____

4. _____ 8. _____

Exercise 19-2: The roles you play

We play distinct roles in the various team environments that make up a part of our lives, whether it's the caretaker, the overachiever, or the rules follower.

What role do you play in your family?

_____

_____

What role do you play on your team, if applicable?

_____

_____

What role do you play in your office, if applicable?

_____

_____

20

Passion Fosters Perseverance

*I do not think there is any other quality so essential to success
of any kind as the quality of perseverance. It overcomes
almost everything, even nature.*

John D. Rockefeller
American Tycoon, Businessman, Philanthropist, and
Cofounder of the Standard Oil Company

Perseverance is defined as steady persistence in a course of action, a purpose, a state, especially in spite of difficulties, obstacles, or discouragement. Interestingly, in theology, perseverance is defined as continuance in a state of grace to the end, leading to eternal salvation. So persevering all the way to the finish line brings great rewards.

In Chapter 10, we discussed the topic of overcoming obstacles. Perseverance is the quality that helps you overcome obstacles, make progress in life, and achieve your dreams. If you have discovered your true north, you will be passionate about your activity or vocation, and that passion will fuel your perseverance, even when the obstacles seem insurmountable and when detractors believe you will fail.

Finding the Love in What You Do

The book titled Way of the Peaceful Warrior: A Book That Changes Lives *is Dan Millman's story about himself—a world-champion college gymnast who sought wisdom from an old night gas-station attendant he called Socrates. The movie based on the book is titled* The Peaceful Warrior. *In one scene, Millman begins to cry. He has been injured in a car accident and has lost his career in gymnastics. Socrates says to him, "A warrior does not give up what he loves; he finds the love in what he does." Essentially, Socrates is telling his young friend to persevere.*

How can we persevere when the going gets tough? We search to find the love in what we're doing. I believe that if we can find the love in what we do, then we're in sync with our calling. If we can't find that love in what we're doing when the going is hard, then we may not truly be in sync with what we're destined to do. That is why the exercise in Chapter 1 is so critical to our success and happiness. If you can find what you're passionate about, what you want to spend the rest of your life doing, then you will be able to find the love in what you're doing.

What Perseverance Looks Like

Irwin W. Rosenberg

Junior officer Irwin W. Rosenberg was discharged from the navy when he was diagnosed with cancer. That was the standard military procedure at the time, but he was determined to get back both his health and his job. At one point, he was given only two weeks to live. But through faith and dogged determination, his cancer was eventually brought under control.

Rosenberg then focused his attention on becoming a naval officer again, but he discovered that navy regulations forbade reinstatement of a person discharged with cancer. Everyone around him said, "Give up. It can't be done. It would take an act of Congress to get you reinstated." Their advice gave him an idea—to pursue an act of Congress.

After years of waiting, petitioning, cutting through red tape, and battling bureaucracy, Irwin Rosenberg was allowed to reenlist in the navy because President Truman eventually signed a special bill into law. Rosenberg went on to become a rear admiral in the US Seventh Fleet.[99]

Dr. David Hartman

When David Hartman, a twenty-six-year-old Philadelphian, was handed his medical degree at Temple University in 1976, he became the first blind American ever to complete pre-med and medical studies. He was born in suburban Haverford, Pennsylvania, with malformed lenses that impaired his vision. At age eight, he developed glaucoma and detached retinas. After three operations, young Hartman learned that he would never see again.

---

99. Norman Vincent Peale, *You Can if You Think You Can* (New York: Fireside/Simon & Schuster, 1986), 117.

The obstacles to becoming a doctor looked insurmountable to everyone but David. His mother suggested less demanding careers, and he politely demurred. He was looking for the toughest challenge he could find. He plunged into pre-med at Gettysburg College. Nine medical schools turned him down before Temple University decided to give him a chance. From the first semester on, Hartman stayed in the top fifth of his class. His success required a massive collaboration of effort, not only from classmates and professors but from volunteers who taped seven hundred hours of medical textbooks and exams.

When David Hartman, a twenty-six-year-old Philadelphian, was handed his medical degree at Temple University in 1976, he became the first blind American ever to complete pre-med and medical studies.

Hartman went on to complete a one-year internship at Temple University Hospital, followed by three years of residency at the University of Pennsylvania hospital and two more at Temple. He now specializes in psychiatry and rehabilitative medicine.[100] As a member of the Board of Trustees at Temple, not only am I proud to tell Dr. Hartman's story, but I can attest to the egalitarian culture of this incredible institution. This is one of many reasons why Temple University is one of the five nonprofits I have chosen as beneficiaries of my profits from this book. The institution was started by another persistent American, Russell Conwell, a Baptist minister who served as a colonel in the Civil War. His legacy lives on in everyone who attends Temple, and he no doubt is looking down from heaven with a smile on his face, knowing that thousands of the less fortunate attend this institution every year.

Johnny Unitas

Another great example of persistence is Johnny Unitas, who was considered too small to play football for Notre Dame. The Pittsburgh Steelers cut him from their team. So Unitas sent a two-penny postcard to Weeb Ewbank, coach of the Baltimore Colts, and pleaded for a chance. Ewbank gave him a tryout and hired him, and that year they won the world football championship. Unitas was later

---

100. Lenora Berson, "'Everyone Is Handicapped in Some Way,' Says David Hartman, Phi Beta, Husband, Doctor—And Blind," *People* Blog, last updated October 11, 1976, accessed on December 1, 2013, http://www.people.com/people/archive/article/0,,20066974,00.html.

inducted into the NFL Hall of Fame. His record of throwing a touchdown pass in forty-seven consecutive games (between 1956 and 1960) remains unsurpassed. Not bad for someone considered too short. Persistence truly was one of his gifts. Ignoring detractors had to be another one.

He absolutely wouldn't give up on himself when the whole world seemed to. Nobody knew he existed. He continued to work out when nobody wanted him after college and ended up leading the Colts to the world championship in football. A primary lesson from that story is this: Don't use other people's opinions to come to conclusions about yourself. Your inner strength, perseverance, and will to win should supersede the opinions of other people.

Larry Holmes

Larry Holmes is the former heavyweight boxing champion of the world; he held the title longer than any heavyweight fighter in history. Larry grew up in the low-income housing projects of Easton, Pennsylvania. After dropping out of school in the seventh grade, he began working as a delivery person and an occasional sparring partner for Cassius Clay (now Muhammad Ali). Larry once told me that he would train for his fights by running four miles down the canal trail in Easton. While he knew it was very hard for him to run the four miles back home, he would do so by pushing himself to the brink. He'd begin breaking down. As tears rolled down his face, he would pray to God and thank Him for giving him two healthy legs to run on and for the chance to box. He persevered through each run. Larry believed that those moments helped him persevere in his championship fights, too.

Larry Holmes once worked in a clothing factory as a sixteen-year-old "bundle boy," carrying piles of men's pants from one workstation to another. Another employee of Friedman's Pants factory was my mother, Sara Lipari Richards. Years later, my mom and I happened to be in the Alpha Building in Easton, closing on her house, when my mother suddenly called out, "Larry, Larry, come here! I want you to meet my son." Larry Holmes approached us, saying "Hi, Mrs. Richards."

After the encounter, I thought, *What a remarkable man.* Larry Holmes, the reigning world heavyweight boxing champion, still politely addressing my working mom as "Mrs. Richards," while she fondly called him "Larry." What a class act this champion is.

Sharon Woods

Sharon Woods is the first woman from North America to ever get to the top of Mount Everest. She said, "It is not the mountain that we have to conquer, nor the elements, but rather those self-imposed barriers, those limitations in our minds." To persevere to the top of the world, we must break through our barriers like Sharon did.

> "It is not the mountain that we have to conquer, nor the elements, but rather those self-imposed barriers, those limitations in our minds."

Ben Feldman

Another remarkable account is of Ben Feldman, a salesman for The New York Life Insurance Company, who many refer to as the greatest salesman of all time, having led that company's sales for many years. Ben was an introvert. On paper he probably would not have been hired by most firms, yet he overcame through perseverance.

On a few occasions, the Million Dollar Round Table asked him to address its worldwide convention of many thousand salespeople, an incredible honor. His fear of speaking and of large groups did not prevent him from giving back to his industry; he simply gave his presentations from behind the curtain, out of view of the audience. He was later rewarded by being named the recipient of The John Newton Russell Memorial Award, the highest honor that can be bestowed upon an individual in the life insurance and financial planning industry. Later he was joined in that same elite group by his son, Marvin H. (Marv) Feldman, the current CEO of The Life and Health Insurance Foundation for Education (LIFE). This is a wonderful example of persistence being punctuated by a remarkable legacy.

Bill Kelly

As a senior in high school, I served as the captain of my wrestling team. We had a sophomore on the team named Bill Kelly. We were the 138- and 133-pound division wrestlers, respectively. After being undefeated through our first twelve bouts together, we traveled to Pottstown, Pennsylvania, to wrestle Hill Preparatory School, which had won the national championship for three years in a row. The two wrestlers we were going to oppose were both national prep-school champions. All four of us had 12–0 records on that day.

The 133-pounder for Hill Preparatory was a senior named Hiram Mercereau. Mercereau, who had been a three-time national prep-school champion and who had never been beaten in high school, found himself wrestling against Bill Kelly, an inexperienced sophomore from Easton High School. At the end of the second period (out of three), Mercereau was handily beating Kelley 6–2 when he broke Kelly's arm. On examination, it was obvious that the little bone on Kelly's left elbow was in there just floating around.

Our wrestling coach, John Maitland, was also our high school biology teacher, and when he discovered the broken bone, he took a towel, tied it into a knot, and threw it up into the air—the universal sign of submission. Kelly jumped up, and with his good arm, grabbed the towel before it hit the mat, handed it back to Maitland, and said, "Coach, I'm going to beat this guy." As team captain, I stood in the midst of these two not believing what I was hearing.

Maitland said, "Bill, you have a broken arm."

Kelly was persistent. "Coach, I'm going to beat him."

"Bill, you couldn't beat him with two good arms on your best day," the coach replied, "and you have a broken arm."

Kelly repeated, "Coach, I'm going to beat him."

And he did! He went out there with a broken arm and beat a three-time national prep-school champion 7–6 in the third period. That was Mercereau's only loss in his entire four-year career—to a sophomore with a broken arm.

I wouldn't tell you that story if I didn't have the newspaper article to prove it. It was incredible. If Bill had wrestled Mercereau a thousand times, he probably would have lost, all but on that day, which was the one day that he had a goal.[101] Not only was it one of the greatest acts of determination and persistence I have seen to this very day, but it changed my life. I knew, without a doubt, that anything in this world is possible if only you believe in yourself.

Sustained Perseverance

Sometimes we think of perseverance as being the quality that helps us overcome great odds to finish a monumental task or race. But perseverance also can mean a sustained period of action that leads to success. I think of a man named Joe Anders, who lived

---

101. Phillip C. Richards, *Twenty-Five Secrets to Sustainable Success* (Falls Church, Virginia: GAMA International, 2007) 83–84.

across the street from me in Phillipsburg, New Jersey. He worked at the industrial company Ingersoll Rand. Every day for years, he would get up and go to work in the factory. He also worked as a carpenter, roofer, and window installer. He was always working. There had to have been times when he didn't want to go to work. But he demonstrated perseverance because he wanted to provide for his family. So many people persevere in this way on a daily basis, and I admire them greatly.

Perseverance also can mean a sustained period of action that leads to success.

In the classic movie *The Magnificent Seven*, there is a scene toward the end of the movie in which Charles Bronson's character is dressing down one of the young guns who wants to be a champion gunfighter. Bronson points at the Mexican farmers who use pitchforks instead of rifles to defend their farms and families. He tells the young man that the gunfighters are not the heroes; instead, the heroes are the farmers who work sixteen hours a day in the fields to feed their families. The heroes are not the hired gunfighters who are there for the dollars, but the farmers who are prepared to pay the ultimate price for their families.

So Close to Victory

Thomas Edison said, "Many of life's failures are people who did not realize how close they were to success when they gave up."

Recently I wrote an article for my company magazine and began by saying, "The job of a financial planner is the hardest $50,000 job in America; however, it's the easiest $250,000 job on earth." That means that if you can persevere in the career, then by the time you're earning that kind of money, you're on the golf course every day, if you want to be. What amazes me is when people are so close to victory and they throw in the towel. It's that extra little bit of effort at the end that makes all the difference in the world.

Yet, for some reason, people get to the edge of victory and don't cross the finish line. This happens more often than it should, in my experience.

I often see that in sports. Someone will have great talent and skills and be right on the brink of success. They could do something amazing, but they don't. Something is holding them back. Often it's because people simply reach a level of success they want. It's what they had in mind. It's their plateau, and they can't stand it any better because they haven't envisioned it. This is not a bad thing, per se. If someone reaches a certain level of contentment and is operating within their comfort zone, it is a wonderful thing if they truly are content. But if they think there's still more inside of them that the world hasn't seen, that could be cause for concern. That individual will need to find the strength within himself or herself to persevere and operate outside of their comfort zone.

Obstacles Can Be Fuel for Perseverance

Often, obstacles we've overcome during our life's journey become fuel for us to persevere. For example, someone who grew up in abject poverty may vow to overcome poverty and provide a good living for his family.

> Often, obstacles we've overcome
> during our life's journey become fuel for
> us to persevere.

I think it's important for us to identify three personal things that fuel our perseverance. What is it that drives us so hard? You'll find that, for nearly every person who is successful in a particular area, something drove them to succeed. Albert Einstein struggled as an academician but became perhaps the greatest mathematician of all time; his struggles in that area ended up fueling his success. As I've mentioned, I call this "turning your mess into your mission." A lot of inspiration can come from doing just that. As we have more and more success at turning our mess into a mission, we become excited because we realize we are succeeding, and possibly even influencing other people.

In 1905, the University of Bern in Switzerland rejected Einstein's dissertation, saying it was irrelevant and fanciful. He may have been disappointed, but he persevered.

"Willing" Success to Happen

John Maitland, my wrestling coach at Easton High School in Pennsylvania, used to talk about "willing" success to happen. Some athletes *will* something to happen without regard for the obstacles placed in their way. Often, they will put themselves into an illogical trance by convincing themselves of illogical conclusions. It's an intentional deception of one's mind. For example, an athlete may say to himself, "I am unbeatable." Well, that's not true, but the person who ends up unbeaten is the person who really did believe he was unbeatable, psyched himself up, and willed success to happen.

John Maitland is a quintessential example of the more than 350,000 high school coaches in America who routinely launch the careers and successes of thousands of our youngsters. They are truly some of the unsung heroes in our society and, for that reason, the National High School Coaches Association is one of my five passions in the not-for-profit arena.

Don't Let Giving Up Be an Option

Some people give up in life and never find ways to motivate themselves to persevere.

Benjamin Franklin said, "Most people die at twenty-five but aren't buried until they are seventy-five." When I was a speaker with the Collegiate Empowerment Company, we often used that quote when inspiring college students to follow their vision for their lives. We told them to clarify what their dreams are because many people give up on their hopes and dreams. They lose their passion, and they go through their lives just looking forward to retirement.

In 1966, I was reading an article in *The Wall Street Journal* and saw a full-page ad. The page was overwhelmingly blank, but in the middle of the page was a quill pen in a small inkwell. Beneath the inkwell, the text said, "How would you like to retire at age thirty-five?" This was followed by a short paragraph that said, "You can, you know. Millions of people do it every year. Oh, they go on working, but they've given up. They've retired." At the bottom of the ad, in very small print, it said "Marstellar and Co."

I called the phone number for Marstellar and Company, which turned out to be a public relations/advertising firm in New York, and spoke with Mr. Marstellar, who actually took the call himself. I asked him about the ad, and he said, "I get these thoughts now and then, and I just buy a page in *The Wall Street Journal* and hope that it affects somebody." He was right on the money; it sure affected me! There are people who give up at age thirty or thirty-five. Financially they can't stop working, so they stay in the workforce, and they don't retire, but they really have, mentally. The perseverance isn't there. They haven't found their passion. My hope is that this book finds them.

Some people get locked into their careers, and they feel they have too much at stake to leave and begin doing what they are really called to do. They're scared to find their passion. So they retire, mentally. They stay on the job and collect their checks, but they retire mentally. The truth is, no matter what—no matter how much you've invested in a career that is wrong for you—you always have choices. You may say, "I can't afford to quit my job," but you can. If you really want to, you can do it. You may think you're in prison, but you're not. If you can find your passion and then follow it, the probability is that perseverance will follow. Find what you love to do, and don't let giving up be an option. We should all substitute the word "rewire" for "retire."

> No matter how much you've invested in a career that is wrong for you—you always have choices.

Weathering the Doubt

Even for the most passionate person, along the journey there will be moments of weariness, doubt, negativity, or frustration. You just have to weather those emotions and persevere. One way to do that is to reach out and get an encouraging word from somebody who has done the same thing that you're trying to accomplish.

When I had only one year of coursework remaining to finish my doctorate, I experienced mental burnout and felt as though I didn't want to continue any further in my studies. I really felt like quitting. So I reached out to a mentor named Dr. Jack Emery, who was one person from my home town of Phillipsburg who I knew had a PhD. I said to him, "I'm at the end of my doctoral studies, but I'm struggling here. Might you give me some words of wisdom about how you got through your doctorate?" He sent me a couple of e-mails of encouragement, which I taped near my computer so that each time I didn't feel like studying, I would look at those e-mails and find the encouragement to persevere. Sometimes we will experience those feelings—a lack of perseverance. They are fleeting, and we just have to weather them. Getting encouragement from people who have done it really helps.

Athletes often experience waves of fatigue that come over them. I tell them that mental toughness is, in part, just being able to weather that wave of fatigue long enough to come out on the other side, get their second wind, and move forward again.

Pioneering American psychologist and philosopher William James had a quote about that: "If an unusual necessity forces us onward, a surprising thing occurs: The fatigue gets worse, up to a certain point, when gradually or suddenly it passes away, and we are fresher than before. We have evidently tapped a new level of energy. There may be layer after layer of this experience, a third and fourth wind. We find amounts of ease and power that we never dreamed ourselves to own, sources of strength habitually not taxed because habitually we never push through the obstruction of fatigue."

In Outliers, *Malcolm Gladwell talks about the role of perseverance in solving math problems. He wrote, "Success is a function of persistence and doggedness and a willingness to work hard for twenty-two minutes to make sense of something that most people would give up on after thirty seconds."[102] Whether it's in math or life, success gives you the motivation to keep trying, to keep going.*

Developing Positive Self-Talk

Positive self-talk can help us develop perseverance. We have to develop it before we get to that moment when we want to give up. One sports-psychology technique I often use with distance runners or cyclists is to recite poetry or repeat mantras, which are words or phrases we say to ourselves to bring about a desired emotional state. UCLA head basketball coach John Wooden was a big fan of this technique. Poems and mantras can help us improve our self-talk. One cyclist I knew recited the poem titled "Don't Quit." The poem says, "When things go wrong, as they sometimes will, when the road you're trudging seems all uphill, when the funds are low and the debts are high, and you want to smile, but you have to sigh, when care is pressing you down a bit, rest if you must, but don't you quit."

An extremely successful CEO I know has a mantra that he repeats to himself many times a day. He talks about himself in the third person, saying silently to himself: "He's tough as nails. I wouldn't want to compete with him." He says that to himself tens of times a day, and he has been doing it since he was a child. That's where his inspiration and competitiveness come from.

Self-talk really does make a difference.

---

102. Gladwell, 246.

Perseverance Is Not About IQ

Perseverance—never quitting on your dreams—can lead to success, and it's not all about intelligence. In fact, Bob Senkler, CEO and Chairman of Securian Financial, says that an IQ above 125 is unneeded. You need some degree of intelligence to succeed, but above a certain IQ level, there are as many unsuccessful people as there as there are successful ones. It's evident that there's something more to it than just IQ. Part of it is the adversity quotient—the ability to cope. Another part of it is probably the emotional quotient. I believe a big part of it is perseverance, and I think perseverance is correlated to desire, passion, and competitiveness.

> Intellect isn't as critical to giftedness
> as perseverance is.

Shawn Achor, whom we mentioned earlier, taught the most popular course at Harvard University titled "Science of Happiness." His decade-plus of research revealed that there is no correlation between happiness and one's grade-point average. The single most important contributor to one's happiness, based on research done in forty countries, is social cohesion—strong support groups. The takeaway is to find your passion, your calling, which contributes to contentment in what you do and makes you fun to be around. Social cohesion is the result. Never underestimating the importance of friends and family is simply good advice! Being a team player is a prescription for success.

A 2005 PsychologyToday.com article mentions an often-cited paper that found that intellect isn't as critical to giftedness as perseverance is. University of Connecticut psychologist Joseph Renzulli, Director of the National Research Center on the Gifted and Talented, reported that "task commitment"—characterized by perseverance, endurance, and hard work—is one of the three essential components of giftedness. The other two components are ability and creativity. Renzulli said that the evidence that these nonintellectual factors are critical to giftedness is "nothing short of overwhelming."[103]

The article also reported that "grit" is largely responsible for the success of a group of subjects in a University of Pennsylvania research study. Martin E. P. Seligman, director of the university's Positive Psychology Center, identified high achievers in various fields, interviewed them, and described the characteristics that distinguished them.

---

103. Peter Doskoch, "The Winning Edge," PsychologyToday.com, last reviewed July 20, 2012, accessed on December 1, 2013, http://www.psychologytoday.com/articles/200510/the-winning -edge.

He found that a large number of the successful people had tenacity, a characteristic he dubbed "grit," or the determination to accomplish an ambitious, long-term goal despite the inevitable obstacles. He found that people with grit are more likely to achieve success in school, work, and other pursuits—perhaps because their passion and commitment help them endure the inevitable setbacks that occur in any long-term undertaking.[104]

I think spiritual intelligence is related to success as well. As we delve into that deep spiritual realm, we can find greater resources for perseverance.

In the spiritual realm, we also can find a compulsion to use our talents wisely. The Bible clearly admonishes us to use our talents and assures us that we're going to be held accountable for not using them. In the Parable of the Talents (Matthew 25:14–28), three servants were given five talents, two talents, and one talent, respectively (in those days, a talent was a unit of money). The first two men used their talents and doubled what they had started out with. The third man buried his talent in the ground to keep it safe, but his master was displeased with him. He was called "wicked" and "lazy." God has given us each different talents and abilities that He expects us to put to good use. Often, that requires perseverance. It should always warrant gratitude.

The Hill You Will Die On

When first going into business, I looked for candidates who could persevere. When questioning a young college graduate, I would explain what type of candidate I was looking for. I wasn't looking for the guy who can walk into a barroom and knock somebody else out. I was looking for the guy who gets knocked down and gets up—time after time. It finally occurs to the guy who's knocking him out that unless he kills the one who keeps persevering, that guy is going to win because he's not going to give up. When you can find that person who gets knocked down and keeps getting up, you've got a great future team member in your company or on your team. You can find out a lot about a person by asking what kind of adversity he or she has overcome.

So the question is, what is it for each of us that would make us get up again? It's important to determine what would make you say, "I don't care how many times you knock me down; I'm going to get up. This is a fight I will not lose." What is it that you're willing to fight for? Alf Halverson, a friend of mine who is a pastor, often says, "What is the hill you are willing to die on?" Is this the hill you're willing to die on? If it is, then you have

---

104. Ibid.

found your source of perseverance. But if that is not the hill you're willing to die on, then sooner or later you're not going to get back up again.

We must ask ourselves what it is we're persevering for. When we ask and answer that question, we're in essence discovering the one thing or the few things that motivate us in life. It could be our family, our business, our career, or something else.

The person who has no desire to persevere simply has not found the right hill—he or she has not found their passion in life. That's the point of the exercise in Chapter 1—you must find your hill, your passion, your true north. If you can find that, then perseverance is a natural outflow. Success is the predictable outcome.

It's Your Turn

Exercise 20-1: What fuels your perseverance?

What drives you? For nearly every person who has success in a particular area, something drove him or her to succeed. Identify three things that fuel your perseverance:

1. _____

2. _____

3. _____

Exercise 20-2: For what or whom are you persevering?

It's important to determine what would make you say, "I don't care how many times you knock me down, I'm going to get up. This is a fight I will not lose." What is it that you are willing to fight for? For whom or for what are you all in?

1. _____

2. _____

3. _____

Chapter

21

Because the Clock Is Ticking

*So you, too, must keep watch! For you do not know
the day or hour of my return.*

Matthew 25:13

The concept of a ticking clock is quite prevalent in sports. It's a concept I use with athletes a lot, especially in their senior year of high school or college. Lafayette College's football team has a countdown clock in its locker room that counts down to their season's end-of-the-year rivalry game against Lehigh University, which is the longest-played rivalry in college football. It reminds the team members that the clock is ticking, and they must make every moment count.

The clock is ticking for each of us. Keeping that in mind can motivate us to spend our time wisely, doing the things we love to do.

None of us knows how much time we have left in life to discover and use our talents. The sooner we discover our true north, the sooner we can begin doing the things we love to do and living the life we have always dreamed of living. Our time here is indeed short, and it is our responsibility to find our talents and use them wisely. Voltaire said, "Every person is guilty of the good he didn't do."

As a director on boards for many charitable foundations, I often hear the staff members who work for those organizations talk about the three T's: time, talent, and treasure (sharing monetary or material gifts). That's one of the main things they're hoping for from board members. That's also what we should be contributing to our own endeavors and to those around us. Serving these not-for-profit organizations with passion is so much more challenging than being on the board of a for-profit organization. In the latter, fellow board members are serving for financial gain, whereas in charitable organizations, it's the passion that drives the work and even the emotional disagreements. The statement that we get far more from giving than from receiving is evident in so many of my colleagues serving on these not-for-profit boards.

Only God knows how much time each of us has left, so we have to live as though each day could be our last. Doing so develops in us an attitude of gratitude, which is the catalyst for productivity because it provides us with a positive fuel source. Gratefulness goes a long way toward getting us to do that which we love—or finding the love in that which we do.

One day, I am going to stand before the Lord. I imagine that He will hold me accountable to the question "What have you done with the gifts I've given you to expand My kingdom?" You might also believe you'll be in this situation. Maybe one of the gifts you've had in life is money. Maybe it's the ability to organize people. Maybe it's the ability to be an effective public speaker. If you squandered those gifts, you are guilty of the good you didn't do. So we've got to use those higher-level gifts for His greater good before the clock runs out.

> Only God knows how much time each of us has left, so we have to live as though each day could be our last.

You need to find out who you are and what you're good at as quickly as possible so that you can make the most of your life, help other people, be happy doing what you love, acknowledge and focus on your blessings, and delegate the rest.

Our Elders Were Correct

When many of us were children, our elders told us, "Enjoy yourself because you'll be old before you know it." I don't know if a child has ever lived on this earth who ever believed that or took it seriously. As kids, we minimized it and thought at the time how little they knew. But I can tell you that at age seventy-three, those lessons we heard from older people when we were children could not be more accurate. Life does happen quickly, and all of a sudden you reach a point in your life where you say, "I'm still looking forward to what's ahead, but on the other hand, where did all those years ago? What happened to them?"

A catchy quote by Lily Tomlin says, "We're all in this alone." We come into this world alone, and we're going to leave it alone. Another quote I like is "Death was Patrick Henry's second choice." And Gandhi said, "Live your life as if you were going to die tomorrow; plan your life as if you were going to live forever." These bits of wisdom have withstood the tests of time only because they are true.

What Older People Would Do Differently

Dr. Tony Campolo,[105] a sociologist at Eastern University, a Christian university in St. Davids, Pennsylvania, conducted a study among fifty people over the age of ninety-five. The subjects were asked what they would do differently if they had life to live over again. They said they would do three things differently:

1. They would risk more.
2. They would reflect more.
3. They would do more things that would live on after they were dead.

In a sermon he delivered on January 1, 2000, Dr. Campolo explained how those responses can provide direction for how we should live life.[106]

Dr. Campolo asks, "What do you want on your tombstone? How do you want to be remembered?" Your answer to that question is your purpose in life. All you need to do is work backward from the words you want on your tombstone to the present moment. We all should live our lives so purposefully that no one has to wonder what to inscribe on our tombstones—our loved ones will know what to write because our purpose was obvious and so apparent from the way we lived our lives.

This message was so powerful that when I was honored to give the commencement speech to the Fox School of Business of Temple University in 2011, I chose to use it as the centerpiece of the talk. The night before, I boarded a flight from Fort Myers to Philadelphia with intentions of polishing the talk on board. Sitting in seat 4C, I was joined in seat 4D by another man who was also wearing blue jeans. Before I could place my Bose headset on, he asked, "So, are you going home?"

---

105. Tony Campolo, PhD, is a professor emeritus of sociology at Eastern University, a former faculty member at the University of Pennsylvania, and the founder and president of the Evangelical Association for the Promotion of Education. He has written more than thirty-five books, and he blogs regularly on his website, redletterchristians.org.

106. The sermon is available at http://tonycampolo.org/sermons/2000/01/if-i-had-to-live-it-over -again/.

My brief "no" simply prompted his second question: "So why are you going to Philadelphia?"

Continuing to read my script didn't deter more questions from 4D. "So why?"

Finally, I said I was heading to Philadelphia to give a talk.

Immediately he said, "Who are you speaking to?"

I said I was giving the commencement speech to Temple Fox School. Wrong answer!

His next question was, "Oh, can I read it?"

Unbelievable! I thought. I handed 4D the paperwork and almost immediately heard, "There's a mistake here."

"What's the mistake?" was my answer.

He said, "It's Eastern University, not Eastern Baptist College" (the institution at which Dr. Campolo teaches).

"Really?" I asked. "How do you know?"

"I'm the president," he said. And he was! Sitting next to me was Dr. David Black, a perfectly delightful man and a friend and employer of my idol, Dr. Tony Campolo. Our exchanged promise for the two of us to have dinner with David and our spouses is, as yet, an unfulfilled one. To me, dining with Dr. Campolo would be like being with the pope. His insightfulness, faith, devotion, and wisdom are legendary.

It has a lot to do with legacy. We need to live our lives focused on the legacy we want to leave behind.

Doing What You Love Creates Exponential Energy

When we discover our life's calling, our true north, we get a lot of energy from it, and that energy is exponential. Let's look at our emotional energy on a scale from 1 to 100, with 100 being the highest measure. If our emotional energy—our psychological where-withal to deal with stressors—is in the 90s, that's like a letter grade of an "A." We feel great. The 80s are a "B," and so forth. When we're focusing on those top three things on our list from Chapter 1, we actually get so energized from doing those things that our energy stays up in the 90s. The more you do those things you love and the more your energy is in the 90s, what ends up happening is that you continue to feel good, and that energy transfers into other aspects of your day.

First, you feel good because you are energized from doing what you love, so then you get a workout in, and your workout is actually better than usual because you are feeling good. Then you decide to eat a healthier meal, and you feel even better. Next thing you know, you're having better conversations, and you're resolving conflicts better at work and as a parent and spouse. I've seen people who are extremely energized in every aspect of their lives. It's because they are living in that realm of exponential energy; they're in that sweet spot, and the things they do are feeding themselves energy. It's fascinating to see it happen.

Exercising provides us with energy and can actually increase our longevity. In the book *Younger Next Year*, authors Chris Crowley and Henry S. Lodge, MD, encourage people to exercise six times a week to optimize their health. They say the most important factor in good health is exercise, and the second most important factor is diet. They note that a fifty-year-old who is thirty pounds overweight and smokes one pack of cigarettes a day but exercises for six days a week can expect to live eight years longer than a fifty-year-old nonsmoker who doesn't exercise at all.

Age has nothing to do with following your calling. It's never too late.

It's Never Too Late to Find Your True North

There are many stories about people who didn't find their calling until late in life and went on to have successful careers in an entirely new field than they had been involved in as younger people. Age has nothing to do with following your calling. It's never too late. Many people may be retiring in their fifties or sixties and just beginning to explore their true calling, and I think that's wonderful. Finding your true north isn't time-limited; you can get to it whenever you want. Consider these success stories of people who discovered their calling later in life than their peers:

- *Athlete Kurt Warner didn't enter the NFL until age twenty-eight, and he went on to become a two-time MVP and Super Bowl champion.*
- *Singer K. T. Oslin released her first album at age forty-seven and became a major country-music success.*

- *Eugène Ehrhart started publishing in mathematics in his forties and finished his PhD thesis at the age of sixty.*

- *Frank McCourt didn't publish his first book,* Angela's Ashes, *until he was sixty-six; the book won the Pulitzer Prize.*

The number two person at the New York Life Insurance Company in New York, one of the largest companies in the world, was Fred Sievert. We became friends when we both served on the Board of Trustees of The American College. When Fred retired from New York Life, he rewired himself by enrolling at the Princeton Theological Seminary to become a minister. He will no doubt do even more good in the remaining years of his life than he did during his working years at New York Life, which is really saying a lot because he's an icon in our industry. Fred's example is why they should retire the word "retirement." His book, *God Revealed: Revisit Your Path to Enrich Your Future*, tells how he received an unexpected visit from God when he was twelve. His spiritual longing from that important boyhood encounter has influenced his decisions since that time.[107]

Karsten Lundgren, my good friend at Thrivent for Christians (formerly Thrivent for Lutherans), is past retirement age. He recently answered the question "When are you going to retire?" with the answer "I retired ten years ago. I'm just doing what I love."

What an inspiration for the many.

Catalytic Moments That Make Us Appreciate Life Even More

We may plan to do that which we love and are gifted with, but sometimes we just never make it happen. Then we hear about people who make dramatic shifts in their lives, and we wonder what happened. Quite often, the shift was precipitated by a crisis. Maybe the person had a heart attack and decided to make some changes in his life. Or maybe he lost a loved one. Catalytic moments like those make us realize how precious life is and motivate us to make shifts in our lives.

I have had two such catalytic moments in my life. They have served, and continue to serve, as motivators for me to live my best life possible.

---

107. Fred Sievert, *God Revealed: Revisit Your Path to Enrich Your Future* (New York: Morgan James Publishing, 2014).

The first happened while I was in college. One evening, I was driving in my old Camaro with a teammate of mine, Deon, to another teammate's house in inner-city Baltimore. We got lost in a very bad neighborhood. (This was before cell phones and GPS devices were available.) We drove down a wrong street, not knowing that there were major crack houses on that street, where many deals were being made. A car pulled up behind us, and the driver began flicking the beams at us. We thought it was our friend, Trey, coming to help us. We pulled off to the side of the road, and the car pulled up along the side of us, revealing that it was some guys from the crack house who thought we were there looking for some drugs.

I know that little kids grow into adults in the blink of an eye, so I cherish every day with them.

As one of the guys began talking, Deon and I realized that these guys were threatening to kill us. One guy reached into his sweatshirt with a movement clearly indicative that he was pulling out a gun. I was petrified. I thought, I can't believe I'm going to die right here, right now, like this. This isn't the way I expected it to end. *I was enraged but completely powerless in that situation; there was nothing I could do. I closed my eyes, placed my hands on the steering wheel, and waited for him to shoot me. A few moments later, their car sped off in front of us. Deon and I were thankfully able to leave that neighborhood, get to our friend's house, and find safety. After that, the thought kept crossing my mind that I could have died that night. It made me self-reflect on what I really wanted to do with my life. I realized then that the clock is ticking.*

A second catalytic moment that changed my perspective happened after I was married, when our daughter, Ellie, was four years old. She began experiencing some chronic belly pain. One night, we were up all through the night and even tried to go to the ER twice, but they were full. The next morning, we went to our pediatrician, and he admitted her into St. Luke's hospital in the Lehigh Valley. We were there for several days. We had a four-month-old son at home who was nursing, as well as a two-year-old son, so it was difficult for my wife to bring the baby around and for her to be at the hospital.

Eventually they realized that my daughter had several large kidney stones. They were now showing up on an x-ray, and she had developed a kidney infection from them. Everyone was seriously concerned for her life. At 2:00 a.m., we had to rush her to the Children's Hospital of Philadelphia in an ambulance. Doctors didn't tell us that she could die, but that was the implied message. Seeing the most valuable, precious thing in all the world to me lying there, fighting for her life, again made me realize that the clock is ticking. She spent the next few days in the children's hospital, where she had surgery to remove some huge kidney stones. Throughout those days and nights, I kept thinking, This could be it. She could die. How precious life really is. How grateful I am to God to be with her. *She survived that experience, and because of it, every single day, I'm so grateful that I get today with my kids because for a short while there, I thought I might not have my daughter. I know that little kids grow into adults in the blink of an eye, so I cherish every day with them.*

Suffering is one of the main things that we have in common with everybody across all of civilization, anywhere in the world.

I have had two catalytic moments in my life that changed my perspective as well. Years ago, I was fishing with a friend in northern Minnesota. We were out on a lake in a boat when a man began shooting at us with a high-powered rifle. Each bullet that came at us was only a foot or two above our heads. We could hear each bullet coming, just like I heard, as a kid, a freight train that wasn't going to stop at the Lehigh Valley Station. The sound of the bullets was loud and powerful, and we lay in the boat with our heads down and possibly our hands clasped in prayer, though I'm unsure of the latter.

I was keenly aware that each bullet that came our way could be the end, that it could pierce right through the boat. It reminded me that things happen that you can't control. The only thing you can control is how you live your life. Your attitude, as Viktor Frankl says—how you perceive things and what you think—is all that's within your control, and little else is. That experience has often made me think about all of our young people in the military who go through months, or even years, of similar experiences, dodging bullets that sound like oncoming freight trains. They are true heroes. Winston Churchill said, "There's nothing so exhilarating as having been shot at without effect." Clearly that feeling was not felt until long after the ordeal.

Then, four years ago, I had a second catalytic moment that made me realize how short life really is. Our son, Scott, was in the intensive-care ward at the Mayo Clinic in Rochester, Minnesota. The head of intensive care was a physician from Ireland. He and Scott's cardiologist approached me, and the internist said, "I want you to know, we're going to do everything we can to save Scott. At the same time, please know that he is the sickest person in this hospital." Then the cardiologist said, "And part of that is not the leukemia as much as it is the heart." He went on to tell me more about that.

I asked him, "On a scale of one to ten, how worried are you?"

He said, "I'm an eight." That was the most frightening moment of my life; Scott was called back to his Creator the very next day.

I remember riding back to Minneapolis by car with Kip, Scott's younger brother. Kip vowed that he would spend the rest of his life knowing that Scott was right there living his life with him. As you might imagine, Scott's death has had a profound effect on Kip, not only because they were brothers, but also because Scott was his best friend. This last time, Scott was in intensive care for eight straight days. Kip never left his room except to go get pizza at night. He slept in the room on a couch that the Mayo Clinic graciously provided, and he was Scott's constant advocate. Kip was engaged at that time to Stephanie, the woman who is now his wife, and they now have two children, Cam and Phil III. Much of Kip's happiness today stems from his conviction that he will be with his Scott again.

The pain associated with that loss has obviously been devastating for Sue and me as well. Of the more than 32,000 hits on Scott's Caring Bridge website, the most-used phrase was "I can't imagine... ." I have noticed that when people who have lost a child meet others who also know that loss, a bond forms, and there is a shared affinity, friendship, and trust. You feel an instantaneous empathy for the other family, knowing that "I can't imagine..." is known to the other. In cases in which I've learned that somebody else has lost a child, we often become friends because the pain is so outrageous, so surreal, so indescribable that, unless you've lived it, you cannot imagine how horrible it is. And if someone else lived it, you know you're brothers or sisters beneath the skin. I've seen people who have stopped smoking, stopped drinking, changed their lives, after the loss of a child. I've also seen people who have withdrawn into their shell forever. It changed their life, but I'm not sure it was always for the better. My deepest sympathies are reserved for those who have had such a loss without a strong faith to comfort them. Yes, time is short, and the clock is ticking, for all of us.

A situation like that brings you face to face in an uncomfortable way with your mortality and makes you examine how you have lived your life. I'm proud to say that Scott lived a great life. His biggest decision in life was whether to stay at North Star or become a minister, and he figured out a way to do both. He was president of the company, and he spent the last ten years of his life ministering to anybody who would listen (and even to those who wouldn't). His life was surely not in vain.

He left behind a beautiful wife, whom we now call our daughter, and two beautiful children, Nick and Lauren, who are now nine and thirteen. Should Michelle someday choose to remarry, I hope to walk her down the aisle and give her away. Because her own dad is gone, I'd be honored to play a part in the happiness of our "daughter."

There is no greater emotional pain than to bury your child. It's just not the way it's supposed to be. Suffering is one of the main things that we have in common with everybody across all of civilization, anywhere in the world. We all connect around the topic of suffering, and the greatest of all suffering is to experience the loss of a child.

Any time we're at a funeral, I think most of us are reminded that life is short. It makes us want to get to the life experiences that are really important to us. A funeral can actually be a powerful motivator to engage in those activities we love the most.

Legacies and love live on.

Having friends or family members who are serving in a war also reminds us that the clock is ticking. Two of my friends have served overseas, and I am closely connected with their families. Gerald Finnegan graduated from Annapolis and served in Iraq, and Marcus Millen graduated from West Point and served in Afghanistan. In both cases, their families and I prayed daily and eagerly awaited to hear news from them regarding their well-being. You really appreciate how valuable time is when you have a loved one serving in combat.

When friends of ours leave us, the wreaths we send are inscribed with the words, "When she lived, she lived for you; now that she is gone, she lives in you." Surely, Scott lives on in his children as well as the rest of our family. Legacies and love live on.

Leave Your Legacy Behind

What are the gifts that God gave you, not just in terms of talents but also in terms of children and grandchildren? How will you be remembered? One of the greatest gifts we can share with our loved ones is a picture of who we are—a tangible remembrance of our legacy. Leave your children and grandchildren something tangible that indicates what your values were during your life—maybe a book, a video, or a collection of keepsakes.

The clock is ticking for each of us. The good news is that your true north is waiting to be discovered and optimized, and if you do that, then the sky is not the limit in terms of what you can accomplish, regardless of your age. Once you find the right vocation, you will find that your work can be fun and energizing.

In 1932, English educator, philosopher, and Unitarian minister Lawrence Pearsall Jacks (1860–1955) wrote this often-repeated passage: "A master in the art of living draws no sharp distinction between his work and his play, his labour and his leisure, his mind and his body, his education and his recreation. He hardly knows which is which. He simply pursues his vision of excellence through whatever he is doing and leaves others to determine whether he is working or playing. To himself he always seems to be doing both. Enough for him that he does it well."[108] This quote hangs outside my office so that all who are about to enter can see it. This book is intended to give you an opportunity to live the happy life described in this quote.

That is our prayer for you—that you are able to sift through all of the cues that life hands you and find your precious, God-given talents so that you can enjoy the activities you engage in and be fulfilled by them. We wish you all the best as you set out on your journey to find your true north and to create a legacy of success.

It's Your Turn

Exercise 21-1: Your catalytic moments

Catalytic moments like suffering a great loss make us realize how precious life is and motivate us to make shifts in our lives. What specific catalytic events have occurred in your life that changed your perspective and made you realize the clock is ticking?

1. _____
2. _____
3. _____
4. _____
5. _____

---

108. Lawrence Pearsall Jacks, *Education through Recreation* (1932), 1.

Exercise 21-2: The gifts God has given you

What are the gifts that God has given you, not just in terms of talents but also in terms of friends, partners, siblings, children, and grandchildren?

1. _____

2. _____

3. _____

4. _____

5. _____

6. _____

7. _____

8. _____

9. _____

10. _____

Notes

Notes

Notes

Notes

Notes

Notes